CHILDREN'S LANGUAGE

Volume 9

CHILDREN'S LANGUAGE

Volume 9

Edited by

CAROLYN E. JOHNSON
JOHN H. V. GILBERT
University of British Columbia

LAWRENCE ERLBAUM ASSOCIATES, PUBLISHERS
1996   Mahwah, New Jersey

Lawrence Erlbaum Associates, Inc., Publishers
10 Industrial Avenue
Mahwah, New Jersey 07430

Library of Congress Cataloging-in-Publication Data

ISBN: 0-8058-2054-X
ISSN: 0163-2809

Books published by Lawrence Erlbaum Associates are printed on acid-free paper,
and their bindings are chosen for strength and durability.

Printed in the United States of America
10 9 8 7 6 5 4 3 2 1

Contributors

DONELLA ANTELMI
University of Venice, Italy

ANNE E. BAKER
University of Amsterdam, the Netherlands

BARBARA BERNHARDT
University of British Columbia, Vancouver, Canada

BEPPIE V. D. BOGAERDE
University of Amsterdam, the Netherlands

BARBARA BOKUS
University of Warsaw, Poland

MIREILLE BRIGAUDIOT
Université Paris III, France

PAUL VAN DEN BROEK
University of Nijmegen, the Netherlands

JAN BROKX
Instituut voor Doven, St. Michielsgestel, the Netherlands

EVE V. CLARK
Stanford University, California

JANE A. COERTS
University of Amsterdam, and University of Nijmegen, the Netherlands

MARGARET DEUCHAR
University of Wales, Bangor, Wales

CHRISTLIEBE EL MOGHARBEL
University of Hamburg, Germany

JERRY FRIEDMAN
San Francisco State University, California

JOHN H. V. GILBERT
University of British Columbia, Vancouver, Canada

GISELA HÅKANSSON
Lund University, Sweden

ELLIOT HELMAN
San Francisco State University, California

CAROLYN E. JOHNSON
University of British Columbia, Vancouver, Canada

GUNLÖG JOSEFSSON
Lund University, Sweden

MARLON KUNTZE
San Francisco State University, California

YONATA LEVY
The Hebrew University, Jerusalem, Israel

CONXITA LLEÓ
University of Hamburg, Germany

ANTONIO MALDONADO
Universidad Autónoma de Madrid, Spain

ALLYSSA McCABE
University of Massachusetts, Lowell, Massachusetts

INGMARIE MELLENIUS
Lund University, Sweden

ALIYAH MORGENSTERN
Université Paris III, France

PRISCILLA POYNOR MOYERS
San Francisco State University, California

ULRIKA NETTELBLADT
Lund University, Sweden

CATHERINE NICOLAS
Université Paris III, France

CAROLE PETERSON
Memorial University, St. John's, Newfoundland, Canada

MICHAEL PRINZ
University of Hamburg, Germany

PHILIP M. PRINZ
San Francisco State University, California

CAROL STOEL-GAMMON
University of Washington, Seattle, Washington

MICHAEL STRONG
San Francisco State University, California

SUSAN M. SUZMAN
University of Witwatersrand, Johannesburg, South Africa

JAMES VINCENT
San Francisco State University, California

Contents

Preface

The International Association for the Study of Child Language (IASCL) was first discussed at the International Colloquium of Paedolinguistics held in Brno, in the former Czechoslovakia, in 1970. After further discussion, IASCL was officially founded at the International Symposium on First Language Acquisition held in Florence in 1972. At that time, the very young *Journal of Child Language* (edited by David Crystal) was adopted as the official organ of the association. One of the major aims of the IASCL was to hold regular international meetings of investigators working in the new field of child language studies; this goal led to its organization of the First International Conference on the Study of Child Language, held in London during the summer of 1975. Since that time, IASCL has met triennially at Congresses held specifically to further the ideals of its founders.

The proceedings of the Florence meeting and subsequent meetings have been published. They form a remarkable historical account of the development and diversity of the field. From the first set of proceedings, published as *Baby Talk and Infant Speech* (edited by Walburga von Raffler-Engel and Ivan Lebrun), the Association has sought to demonstrate the growth of research in child language, through either thematic or eclectic volumes. The meetings in London, Tokyo, Vancouver, Austin, Lund, Budapest, and Trieste represent not only the geographical diversity of the Association's membership, but through their published proceedings draw an interesting thread through almost 25 years of ongoing investigation.

This volume (an eclectic one) contains a selection of papers from the Trieste Congress held in July 1993, and is the ninth to be published in the series *Children's Language,* of which Keith E. Nelson was founding Editor. We believe that this volume neatly represents the membership of IASCL, the intellectual richness of the field, and the endeavours of IASCL.

In their *Preface* to Volume 7 in this series, Gina Conti-Ramsden and Catherine Snow wrote: "It is the aim of the IASCL to continue to foster openness and the exchange of ideas about children's language across national, linguistic, and disciplinary boundaries." Those who have attended the Association's Congresses can attest to its success in meeting this aim. The consistent excellence of presentations is complemented by a high level of organization. Because IASCL is a small organization, there is a warmth and understanding among delegates that does indeed "foster openness and the exchange of ideas" seldom found in meetings of larger organizations. Given that the weight of running the organization falls on the President and the Secretary–Treasurer, and the Congresses are organized entirely by volunteers in the host community, we are indeed privileged to meet every three years with a continuing record of success.

The Trieste meeting continued a tradition of excellence in organization and hospitality. We acknowledge our gratitude to all those who made this volume possible. Former President Jean Berko-Gleason, who served as the IASCL liaison with the Congress organizers in Trieste, current President Ruth Berman, and Secretary–Treasurer Phil Dale, all of whom encouraged us (with their usual enthusiasm) to edit this volume. Of our many colleagues in Italy, we would especially like to thank those who, under the unflagging and committed leadership of Marie-Sylvie Barbiera, formed the organizing committee in Trieste and made the Congress such a success. We recognize that the smooth running of the Congress was only achieved because of the incredible dedication and work of this small group of people. We will remember our bus trip into the hills for dinner and our reception on the Mediterranean coast with great joy. We hope that the special quality of the Trieste Congress and the lively spirit of its participants are reflected in this volume. We would like to thank all of the authors, who kept so closely to our publication deadline. And, finally, we would like to thank our old friend Judi Amsel at Lawrence Erlbaum for her willingness to shepherd us through the preparation of the manuscript and her enthusiasm for this latest volume in the Children's Language series.

As we look back over the seven meetings of IASCL and the special nature of the investigative work in which the members of our association are involved, we conclude with the poet T. S. Eliot:

> We shall not cease from exploration
> And the end of all our exploring
> Will be to arrive where we started
> And know the place for the first time.
>   (*Little Gidding, Part 5*)

Carolyn E. Johnson
John H. V. Gilbert

Introduction

Carolyn E. Johnson
John H. V. Gilbert
University of British Columbia

The 17 chapters in this volume bring together the work of 32 scholars from 13 countries—investigations of children learning 15 different languages, in some instances more than one at a time. The scope of this work, as broad as it is, only partially represents the research interests and approaches of the more than 350 scholars from 34 countries who contributed papers or posters to the Sixth International Congress for the Study of Child Language.

This investigative power and diversity are for the most part focused on topics and issues that have been under discussion for the last 30 or so years of modern day child language research, some even beyond that in early diary studies and philosophers' speculations (e.g., Locke, 1690/1964). For example, in chapter 1, Conxita Lleó, Michael Prinz, and colleagues address the issue of continuity between babbling and speech, which has motivated a considerable body of research since the appearance of Roman Jakobson's *Kindersprache, Aphasie und allgemeine Lautgesetze* in 1941 (see Elbers, 1982; Oller Wieman, Doyle, & Ross, 1976; Stoel-Gammon & Cooper, 1984; Vihman, Macken, Miller, Simmons, & Miller, 1985). In chapter 3, Margaret Deuchar considers whether children's earliest word combinations represent syntactic categories given in Universal Grammar (UG), and whether UG principles are given from the beginning or have to mature. Her questions connect us with the earliest work of Braine (1963) and the lively discussion over more than the next decade about the categorial status of words in children's two-word combinations and the (potential) continuity of development from these first combinations to clearly demonstrable syntactic categories (see, for example, L. Bloom, 1973; Bowerman, 1973; Braine, 1976; Brown, 1973; Miller & Ervin, 1964; Schlesinger, 1974).

Although the issues are mainly familiar ones, the chapters in this volume contribute to the advancement of child language study in several specific ways. First, they represent current theoretical frameworks, both bringing the insights of the theories to the interpretation of language development and testing tenets or implications of the theories with child language data. Second, they contribute substantively to the crosslinguistic study of child language, reflecting both the linguistic diversity of the authors themselves and a recent major shift in the approach to child language study. Third, they build on the now considerable body of knowledge about children's language, both adding to information about the basic systems of phonology, syntax, and semantics and extending beyond to explore aspects of narrative and literacy development, language acquisition by bilingual and atypical children, and language processing. Finally, they contain hints of new directions in child language study, such as increased attention to the impact of phonology on other language systems.

ISSUES AND THEORIES

Differing perspectives on some unresolved issues are directly illustrated by several chapters in this volume. For example, Yonata Levy (chapter 5) appeals to facts from studies of children learning Hebrew, English, German, Polish, and Icelandic to test the predictions of formalist versus functionalist theories about the development of morphological subsystems. She argues that "closed," or autonomous systems—that is, ones that can be learned exclusively on the basis of formal, distributional features—are intrinsically the easiest to learn and, thus, earliest acquired. Although such systems ultimately must be "opened up," dependencies among systems (e.g., between conceptual or semantic distinctions and formal distributional properties) at first complicate the learning task for young children. Eve Clark (chapter 4), on the other hand, uses longitudinal data from three children learning English to argue that young children (1;6–3;0) use their conceptual knowledge of event and state types to categorize verbs according to their inherent aspect, thereby predicting formal properties such as argument structure, inflection, and participation in syntactic constructions. She extends this notion (related to work by, for example, Antinucci & Miller, 1976, and Bloom, Lifter, & Hafitz, 1980) by hypothesizing that children use specific verbs as templates for other, semantically related verbs, for example, using their knowledge of *run* to predict the argument structure and inflections of *walk*, *race*, and *slide*.

The continuing relevance and unresolved status of such issues are to be expected, given the complexity of language itself and the factors that interact in its development and performance, as well as the huge gap that continues to exist between our understanding of neurological structure and function on the one hand and complex behaviors on the other. However, progress in how we address these issues is easy to see in recent language development research, including the chapters in this book. Advances in detail and sophistication of linguistic theory and in the amount and type of empirical data available allow us to focus our questions and arguments much more precisely than we could when these issues were first debated on a wide scale.

Chapters 1 and 2 (Lleó et al. and Bernhardt & Stoel-Gammon, respectively) deal with early phonological acquisition within the current nonlinear phonological framework. Further, Lleó et al. explore the babbling-to-speech continuity issue from a principles and parameters perspective (Chomsky, 1981), which has been applied primarily to the study of syntactic acquisition. Their perspective and results lead them to distinguish between universal grammatical continuity, which predicts aspects of early sound production due to universal constraints on language (the principles of Universal Grammar) before parameterization occurs, and language-specific continuity, which predicts continuity in the sense of sounds and sound patterns converging with the target language, the result of parameter setting. The Principles-and-Parameters model allows Lleó et al. to describe continuity in some aspects of the transition to linguistic sound production that would otherwise appear to be discontinuous.

Barbara Bernhardt and Carol Stoel-Gammon (chapter 2) also frame their study of the earliest words produced by normal and phonologically delayed English-learning children within nonlinear phonological theory. They appeal to the recent notion of Combinatorial Specification (Archangeli & Pulleyblank, 1994) to argue for the importance of separating markedness from specification and default prediction when accounting for children's earliest representations of phonological features, segments, and prosodic structures. Hypotheses based on Combinatorial Specification allowed them to account for aspects of the children's systems due to language-specific characteristics and factors relating to the real-time acquisition process as well as universally unmarked features. Further dialogue is needed to determine the fit of Principles and Parameters with Combinatorial Specification in accounting for the very similar conclusions reached by Lleó et al. and Bernhardt and Stoel-Gammon.

Current syntactic theory provides the basis for chapters 3, 8 and 10. Margaret Deuchar (chapter 3) and Donella Antelmi (chapter 8) both address the acquisition of functional categories within a Government and Binding framework (Chomsky, 1981). Deuchar argues for discontinuity and a maturational approach to early syntax, because some of children's earliest combinatory words—those comparable to Braine's (1963) *pivots*—are acategorial (that is, they cannot be assigned to lexical categories) and appear to reflect cognitive rather than linguistic factors. Antelmi is concerned with a later stage of development, when children are beginning to syntactically combine clauses. She presents Italian acquisition data to demonstrate that COMP (a functional category) is not initially available, but rather develops gradually. Both Deuchar and Antelmi agree with Radford (1990) that functional categories are not initially given in Universal Grammar—*contra* Hyams (1986)—but rather depend on maturation (as well as reanalysis or learning). In chapter 10, Gunlög Josefsson provides evidence of Swedish children's late acquisition of object shift, along with a variety of strategies they use to avoid it, which she explains by positing that learning object shift requires analyzing this syntactic operation as a head-to-head movement of a weak object pronoun to a functional projection to the left of negation or a sentence adverbial.

THE CROSSLINGUISTIC STUDY OF CHILDREN'S LANGUAGE

The coming of age of the crosslinguistic approach to studying language development was signaled by the publication in 1985 of the first two of Dan Slobin's (now four) volumes of *The Crosslinguistic Study of Language Acquisition*. In Slobin's (1985) words, "The world provides us with a marvelous set of 'natural experiments,' in which children with similar endowments master languages of varying forms" (p. 5). These natural experiments have two complementary goals: (a) to identify commonalities of development by children across languages, working toward determining universals of language and language learning, and (b) to describe patterns of development that are language-specific, determining how particular typological characteristics influence the course of language acquisition (with information gained here contributing back to the first goal).

Susan Suzman's chapter 6 is an excellent example of the sort of study Slobin (1985) had in mind when he called crosslinguistic study "a method in developmental psycholinguistics." Interested like Clark (chapter 4) and Levy (chapter 5) in determinants of morphological system acquisition, Suzman uses a crosslinguistic approach (cf. Levy) to examine a single morphological system (cf. Clark). She points out that the noun classification system in Bantu languages provides a "felicitous linguistic framework" in which to carry out such an investigation, in that it interacts only minimally with other systems (partly because very young children hear mainly singular forms, eliminating the complication of number marking in the earliest stage). Suzman demonstrates that the different morphophonological features of the noun class prefixes in Zulu, Swati, Sotho, and Tswana predict both relative ease of acquisition and children's acquisition strategies in these four closely related Southeastern Bantu languages. All Bantu children use noun class prefixes early, Zulu children doing so earliest and with overgeneralization errors due to the regular, vowel-onset shape of the prefixes in the major noun classes and their prosodically prominent full form in object position. Children learning Sotho and Tswana start to learn their less transparent systems later and produce "shadow prefixes," as opposed to overgeneralized forms. Note that Suzman's results provide further evidence for Levy's general claim about system autonomy and ease of acquisition (chapter 5).

Several other chapters depend on crosslinguistic study as a method. Lleó et al. (chapter 1) compare the distribution of place and manner of consonantal production, laryngeal consonants, and syllable structure of infants learning Spanish and German to test their hypotheses about universal versus language-specific babbling-to-speech continuity; the hypotheses could not be tested without data from languages that differed on the relevant parameters. In addition, the authors provide the community of child language scholars with valuable new empirical data on the early sounds and sound systems of children learning Spanish and German. Levy's conclusion about the ease of learning morphological systems (chapter 5) also depends on crosslinguistic study as a method. For several specific systems, she uses data from typologically different languages to show the relative time and rate of acquisition, depending on whether learning the system involves interdependencies with other systems. For example, she compares the relatively late acquisition of the Icelandic gender system, which is complex and plurifunctional, depending in part on semantic encoding of animacy and sex distinctions, with early acquisition of the purely formal Hebrew gender system. Comparisons of a variety of systems across several languages allow her to make a generalization about the ease of acquiring formally autonomous systems that would otherwise not be licensed. Deuchar (chapter 3) features data from her daughter, who is bilingual in Spanish and English, and data from monolingual Spanish acquisition as evidence of equivalent precategorial and acategorial structures in the two languages.

A number of other chapters contribute to the crosslinguistic study of children's language by adding to our knowledge about specific aspects of a variety of languages. Mireille Brigaudiot and her colleagues (chapter 7) describe the development of self reference for three children, two learning French and one learning English. In chapter 8, Antelmi's description of the development of sentence embedding is based on longitudinal data from an Italian child. Josefsson (chapter 10) presents information about Swedish children's acquisition of object shift. Ingmarie Mellenius (chapter 11) also explores Swedish children's language, in this case their acquisition of word formation rules as demonstrated by comprehension of novel compound nouns; she then goes on to compare her results with those from studies of Hebrew- and English-speaking children reported elsewhere (e.g., Clark & Berman, 1984). Håkansson and Nettelbladt's chapter (9) about the development of Swedish word order provides information about both typical and language-impaired children learning Swedish monolingually, but also children learning Swedish as an additional language. In chapter 13, Bokus reports a large group cross-sectional study of Polish children's developing control of narrative space when telling stories, both as monologues and in dialogic discourse.

A different facet of crosslinguistic study—one that also involves bilingualism—is represented by three chapters concerned with children who are learning signed languages. In chapter 14, Anne Baker and Beppie van den Bogaerde compare the language input and attentional strategies used by deaf mothers to their deaf and hearing children learning Dutch and Sign Language of the Netherlands, and the children's attentional behavior when addressed in each of these languages. Jane Coerts and colleagues (chapter 15) also report a study of children learning both Dutch and Sign Language of the Netherlands, in this case an investigation of the progress in both languages made by two deaf children who received cochlear implants at the age of 5 years (the first such children in the Netherlands). Philip Prinz and his co-investigators (chapter 16) present data that show a positive correlation between fluency in American Sign Language and achievement in English reading and writing for nine deaf students between 11 and 13 years old.

EXTENDING THE DOMAIN OF ENQUIRY

Research in child language has progressed to the point where the accumulation of information and research methods support the extension of investigation into aspects of language learning beyond the basic phonological, semantic, and syntactic systems. Represented in this volume are the areas of narrative development and language input (both of which, of course, already have a long history of study), and the newer research areas of language disorders and language processing.

Chapters 12 and 13 contribute to a body of literature that has grown enormously over the past few years—that concerning narrative development. However, in contrast to the bulk of this literature, which deals primarily with thematic and goal-oriented episodic development (change in the ability to deal with the main story line) these two chapters focus on children's inclusion of contextualizing information. In chapter 12, Carole Peterson and Allyssa McCabe continue their systematic exploration of narrative development by focusing on the cause of the wide variation they have observed in the amount of orienting information in children's personal narratives. Peterson and McCabe's 18-month study of 10 young English-speaking children shows that the children who spontaneously provided most information about *where* and *when* in their narratives at age 3;7 were those whose parents prompted most often for contextual information when the children were 2;2. Barbara Bokus (chapter 13) reports the largest group study in this volume—an investigation of 384 Polish children between the ages of 3 and 7 years. Building on her own and Peterson and McCabe's earlier work, she moves away from the narrative line of stories to focus on what she calls *narrative space*, which she discusses in terms of Bruner's (1986) dual landscapes of action and consciousness. She argues that her results, which show that children can produce such dual landscapes in their stories by age 5 or 6, demonstrate the dependence of this achievement on the child's developing theory of mind.

It is by now well established that children whose language is not developing normally are, nevertheless, learning the same language as their more typical peers; development of particular language systems may be slow relative to other systems (e.g. slow phonology but on-schedule syntax), or all aspects of language development may be slowed. In addition, asynchronies may exist within systems, such as phonology or morphology, resulting in an overall profile dissimilar to that of a younger child whose language is developing normally. However, for the most part the constraints and rules operating in each language subsystem are the same for both groups of children (and, of course, typical children also exhibit more advanced levels of development in some language subsystems than others). The state of the art is such that (a) speech-language pathologists have a basis for planning principled intervention, and (b) results from studies of children with delayed language (most often referred to as *specific language impairment*) can be used to test theories and models of language and language development. At the same time, more information about specific aspects of language development by this population is needed.

Four chapters in this volume contribute information about children who show delay in developing language. Bernhardt and Stoel-Gammon (chapter 2) test their hypotheses about phonological markedness with data from both normal children and children with phonological delays. Both groups of children provide support for the notion of Combinatorial Specification. In addition, the analyses based on this notion allow a well-motivated description of the data from both groups of children, including the similarities and differences between the normal children and those with delays in phonological development. It also provides a basis for planning a theoretically motivated intervention program for the children with phonological delays. Levy (chapter 5) uses data from children with neurologically based language disturbances in addition to crosslinguistic data to address her hypothesis concerning morphological development. Combining two ususally disparate research areas, Gisela Håkansson and Ulrika Nettelbladt (chapter 9) examine data from both immigrant children learning Swedish as an additional language and Swedish children with specific language impairment. Their evidence shows that these two groups of children both learn Swedish word-order rules in a rigid, effortful manner, relying on a canonical subject-verb word-order strategy, which contrasts with the rapid acquisition of word order by normally developing monolingual Swedish children.

In chapter 17, Barbara Bernhardt and Carolyn Johnson discuss the production of *filler syllables* by two children with severe phonological and more general language production disorders. They use longitudinal data from one of the children to test the predictions of linear speech production models, in most detail Garrett's (1984) model, which is widely used to account for both adult speech errors and aphasic language production. This chapter (along with two other presentations at the Trieste Congress) begins a new, more formal and specific approach to an old question: How can the difference between what a child knows about language and what the child actually says be explained? This question returns us to the classic studies of language acquisition, such as the exploratory work published in Ursulla Bellugi and Roger Brown's (1964) *Acquisition of Language*, while building on work completed since that time in research areas complementary to those in language acquisition.

NEW DIRECTIONS

The chapters in this volume reflect the current strength of crosslinguistic research, the application and testing of new theoretical developments, a new legitimacy of language disorder data, and a new appeal to the descriptive possiblities of language processing models. In addition, there is a theme that runs quietly through many of the chapters and points the way for important research in the future: the role of prosody in the acquisition of various language structures and systems. For example, Suzman (chapter 6) explains its importance for Zulu children learning noun classifiers, which first appear in the intonationally distinguished object position. Mellenius (chapter 9) discusses the importance of intonation in Swedish noun compounding. Josefsson (chapter 10) notes the dependence of the late-emerging object shift in Swedish on a specific clause intonation, about which very little is known so far, but that is a promising avenue for exploration.

Although it is not the explicit focus of any chapter, prosody is an important theme, one that reflects a new emphasis in research. This research is overdue. Despite consistent individual voices explicating the role of phonological factors in learning words, morphology, syntax, and pragmatics, phonology is often ignored, to the detriment of our collective knowledge. This is illustrated by the neglect of phonological development by a number of—including the most recent—child language textbooks (e.g., P. Bloom, 1994). This neglect is even ironic, considering that the Stanford Child Phonology Project, under the leadership of Charles Ferguson, was the source of much of the vigor of child language research at the beginning of the 1970s. It is possible that some of the impetus for the return of attention to phonological factors has been provided by the recent success of applying nonlinear phonological theory to phonological development, in conjunction with a fine-tuning of research questions about determinants of acquiring other language systems. In any case, we welcome it.

REFERENCES

Antinucci, F., & Miller, R. (1976). How children talk about what happened. *Journal of Child Language, 3*, 167–189.

Archangeli, D., & Pulleyblank, D. (1994). *Grounded phonology*. Cambridge, MA: MIT Press.

Bellugi, U., & Brown, R. (1964). *The acquisition of language*. Chicago: University of Chicago Press. (Originally published in the Monographs of the Society for Research in Child Development, Vol. 29, No. 1.)

Bloom, L. (1973). Why not pivot grammar? In C. Ferguson & D. Slobin (Eds.), *Studies of child language development* (pp. 430–440). New York: Holt, Rinehart & Winston.

Bloom, L., Lifter, K., & Hafitz, J. (1980). Semantics of verbs and the development of verb inflection in child language. *Language, 56*, 386–412.

Bloom, P. (Ed.), (1994). *Language acquisition*. Cambridge, MA: MIT Press.

Bowerman, M. (1973). *Early syntactic development: A cross-linguistic study with special reference to Finnish*. London: Cambridge University Press.

Braine, M. (1963). The ontogeny of English phrase structure: The first phase. *Language, 19*, 1–13.

Braine, M. (1976). Children's first word combinations. *Monographs of the Society for Research in Child Development, 41* (1, Serial No. 164).

Brown, R. (1973). *A first language: The early stages*. Cambridge, MA: Harvard University Press.

Bruner, J. (1986). *Actual minds, possible worlds*. Cambridge, MA: Harvard University Press.

Clark, E., & Berman, R. (1984). Structure and use in the acquisition of word formation. *Language, 60*, 542–590.

Chomsky, N. (1981). *Lectures on Government and Binding*. Dordrecht: Foris.

Elbers, L. (1982). Operating principles in repetitive babbling: A cognitive continuity approach. *Cognition, 12*, 45–63.

Garrett, M. (1984). The organization of processing structure for language production: Applications in aphasic speech. In D. Caplan (Ed.), *Biological perspectives on language* (pp. 172–193). Cambridge, MA: MIT Press.

Hyams, N. (1986). *Language acquisition and the theory of parameters*. Dordrecht: Foris.

Jakobson, R. (1941). *Kindersprache, Aphasie und allgemeine Lautgesetze*. Uppsala: Almqvist and Wiksell.

Locke, J. (1964). *An essay concerning human understanding*. Abridged and edited by A.D. Woozley. Cleveland: Meridian Books. (Original work published 1690)

Miller, W., & Ervin, S. (1964). The development of grammar in child language. In U. Bellugi & R. Brown (Eds.), The acquisition of language. *Monographs of the Society for Research in Child Development, 29* (1), 9–34.

Oller, D. K., Wieman, L., Doyle, W., & Ross, C. (1976). *Journal of Child Language, 3*, 1–11.

Radford, A. (1990). *Syntactic theory and the acquisition of English syntax*. Oxford, England: Blackwell.

Schlesinger, I. M. (1974). Relational concepts underlying language. In R. Schiefelbusch & L. Lloyd (Eds.), *Language perspectives: Acquisition, retardation, and intervention* (pp. 129–151). Baltimore, MD: University Park Press.

Slobin, D. I. (1985). *The crosslinguistic study of language acquisition, Vol. 1: The data, and Vol. 2: Theoretical Issues*. Hillsdale, NJ: Lawrence Erlbaum Associates.

Stoel-Gammon, C., & Cooper, J. (1984). Patterns of early lexical and phonological development. *Journal of Child Language, 11*, 247–271.

Vihman, M., Macken, M., Miller, R., Simmons, H., & Miller, J. (1985). From babbling to speech: A reassessment of the continuity issue. *Language, 61*, 397–445.

Early Phonological Acquisition of German and Spanish: A Reinterpretation of the Continuity Issue Within the Principles and Parameters Model

Conxita Lleó
Michael Prinz
Christliebe El Mogharbel
University of Hamburg

Antonio Maldonado
Universidad Autónoma de Madrid

INTRODUCTION

Recent studies on phonological acquisition have largely discarded Jakobson's hypothesis on the discontinuity of prespeech babbling and early word production (see Jakobson, 1941, p. 20) and have given support to the phonetic continuity of these two utterance forms. It is still controversial, however, to what extent early infant sound production is governed by universal principles or reflects language-specific influences. In recent years research on early phonological acquisition has focused on language-specific characteristics of babbling. Crosslinguistic studies have shown that young children have preferences for sounds and sound structures, which can be correlated with certain characteristics of the respective target languages. For instance, at the babbling stage Japanese children produce more back vowels than English, French, Chinese, or Arabic children (de Boysson-Bardies, Hallé, Sagart, & Durand, 1989), Swedish and English children produce more stops than French or Japanese children (de Boysson-Bardies & Vihman, 1991), and English children produce more closed syllables than French children (Levitt & Utman, 1992).

On the basis of these results, most researchers have argued that there is no evidence for a separation of babbling and first words and, thus, that the Jakobsonian view was incorrect. It is not only the case that features of the target language are already traceable in the babbling stage and that both sound productions temporally coexist, but it is further the case that babbling and first words share phonetic material, so that the sounds that constitute the first words are the sounds preferred during the babbling stage (de Boysson-Bardies & Vihman, 1991; Vihman, 1993; Vihman, Macken, Miller, Simmons, & Miller, 1985). Many sounds and sound structures produced at the babbling stage constitute a common core, contained in the productions of all babbling children and also contained in all languages of the world, like coronals, stops, nasals, and CV syllables (Locke, 1983). These are the sounds and sound structures purported to be less marked.

Concomitantly, if at the babbling stage children produce sounds that are not included in their target languages, but which constitute a unitary set produced by all children independently of their target languages, this might provide some substance to the discontinuity hypothesis. It is thus necessary to ask a fundamental question: Is the production of sounds not belonging to the child's target language an indicator of chaos, that is, lack of phonological organization? In other words, does the presence of such sounds in babbling imply that the phonological component of the lexicon develops according to its own dynamics and runs independently from babbling, that it is formally and functionally separated from it?

A crosslinguistic study is presented here in order to examine the question of the universality versus language specificity of babbling. With this study, a contribution is made to the continuity issue from the point of view of the "Principles and Parameters" model. In this view, children have access to grammatical rules and primitive symbols of the same type as adults do. Continuity thus lies in the qualitative nature of the linguistic abilities, in the formal nature of grammatical rules and representations, and in the way of realizing these in comprehension and production (Pinker, 1984, p. 7f). Under this assumption, the child's intermediate grammars will not fall outside the variation range allowed by the principles of Universal Grammar (UG; Carreira, 1991, p. 4). Accordingly, the child has access to general principles of UG, some of which leave several options open—the so-called parameters—which are then set along the values of the input language. For a more detailed description of the model and some of its applications to syntactic acquisition, see, for instance, Chomsky (1981), Flynn (1987), and Roeper and Williams (1987).

This model was mainly proposed for and has mostly been tested within the syntax. In the realm of phonology there have been some proposals that have been more or less worked out: on the syllable (Kaye, 1989), on autosegmentalization of features (Goldsmith, 1979), on underspecification (Clements, 1985), as well as other parameters related to suprasegmentals, such as stress (Dresher & Kaye, 1990; Halle & Vergnaud, 1987). The present chapter concentrates on parameters relating to phonological feature hierarchy, to spreading of phonological features, and to the structure of the syllable at the transition from babbling to the first words. Having the continuity issue as the background point of reference, two kinds of hypotheses should be tested: (a) Within a universal grammatical-theoretical continuity view, children are expected to acquire only those aspects of *language* allowed by the principles of UG (Carreira, 1991; Pinker, 1984), and (b) a language-specific interpretation of the continuity assumption implies that there must be signs of the target *languages* in the early grammars (de Boysson-Bardies & Vihman, 1991; Vihman et al., 1985).

According to this interpretation of continuity, early sound production will contain sounds and sound structures determined by the principles of UG and then be subject to parameterization, provided that the setting of a certain parameter is allowed by the corresponding stage of development of a particular child. Consequently, babbling and early words should manifest universal characteristics shared by the utterances produced by all children, independently of the target language and stemming from UG, and they should progressively contain language-specific characteristics determined by the target language. According to the hypotheses defended in this chapter, these two aspects should have a different weight in babbling and early words, babbling being more directly controlled by universal principles and words involving a higher degree of parameterization. However, notice that both aspects should be present in both utterance forms, and that the difference is a matter of degree rather than one that is qualitative. If these hypotheses are verified, continuity in its theoretical-grammatical-universal and in its language-specific interpretation will be confirmed.

This chapter makes an empirical as well as a theoretical contribution. On the one hand, research on the transition from babbling to speech is given a larger empirical basis, because crosslinguistic German and Spanish developmental data corresponding to such an early age have never been analyzed before. On the other hand, the chapter makes a contribution to the theoretical body on phonological acquisition by reflecting on the continuity issue, in the sense briefly discussed above.

METHOD

The analysis is based on a longitudinal investigation of five children acquiring German in Hamburg and four children acquiring Spanish in Madrid.[1] The investigation began when the children were between 8 and 9 months of age. The German infants were audio recorded twice a month in their homes using a high-fidelity Sony TCD-D10 PRO cassette recorder and a portable Beyerdynamic microphone concealed in a vest that the children wore. The Spanish infants were both audio and video recorded once a month with a Panasonic video camera, and the same audio equipment used for the German children.

[1]This research was supported by a grant of the German Science Foundation *(Deutsche Forschungsgemeinschaft)* to Lleó (Ll 3/2–1). We thank the children and their parents, our Spanish colleagues Théophile Ambadiang, Juana Gil, Eugenia Sebastián, Pilar Soto, and Margarita Vidal, who registered the Spanish data, and the students responsible for the transcription, namely Marianne Brockmann, Alexandra Döring, Thorsten Frahm, Susann Oberacker, and Rolf Oechsler. The exchange with the Spanish colleagues was sponsored by a grant of the DAAD (AZ 322-AI-e-dr).

The infants were all recorded in unstructured play sessions with the mother and one investigator. In the German sessions, the situational context was noted by a second investigator. Both the German and the Spanish recordings were transcribed by the German research team. Each session was transcribed by at least two trained phoneticians by means of IPA (International Phonetic Association, 1989) symbols, using Revox B215 recorders. IPA symbols were complemented according to the suggestions made by Bush, Edwards, Luckau, Stoel, Macken, and Petersen (1973), and by further signs designed for the purpose of this project. Segments that could not be agreed on for transcription were discarded.

Six sessions for each child were chosen for analysis, corresponding to the following points:

1. babbling only (age 0;9)
2. babbling only (age 0;10)
3. at least 1 word type (age 0;11 to 1;1)
4. at least 4 word types (age 1;0 to 1;5)
5. at least 15 word types (age 1;3 to 1;6)
6. at least 25 word types (age 1;4 to 1;8)

These points coincide in part with those set up by de Boysson-Bardies and Vihman (1991). Thus, our results are, to a high degree, comparable with their crosslinguistic investigation, which encompassed English, French, Japanese, and Swedish. The present study adds two more language groups not included in the database they examined.

The data were submitted to frequency counts of laryngeals, place and manner of supralaryngeal consonants and syllable structure (branching of rhymes). All calculations were done for words and babble separately.

Because the identification of words produced at such an early age may not be straightforward, it is appropriate to refer to the criteria applied. In general, the decision that a particular word had been produced was based on Menn (1978, pp. 21–26) and Vihman and McCune (1994). Menn's minimal requirement consists of the recurrent association of a sound pattern and a meaning, although both may exhibit a certain degree of variation; she thus further requires that a "well-behaved word" be "phonetically consistent" and "semantically coherent" (p. 24). Vihman and McCune (1994) complemented Menn's proposal by trying to formulate an operational method based on more precise requirements, such as the existence of a "determinative context," as well as usage in multiple situations and identification by the mother. Phonetic criteria are also considered necessary, such as a certain degree of phonetic similarity to the target word. In our analyses, an utterance had to satisfy most of these criteria in order to qualify as a word. Imitations—utterances produced immediately after an adult model was provided—were not considered for analysis, except for the additional help they might have supplied to the identification of particular words. So-called "proto-words," like onomatopoetic expressions and imitations of animal sounds, have been included in the analysis, although here the criteria just discussed, especially the phonetic ones, had to be applied in a loose way.

The results presented and discussed later (Figs. 1.1–1.5) show the average language group values for each of the six points listed earlier, thus giving information on the development over time. To test statistical significance, variance measures (two-tailed student-t tests) were conducted on three scores (Tables 1.1–1.2): for babbling, the first and second points (abbreviated B); for the word phase, the fifth point (W1) and the sixth point (W2). They are listed here for ease of reference:

B   babbling only (points 1 and 2)
W1   words from point 5 (15 words)
W2   words from point 6 (25 words)

Probability values were determined on the basis of the percentages for these three scores, calculated separately for German and Spanish. The value $p \leq .05$ will be considered as significant, $p \leq .1$ as marginally significant and $p \leq .01$ as highly significant.

RESULTS

Tables 1.1 and 1.2 contain a summary of the results regarding the distribution of laryngeals, place and manner of supralaryngeal consonants, and closed syllables for the German and Spanish infants, respectively. The values for laryngeals and supralaryngeals are complementary: Both categories together sum up to the total of consonants produced by each group. The class of Fricatives refers to fricatives and approximants. The category Spirants represents an additional subclass under Manner, selected out of fricatives (and approximants), its values being already included within this category. The points illustrated in the tables—B, W1 and W2, correspond to those considered for statistical analyses.

Laryngeals

Besides the information on laryngeals [h] and [ʔ] presented in terms of percentages in Tables 1.1 and 1.2, Fig. 1.1 illustrates their longitudinal development. Here, too, the percentages were calculated out of all consonants produced at each point. In the babbling productions, the Spanish values (B = 33.2%) are higher than the German ones (B = 21.7%), although the intergroup difference is not significant ($p = .185$). In the word data, the Spanish values are also higher than the German ones: At W1 laryngeals reach 16.8% in Spanish and 14.7% in German; at W2 they reach 20.6% in Spanish and 18% in German. Neither of

TABLE 1.1
Summary of the German Data: Numbers and Percentages of Laryngeals, Place and Manner of Supralaryngeals, and Closed Syllables at the Three Statistically Relevant Points (Babbling, 15 Words, 25 Words)

		B		W1		W2	
		n	%	n	%	n	%
	Laryngeals	678	21.7	121	14.7	277	18
SUPRALARYNGEALS Place	Labials	770	29.3	256	40.4	741	48.8
	Coronals	1174	45.2	288	34.1	461	39.2
	Palatals	407	13.4	24	4.0	82	4.0
	Velars	208	7.5	69	10.4	83	6.3
SUPRALARYNGEALS Manner	Stops	1276	50.3	418	63.4	791	56.2
	Fricatives	546	20.3	94	14.6	228	15.0
	Nasals	531	18.5	126	19.7	345	22.5
	Liquids	289	8.4	10	1.9	76	5.4
	Spirants	169	6.1	55	8.6	90	6.5
	Closed syllables	224	12.1	75	14.4	179	17.6

TABLE 1.2
Summary of the Spanish Data: Numbers and Percentages of Laryngeals, Place and Manner of Supralaryngeals, and Closed Syllables for the Three Statistically Relevant Points (Babbling, 15 Words, 25 Words)

		B		W1		W2	
		n	%	n	%	n	%
	Laryngeals	800	33.2	77	16.8	192	20.6
SUPRALARYNGEALS Place	Labials	719	40.4	218	37.1	257	35.8
	Coronals	554	31.5	94	29.2	198	34.7
	Palatals	177	10.4	34	14.2	73	10.9
	Velars	339	17.1	64	19.5	107	17.6
SUPRALARYNGEALS Manner	Stops	564	30.6	115	41.9	393	48.4
	Fricatives	631	34.2	72	29.2	149	23.2
	Nasals	327	20.2	102	21.0	166	23.1
	Liquids	243	14.2	17	4.1	27	7.7
	Spirants	342	19.2	50	11.4	85	11.9
	Closed syllables	168	11.0	17	4.0	16	2.4

German children

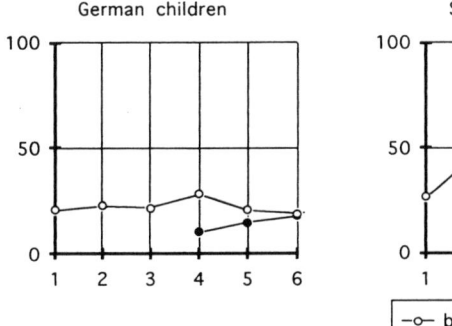

Spanish children

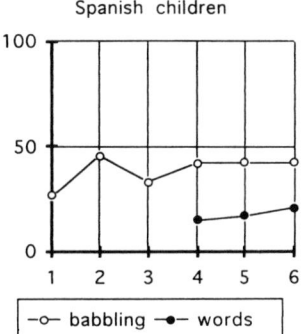

─○─ babbling ─●─ words

FIG. 1.1. Percentages of laryngeals out of all consonants produced at each point.

these intergroup differences is significant, however: $p = .463$ for W1 and $p = .868$ for W2. This lack of significance at all points, in spite of the higher values exhibited by the Spanish children as a group, is due to very high within-group variability, especially within the Spanish data.

A comparison of the babbling and word curves shows a parallel development, especially in the Spanish data: Here at point 3, as the first words appear with a very low level of laryngeals (4.7%), the percentage of laryngeals in babbling drops from 42.2% to 31.3%; both values rise in a parallel fashion, up to 20.6% for words at point 6 and 42.7% for babbling at that same point. In the German data there is a certain parallelism, displaced in time, in the sense that the percentage of laryngeals shows an increasing tendency in the first babbling sessions, as well as in the first word sessions; as soon as words make their appearance, however, the parallelism ceases, laryngeals decreasing in babbling from 28.2% at point 4 to 19.1% at point 6.

Place of Articulation

Supralaryngeal consonants were classified into the categories labial, coronal, palatal, and velar. The results are given in the tables, and by means of line graphs in Fig. 1.2. For purposes of clarity the latter does not include palatals. In the babbling of both language groups, the palatal and velar consonants are less frequent than the coronals and labials. Coronals are more frequent in German babbling (B = 45.2%) than in Spanish babbling (B = 31.5%); this difference is not significant ($p = .192$). On the other hand, labials are more productive in Spanish babbling (B = 40.4%) than in German babbling (B = 29.3%), but this difference is not significant either ($p = .562$). As regards velars, the Spanish infants produce more segments and a higher percentage (B = 17.1%) than the German ones (B = 7.5%), although this is not a significant difference either

Babbling

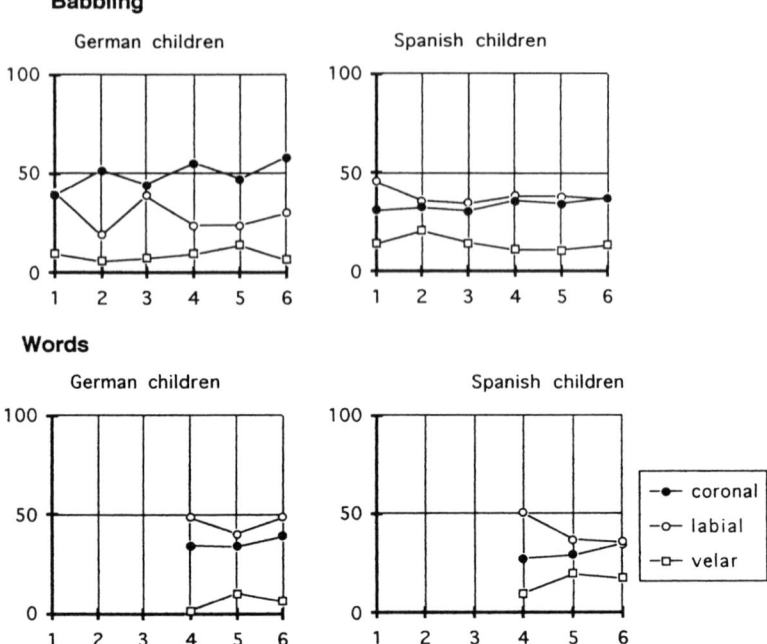

FIG. 1.2. Place of articulation for supralaryngeal consonants: Percentages of coronals, labials and velars along the time axis.

($p = .454$). The minor intergroup difference in palatals is not significant either ($p = .419$); here, the percentages are slightly higher for the German infants (B = 13.4%) than for the Spanish (B = 10.4%).

From babbling to words, the German data show an increase in labials at W1 (40.4%) as well as at W2 (48.8%). This tendency correlates with a general decrease in coronals, as compared with the general tendency in babbling. Nevertheless, within words coronals increase slightly, from 34.1% at W1 to 39.2% at W2. This makes labials the most frequent place of articulation category for words. The Spanish word productions show opposite results as far as labials are concerned: They decrease, from 37.1% at W1 to 35.8% at W2. The values for coronals increase from W1 (29.2%) to W2 (34.7%), although they are lower than those for labials at all points. Consequently, Labial is to be regarded as the most frequent articulation place in Spanish babbling, as well as in the word production of both language groups. There is no significant intergroup difference observed for coronals at W1 ($p = .519$) nor at W2 ($p = .642$). There is none for labials either, at W1 ($p = .932$) nor at W2 ($p = .202$). As regards velars, the values for the Spanish group are always higher than those for the German group, in babbling as well as in words. At W1, the values of both groups increase, to 19.5% in

Spanish and to 10.4% in German, and at W2 they diminish to 17.6% in Spanish and to 6.3% in German. The production of velars does not exhibit a significant difference at W1 (p = .324), but it does at W2, the Spanish being significantly higher than the German (p = .052). The percentages for palatals are also higher within the Spanish word data, reaching 14.2% at W1 and 10.9% at W2; in German palatals reach only 4%, both at W1 and at W2. These intergroup differences are not significant (p = .613 at W1 and p = .448 at W2).

Manner of Articulation

The analysis of articulation manner refers to the categories stops, fricatives, nasals, and liquids. Laryngeals are not included, because they have been considered separately at the beginning of this section. Affricates, with few representatives, have been counted together with the stops, because of their noncontinuant onset. The class of fricatives includes that of approximants. The results are given in the tables, as well as by means of developmental line graphs in Fig. 1.3. The

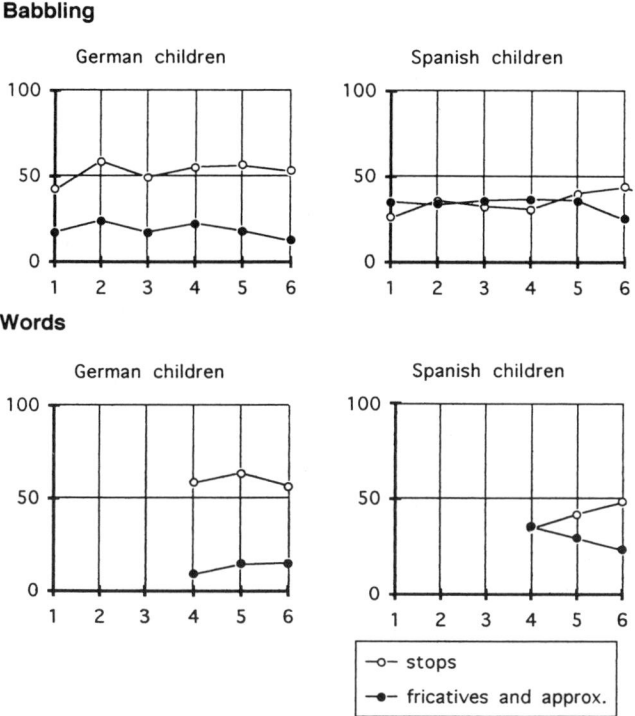

FIG. 1.3. Manner of articulation for supralaryngeal consonants: Percentages of stops and fricatives plus approximants along the time axis.

German data corroborate the high values generally reported for stops, which represent the most frequent manner of articulation in infant speech (cf. de Boysson-Bardies & Vihman, 1991). In our German data, they reach 50.3% in babbling, before they rise to 63.4% at W1 and to 56.2% at W2. In the Spanish data, however, the proportion of stops is much lower, reaching 30.6% in babbling, followed by an increase to 41.9% at W1 and to 48.4% at W2. The difference between the Spanish and the German values for stops is marginally significant for babbling ($p = .075$), significant for W1 ($p = .044$), and marginally significant again for W2 ($p = .102$).

There is an inverse relationship between the values for stops and those for fricatives and approximants: The developmental values of fricatives and approximants are much higher at all points for the Spanish infants (B = 34.2%) than for the German ones (B = 20.3%); they diminish in the German group at W1 (14.6%) and at W2 (15%), whereas in the Spanish group the values decrease successively from 29.2% at W1 to 23.2% at W2. The intergroup difference reaches high significance in B ($p = .001$) and no significance at W1 ($p = .149$) or at W2 ($p = .230$).

A comparison of the babbling and word curves for stops and for fricatives plus approximants shows a fully parallel development. German children produce a much higher percentage of stops than fricatives plus approximants, both in babbling and in words at all points, the values remaining rather stable all along the curves. Spanish children produce similar percentages of stops and of fricatives plus approximants, both in babbling and in words. Starting at point 5 (at the 15-word point), stops exhibit a slightly increasing tendency, whereas fricatives plus approximants have a decreasing one, and this, too, runs in an almost identical fashion in babbling and words. Moreover, the word curves can be described as a subset of the babbling curves, both in German and Spanish.

As is well known, Spanish has a spirantization process, which roughly predicts that voiced obstruents [b, d, g] become [β, ð, γ] medially, if not preceded by a nasal, or by [l] in the case of [d]. To find out whether the high values for fricatives and approximants in the Spanish data were related to the spirantization process of the Spanish target language, those phones that could be realizations of [b, d, g], namely [β, w, v, ð, γ], were extracted from the approximants and fricatives, and their frequencies were examined in both language groups. The results are given in Tables 1.1 and 1.2 under the heading Spirants, and in Fig. 1.4. The consonants [β, w, v, ð, γ] are more frequent in the Spanish data (B = 19.2%, W1 = 11.4%, W2 = 11.9%) than in the German data (B = 6.1%, W1 = 8.6%, W2 = 6.5%). The intergroup differences are significant for babbling ($p = .035$), not significant for W1 ($p = .550$) and significant again for W2 ($p = .06$).

With respect to nasals, the Spanish values are slightly higher than the German ones: B = 20.2%, W1 = 21%, W2 = 23.1% for Spanish, and B = 18.5%, W1 = 19.7%, W2 = 22.5% for German. None of these intergroup differences are statistically significant. As for liquids, the percentages are in general very low,

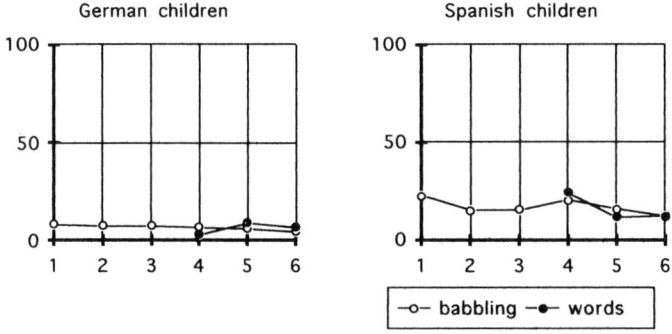

FIG. 1.4. Percentages of spirant consonants [w, v, β, δ, γ] reported from all supralaryngeals produced at each point.

but again higher in Spanish than in German: B = 14.2, W1 = 4.1, W2 = 7.7 for Spanish, and B = 8.4, W1 = 1.9, W2 = 5.4 for German. The intergroup difference in B is significant ($p = .046$), but not at W1 ($p = .501$) or at W2 ($p = .973$).

Syllable Structure: Closed Syllables

The number and percentages of closed syllables are shown in the tables. The percentages were calculated out of all syllables produced. Figure 1.5 illustrates the developmental curves. Although both German and Spanish children exhibit much higher values for open syllables than for closed ones, there is an increasing difference between the two groups, with diverging development: In babbling, the values for closed syllables in German (B = 12.1%) and in Spanish (B = 11%) are quite similar before a constant increase takes place in German, with 14.4% at W1 and 17.6% at W2. In Spanish, the values for closed syllables decrease at W1

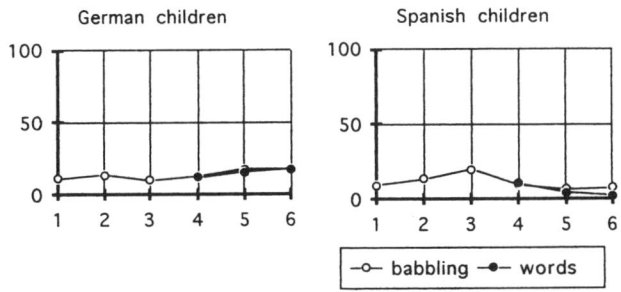

FIG 1.5. Percentages of closed syllables out of all syllables produced at each point.

(4.1%) and at W2 (2.4%). The overall averages give no significant intergroup differences at B ($p = .349$), but a marginal significance at W1 ($p = .103$) and a highly significant value at W2 ($p = .001$).

DISCUSSION

Laryngeals

German has two laryngeals, among which [h] exhibits phonemic status and [ʔ] has only the function of occupying otherwise empty onsets, whereas Spanish has no laryngeals, either phonemically or phonetically.[2] Thus, adult-language influence on babbling and early words should manifest itself in high values for laryngeals in the German data and low ones in the Spanish data; in fact, this is not the case. On the contrary, the average for laryngeals is even higher in Spanish than in German at every point (B, W1, and W2), the intergroup differences not being significant, however, as pointed out in the Results section.

In this domain, no correlation between the adult language and infant sound production can be found. Extensive use of laryngeals is rather a universal feature of infant speech, especially in babbling (see Locke, 1983; Vihman et al., 1985). In word production, laryngeals are less frequent than in babbling, but here again the frequency of production is very similar in both groups and does not reflect a characteristic of the ambient language. If it did, Spanish children should not produce any laryngeals at all. Our finding is comparable to that of Vihman (1992, p. 400), who found [ha] and [he] to be among the most frequent syllables produced by French infants at the 0-word point, even though the target language does not contain laryngeals.

The reason for the universally high number of laryngeals in infant speech has been sought in the physiological correlates of vegetative breathing and, phonetically speaking, aspiration (see Locke, 1983, p. 43). These proposals confront two main difficulties: In the babbling as well as in the word data, laryngeals are produced either with constricted glottis or with spread glottis; the percentage of laryngeals produced with constricted glottis reaches 62.9% in German babbling and 43.2% in Spanish babbling. It is difficult to relate breathing and aspiration to a constriction in the glottis. Moreover, in words, laryngeals appear either as substitutes for a supralaryngeal consonant, or as fillers of an otherwise empty onset, especially in the Spanish data. Even if the vegetative phonetic explanation were to hold for babbling, it does not contribute any insights into the word stage.

The capability of these proposals to account for the data will have to await future interdisciplinary research. At present, without rejecting attempts at harmo-

---

[2]The only surface occurrence of a glottal stop in Spanish can sporadically take place in absolute initial position in very emphatic speech and when articulating at a high intensity level, as when shouting or calling loudly to somebody.

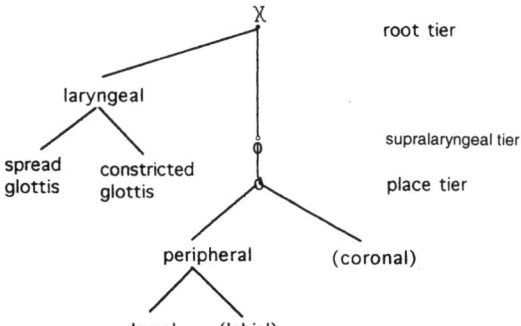

FIG. 1.6. Feature geometry based on Rice (1992).

nizing the physiological and the linguistic hypotheses, we will concentrate on a plausible linguistic explanation, in the following terms. The high number of laryngeals at the initial stages of sound production marks the starting point of a clear tendency for phonological development to proceed from the less complex or unmarked elements to the more complex or marked ones (Carreira, 1991; Rice, 1992, p. 64). The hierarchical representation of features in Fig. 1.6 shows that the phonological structure of laryngeals is the simplest of all consonants: Laryngeals are not specified for place or for any other supralaryngeal feature. Only the features [constricted glottis] versus [spread glottis] are needed to differentiate between /ʔ/ and /h/, but only under the assumption of a distinctive opposition. In Spanish, where there is no adult model to provide a distinction between the glottals [ʔ] and [h], the difference is just fortuitous, as the comparable percentages for [ʔ] (43.2%) versus [h] (56.8%) manifest.

We assume that in the feature representation of Fig. 1.6 depth of embedding in the tree reflects the accessibility of a given feature for acquisition. Thus, laryngeal features, being the least deeply embedded, are also the most accessible to the infant acquiring the phonology of a language. Further, for the early word stage, we assume that lexical items receive less specification in the children's output lexicon than in the adults' lexicon (Iverson & Wheeler, 1987). This simplified representation of lexical items obeys several constraints: (a) acquisition constraints, since many features have not yet been activated, and (b) psycholinguistic contraints, based on memory load and limited storage capacities. If a segment associated with a C-position on the skeletal tier is not specified for any consonantal feature, it will receive the universally simplest specification, that is, [laryngeal], per default.[3] Consequently, the interaction of underspecification and a certain geometrical representation of features explains that German and Spanish children produce a similar proportion of laryngeal consonants at the beginning of

---

[3]There is a lot of synchronic as well as diachronic evidence in favor of the default status of laryngeals. A phonological process by which supraglottal features are delinked and only the remaining laryngeal features are associated to a C-node appears in the historical development of many languages, such as English and Greek. It is known as *debuccalization* (Clements, 1985, p. 233).

the word stage. Later on, as children activate more feature specifications and overcome constraints leading to underspecification, two different developments are predicted: Spanish children will progressively abandon laryngeals, whereas German children will only abandon the ones corresponding to default, but will keep the laryngeals specified as such in the input words, as well as those aimed at filling empty onsets.

A comparative analysis of the babbling and word curves (Fig. 1.1) gives substance to the claim made in the introductory section that babbling is more directly constrained by universal principles than word production. This is manifested by the higher laryngeal curves in babbling, which is especially clear in the Spanish data showing a significantly higher proportion of laryngeals at B than at W1 ($p = .0267$). In German, the higher proportion of laryngeals at B than at W1 is not significant ($p = .2238$), and the babbling curve converges with the word curve, exhibiting an influence of words on babbling.

Place of Articulation

The hierarchy of place features frequencies in the German babbling data once more reflects the view that phonological development proceeds step by step from simpler to more complex elements, that is, from less embedded features to more deeply embedded ones. Drawing on a large body of literature (see, for instance, Paradis & Prunet, 1991), we assume Coronal to be the simplest or unmarked articulator. In other words, once a segment is specified for some supralaryngeal node, it has to be assigned the Place node; and if it is not specified for any particular articulator under Place, it is automatically defined as Coronal. This is usually taken as the default place node, followed by the unmarked peripheral node Labial; the more marked peripheral place node Dorsal is the least frequent. However, one German child and three of the four Spanish subjects produced more labials than coronals in babbling. This variation does not seem to be language specific, but rather an individual factor, as the frequencies of labials and coronals in the German and Spanish adult languages hardly differ from one another (see Table 1.3). How, then, can we explain this apparent deviation from the universal sequencing of features?

Before answering this question, let us turn to the word data. Here all subjects, except one Spanish child, produced more labials than in babbling. This preference for labials in early word production parallels the findings of de Boysson-Bardies and Vihman (1991) for French, English, Japanese, and Swedish (see also Montes Giraldo, 1970, for Spanish). In our Spanish data, the stronger preference for labials in words is less striking than in the German data, due to the already very high values of labials in the Spanish babbling.

The assumption that in phonological acquisition Coronal is the first activated Place node, followed by Labial, provides an explanation for the high proportions of labials at the early word stage. During late babbling, Coronal is activated,

TABLE 1.3

Proportion of Articulation Places and Manners in German According to Ortmann (1975) and in Spanish According to Quillis and Esgueva (1980)

	German	Spanish
Coronal	68.7%	69.3%
Labial	15.7%	16.8%
Velar	8.1%	11.1%
Palatal	5.6%	2.7%
Stop	31.5%	37.1%
Fricative	27.3%	21.6%
Nasal	23.2%	20.9%
Liquid	17.6%	19.5%

whereas the production of early words coincides with the point at which Labial is activated. This leads to a high proportion of labials involved in the production of the first words. Most data on early word production provide independent evidence that Coronal is the default articulator for most infants, even though some might prefer Labial. At a later stage in phonological acquisition, the default function that some infants might have attributed to labial is abandoned, since in the corresponding target languages, German and Spanish, only coronal functions as default. Arguing thoroughly in favor of this last claim would go beyond the purpose of this chapter. We will simply back our claim by means of two relevant observations. In German, if there are two or more obstruents after a vowel, at least the last one has to be coronal (Moulton, 1956). In Spanish, the consonants available for the coda position are almost exclusively coronal.[4]

As stated earlier, velar and palatal consonants are rare with respect to the other articulation places at all sampling points. This is to be seen as good evidence for the status of coronals and labials as less marked for place, whereas velars and palatals are more marked. Our results confirm this universal tendency. On the other hand, the proportions of velars are higher for the Spanish data than for the German data at all points, resulting in statistical significance at W2. This signifi-

---

[4]In general, codas in Spanish are either coronal—liquids [l] and [r] as well as the nasal [n] and the strident [s]—or share the point of articulation of the following obstruent, as is the case for nasals, which attain their articulation place by leftwards spreading. Interestingly, underlying /p/ and /k/ are dialectally produced as [θ] in connected speech, in large areas of Castilla and León. This phenomenon is already documented in Cuervo (1898, pp. 305–306). The obvious generalization underlying these facts is that codas in Spanish, at least in certain dialects, do not license any place features, provided that coronal is unspecified.

cant difference is to be attributed to the different proportions that these articulation places have in the target languages. As listed in Table 1.3, Spanish has more velars than German. Accordingly, velars support both (a) the universal aspect of continuity via unmarkedness, by being less frequent than coronals and labials, *and* (b) continuity as influence of the target language, by being more frequent in Spanish than in German. With regard to palatals, the higher percentage they exhibit in the target language German, according to Table 1.3, is not reflected in the data: The proportions of palatals are higher for the Spanish infants than for the German ones at the early word stage; no significant intergroup difference was found.

Manner of Articulation

In infant as well as adult language, stops are universally the most frequent category of articulation manner (see de Boysson-Bardies & Vihman, 1991). This tendency is reflected in the German data, but not in the Spanish. Compared to the German group, the latter show significantly lower values for stops, corresponding to significantly higher values for fricatives and approximants. The Spanish data contain similar percentages for stops and for fricatives plus approximants.

An explanation for the Spanish children's deviation from the universal trend can be found in the spirantization process in Spanish, which applies to voiced obstruents: [b, d, g] become [β, ð, ɣ] after [+cont] segments. Spanish voiced obstruents are lexically unspecified for the feature [cont] and the specification is given by spreading from the preceding segment (see, for instance, Harris, 1984). This represents a fundamental phonological difference from German voiced stops, which are lexically specified for [cont]. As shown in the Results section, there is a direct reflection of spirantization in the higher percentages of Spirants in the Spanish data. It was pointed out there that the higher values for Spanish spirants over German spirants are statistically significant at B and at W2. The high number of fricatives and approximants in Spanish, especially [β, w, v, ð, ɣ], is to be seen as evidence that, in this case, there is indeed an influence of the ambient language on infant sound production: Supposing that the spreading of [cont] in Spanish is controlled by a parameter in the sense of Clements (1985, p. 247)—that is, by defining, in a language L, which features are left unspecified—this parameter is already beginning to be set at the babbling stage.

Nasals are the second most frequent consonantal category in the German data, ranging after the stops at the word phase, whereas in Spanish they range after the fricatives at all points, and thus constitute the third most frequent category. The proportions of nasals do not differ essentially between both sets of data, and an intergroup comparison shows no statistical significance, which has to be attributed to the similar percentages they exhibit in both target languages (see Table 1.3). In both data sets, their proportion grows slightly, in a constant way, and there is thus no tradeoff with the stops. That is, in both language groups, the increase in stops implies a reduction of fricatives, but no reduction of nasals. This is a relevant point for the definition of manner features. Although a treatment of these features is beyond the scope of this chapter, the data suggest that stops and nasals should share some manner feature, specifically, noncontinuancy, to identify them as a class and separate them from the fricatives.

Syllable Structure: Closed Syllables

Under the hypothesis of adult language influence, we would expect higher values for closed syllables in German than in Spanish infant productions according to Meinhold and Stock (1980), who found out that 67% of German syllables end in a consonant, compared to only 26.5% in Spanish. Furthermore, German allows codas in a basically unrestricted way, while Spanish codas are phonologically highly restricted (see footnote 4). On the other hand, we should not expect closed syllables to be produced at all at the earliest stages of phonological acquisition, as the universally unmarked syllable type is [CV], and the closed syllable structure is generally acquired later (see, e.g., Branigan, 1976; Kent & Bauer, 1985; Lleó, 1986; Vihman, 1992). In fact, closed syllables occur rarely in both data groups. This is especially clear at B, where the proportions of open syllables are comparably high in both groups, reaching the highest value of all three points in German. Closed syllables are significantly more frequent in the German data— especially in word production. Spanish children produce fewer closed syllables, because their input of closed syllables is far less frequent. German children, being exposed to a language with a dominance of closed syllables, integrate this trait of their ambient language in their babbling and early words, although the production of closed syllables is far from reaching the proportion found in the adult language. Consequently, the values for closed syllables increase successively from point to point in the German data.

The incorporation of the data from 1;8 to 2;0 into the study of syllable structure confirms the results obtained in early word production, as can be seen in Fig. 1.7, where the values for closed syllables are clearly higher in German than in Spanish, leading to a highly significant result ($p = .004$). From 1;8 to 1;9 there is a slightly decreasing tendency in both language groups, and from 1;9 to 1;10 the percentages grow in a parallel fashion. From this point on the German children tend to produce increasingly more closed syllables than the Spanish children. These results suggest that the syllabic parameter that controls the branching of the rhyme is already set at the end of the second year of age, a conclusion confirmed by our further work on correct cluster realization (Lleó & Prinz, in press).

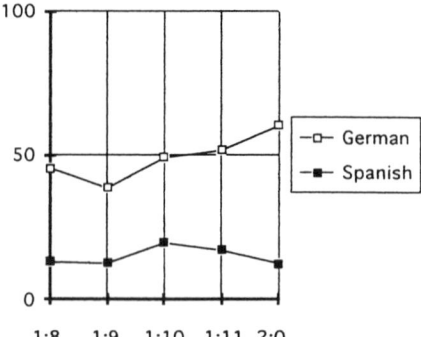

FIG. 1.7. Percentages of closed syllables in later word production from 1;8 to 2;0.

SUMMARY

The developmental study of feature acquisition and closed syllables in babbling and early word production, as presented here, has brought about a refinement of the continuity hypothesis as a twofold question. On the one hand, continuity relates to universally predetermined ordering of acquisition. On the other, continuity implies target language convergent parameterization. Acquisition of phonological features as well as of syllabic structure has been shown to proceed from unspecified elements to more specified ones. In the domain of the structure of phonological features, the universally unmarked feature is the one first acquired and most frequently produced in child language: The unmarked place feature is coronal, an observation also made for the adult language. This is also the feature most frequently produced in babbling. Labials are far more frequent than the other peripheral feature, dorsal: Their frequent activation in the phonological component coincides with the beginning of the word stage. This hierarchy is also predicted from the representation of segment structure offered in Rice (1992, p. 62). Stops are universally supposed to be the most frequent manner of articulation in infant speech. However, only the German infants reflect this universal tendency, whereas Spanish infants produce a large number of fricatives and approximants.

In the domain of syllable structure, it is obvious that, according to our data, the default syllable type consists of one prevocalic consonant and one vowel, that is, CV. This observation is compatible with statements made within metrical phonology, where CV is regarded as the core syllable. Subsequently, closed syllables are introduced in the German productions at a much faster rate than in the Spanish productions, which supports the early setting of the rhyme parameter in German, in a target-language converging fashion.

In some cases, we find traits characteristic of early child sound production deviating from the target language. Laryngeals have to be mentioned here. They are very frequent in Spanish babbling, although the target language does not contain them. This is not surprising, because laryngeals are the least marked segments: In contrast to other consonants they are not specified for place or any other supralaryngeal feature. This is thus in accordance with the continuity assumption stated in terms of UG, which determines the ordering of acquisition from less marked to more marked, and from less specified to more specified.

In yet other cases, parameters specific for the ambient language are already beginning to exert an influence on infant production. The Spanish children make use of many fricatives and approximants, which have to be related to the spirantization rule of the adult language; that is, they have to be attributed to the influence of the ambient language already operating at the babbling stage. Also due to a language specific factor is the higher number of closed syllables in German than in Spanish babbling, and early words. These traits are in accordance with the language-specific continuity assumption, which predicts a convergent development to the target language.

In summary, our results allow a distinction between those aspects of early sound production due to continuity in the sense of UG and those aspects due to continuity in the sense of target language convergence. Some aspects of early sound production not relatable to target language influence might be seen as discontinuous from a pretheoretical perspective. This concerns the production of laryngeals by Spanish infants. In fact, as pointed out in the course of the discussion, these traits have to be viewed as continuous in the sense of universal grammatical continuity; that is, they are explainable as a direct application of phonological principles, before parameterization takes place. Accordingly, laryngeals are produced as the simplest segments, lacking any feature specification. As a result of the analyses presented here the two interpretations of continuity that we posited in the introduction—universal grammatical and language-specific continuity—are elucidated and lie on a well-founded empirical base.

REFERENCES

de Boysson-Bardies, B., Hallé, P. A., Sagart, L., & Durand, C. (1989). A crosslinguistic investigation of vowel formants in babbling. *Journal of Child Language, 16,* 1–17.

de Boysson-Bardies, B., & Vihman, M. M. (1991). Adaptation to language: Evidence from babbling and first words in four languages. *Language, 67,* 297–319.

Branigan, G. (1976). Syllabic structure and the acquisition of consonants: The great conspiracy in word formation. *Journal of Psycholinguistic Research, 5,* 117–133.

Bush, C., Edwards, M. L., Luckau, J. M., Stoel, C., Macken, M., & Petersen, J. (1973). *On specifying a system for transcribing consonants in child language: A working paper with examples from American English and Mexican Spanish.* Stanford, CA: Stanford University, Child Language Project.

Carreira, M. (1991). The acquisition of Spanish syllable structure. In D. Wanner & D. A. Kibbel (Eds.), *New analyses in Romance linguistics* (pp. 3–18). Amsterdam: John Benjamins.

Chomsky, N. (1981). *Lectures on government and binding.* Dordrecht: Foris.

Clements, G. (1985). The geometry of phonological features. *Phonology Yearbook, 3,* 225–252.

Cuervo, R. J. (1898). Disquisiciones sobre antigua ortografía y pronunciación castellanas, II [Comments on old Castilian orthography and pronunciation]. *Revue Hispanique, V,* 273–313.

Dresher, B. E., & Kaye, J. (1990). A computational learning model for metrical phonology. *Cognition, 34,* 137–195.

Flynn, S. (1987). *A parameter setting model of L2 acquisition. Experimental studies in anaphora.* Dordrecht: D. Reidel.

Goldsmith, J. (1979). The aims of autosegmental phonology. In D. Dinnsen (Ed.), *Current approaches to phonological theory* (pp. 202–223). Bloomington: Indiana University Press.

Halle, M., & Vergnaud, J.-R. (1987). *An essay on stress.* Cambridge, MA: MIT Press.

Harris, J. W. (1984). La espirantización en castellano y la representación fonológica autosegmental [Spirantization in Spanish and autosegmental phonological representation]. In *Estudis Gramaticals 1. Working Papers in Linguistics* (pp. 149–167). Bellaterra, Spain: Universitat Autònoma de Barcelona.

International Phonetic Association (1989). Report on the Kiel Convention. *Journal of the International Phonetic Association, 19,* 67–80.

Iverson, G., & Wheeler, D. (1987). Hierarchical structures in child phonology. *Lingua, 73,* 243–257.

Jakobson, R. (1941). *Kindersprache, Aphasie und allgemeine Lautgesetze* [Child language, aphasia, and phonological universals]. Uppsala, Sweden: Almqvist & Wiksell.

Kaye, J. D. (1989). *Phonology: A cognitive view.* Hillsdale, NJ: Lawrence Erlbaum Associates.

Kent, R., & Bauer, H., (1985). Vocalizations of one-year-olds. *Journal of Child Language, 13,* 491–526.

Levitt, A., & Utman, J., (1992). From babbling towards the sound system of English and French: A longitudinal two-case study. *Journal of Child Language, 19,* 19–49.

Lleó, C. (1986). The evolution of syllabic structure as an example of the interaction between universal restrictions and individual strategies in first language acquisition. In M. Brame, H. Contreras, & F. Newmeyer (Eds.), *A Festschrift for Sol Saporta* (pp. 275–288). Seattle: N. Amrofer.

Lleó, C., & Prinz, M. (in press). Consonant clusters in child phonology and the directionality of syllable structure assignment. *Journal of Child Language, 23.*

Locke, J. L. (1983). *Phonological acquisition and change.* New York: Harcourt Brace.

Meinhold, G., & Stock, E. (1980). *Phonologie der deutschen Gegenwartssprache* [Phonology of the German language]. Leipzig: Bibliographisches Institut.

Menn, L. (1978). *Pattern, control, and contrast in beginning speech: A case study in the development of word form and word function.* Bloomington, IN: Indiana University Linguistics Club.

Montes Giraldo, J. J. (1970). Dominancia de las labiales en el sistema fonológico del habla infantil [Dominance of labials in the phonological system of child speech]. *Boletín del Instituto Caro y Cuervo, 25,* 487–488.

Moulton, J. F. (1956). Syllable nuclei and final consonant clusters in German. In M. Halle, H. C. Lunt, H. McLean, & C. H. v. Schoenefeld (Eds.), *For Roman Jakobson* (pp. 372–381). The Hague: Mouton.

Ortmann, W. (1975). *Beispielwörter für deutsche Ausspracheübungen. 7951 hochfrequente Wortformen der Kaeding-Zählung, rechnersortiert nach Einzellauten, Lautverbindungen, Silbenzahl und Akzentposition* [Examples of words for German pronunciation drills. 7951 highly frequent word forms of the Kaeding count, computerized according to single sounds, sound combinations, number of syllables and stress position]. München: Goethe Institut.

Paradis, C., & Prunet, J.-F. (Eds.). (1991). *Phonetics and phonology: The special status of coronals. Internal and external evidence.* New York: Academic Press.

Pinker, S. (1984). *Language learnability and language development.* Cambridge, MA: Harvard University Press.

Quilis, A., & Esgueva, M. (1980). Frecuencia de fonemas en el español hablado [Phoneme frequencies in spoken Spanish]. *Lingüística Española Actual, II,* 1–25.

Rice, K. (1992). On deriving sonority: A structural account of sonority relationships. *Phonology, 9,* 61–99.

Roeper, T., & Williams, E. (Eds.) (1987). *Parameter setting.* Dordrecht: D. Reidel.

Vihman, M. M., Macken, M. A., Miller, R., Simmons, H., & Miller, J. (1985). From babbling to speech: A reassessment of the continuity issue. *Language, 61,* 395–443.

Vihman, M. M. (1992). Early syllables and the construction of phonology. In C. A. Ferguson, L. Menn & C. Stoel-Gammon (Eds.), *Phonological development: Models, research, implications* (pp. 393–435). Timonium, MD: York Press.

Vihman, M. M. (1993). Variable paths to early word production. *Journal of Phonetics, 21,* 61–82.

Vihman, M. M., & McCune, L. (1994). When is a word a word? *Journal of Child Language, 21,* 517–542.

2 Underspecification and Markedness in Normal and Disordered Phonological Development

Barbara Bernhardt
University of British Columbia

Carol Stoel-Gammon
University of Washington

Jakobson (1941/1968) proposed that markedness predicts the types of phonemes and word structures that appear in children's early phonologies; that is, they contain the least marked phonemes/word structures crosslinguistically. Other phonologists following in the generative grammar tradition have further developed this learnability hypothesis: that a child will produce structures with unmarked values until positive linguistic evidence triggers the setting of the marked value for a grammatical parameter (White, 1989). Research in the past five decades, although somewhat encouraging initially (e.g., Cairns & Williams, 1972; Leopold, 1947; Menyuk, 1968), has failed to confirm this prediction (e.g., Ferguson & Farwell, 1975; Macken, 1980; Pye, Ingram & List, 1987; Stoel-Gammon, 1985). Both individual variation and lack of predictive clarity weaken the markedness hypothesis substantially as an explanation for patterns seen in early phonology.

Archangeli and Pulleyblank (1994) have proposed a somewhat different perspective on markedness in relation to their most recent theory of underspecification, combinatorial specification. In this chapter we examine feature and word structure data from children with normal and delayed phonological development from the perspectives presented in Archangeli and Pulleyblank (1994). In the first section we discuss major tenets of the Archangeli and Pulleyblank framework and derive predictions for phonological development in accordance with it. We then describe data from the first 10 words of 52 typically developing children and from a later phonological acquisition period of 22 children with delayed phonological development, concluding with a discussion of the data in terms of the Archangeli and Pulleyblank proposal.

COMBINATORIAL SPECIFICATION

Combinatorial Specification relates to complexity of underlying representation and is an outgrowth of *Radical Underspecification* (Archangeli, 1988). According to the Radical Underspecification view, underlying representations include "only unpredictable values for features, . . . [whereas] predictable [default] values are inserted by rule during the course of the derivation" (p. 192). For example, a segment (phoneme) that is [+sonorant] does not need to be specified for [voice]. All sonorants are voiced, and thus the [+voice] feature is predictable, given the [+sonorant] feature. Key concepts of the Combinatorial Specification proposal concern both the phonological elements themselves and phonological operations. Key concepts concerning phonological elements are:

    1. F-Elements: The primitives of representation are called *F-elements*. F-elements include both features (such as [+continuant]) *and* association lines, which link phonological elements (see Fig. 2.1).

    2. Combinations of F-elements: Representation results from the combinations of F-elements. A segment (=phoneme) is a complex of cooccurring features. A word is a sequence of these feature complexes (see Fig. 2.1).

    3. Default feature/values: Some features and feature values are present in underlying representation, and some are predictable or redundant, and therefore not present in underlying representation. Those predictable features or feature values (+, −, or 0) that need to be present in surface forms but that are *not* present in underlying representation, are inserted during the course of the derivation.

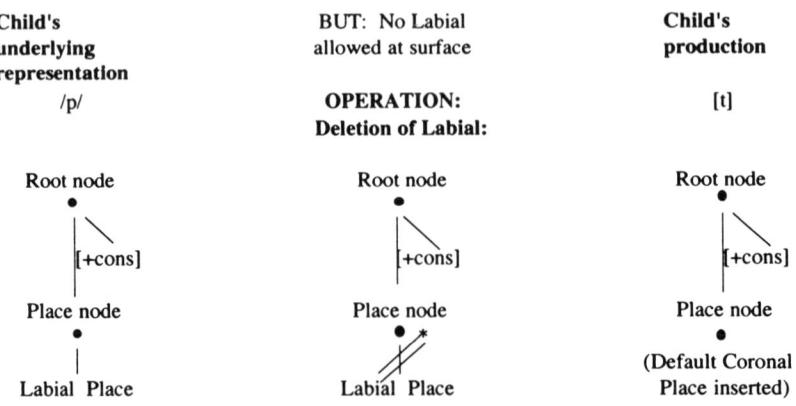

*Double lines indicate deletion of feature through "delinking."

    FIG. 2.1. Example of specified feature deletion and default feature insertion.

Phonological operations involve both insertion and deletion of structure.

1. Insertion or deletion of a structural position, feature or feature value (+, −, or 0): Insertion results in new links (association lines) being formed between phonological elements. Deletion results in delinking (removal of association lines) between elements. For example, a feature such as [Labial] may be "inserted" or "deleted," as is shown in Fig. 2.1. Through exposure to labial segments in the input, [Labial] is "inserted" into a child's underlying representations. If surface constraints inhibit production of [Labial], the feature will be "deleted" during derivation. What surfaces in place of the labial place segment will depend on other constraints in the phonological system. If there are no other constraints, the default place feature [Coronal] may be inserted during derivation. Thus /p/ will surface as [t].

Similarly, feature values may be deleted, and redundant values inserted. For example, the negative value of [anterior] may be inserted in underlying representation as a response to input that includes palatoalveolars ([−anterior] segments). However, surface constraints against production of palatoalveolars result in deletion of the negative value, leaving an unspecified [anterior] feature. Because unspecified [anterior] is redundantly [+], the positive value is inserted during the derivation, resulting in a [+anterior] production. Thus /ʃ/, which is [−anterior], surfaces as [+anterior] [s].

2. Linkings and delinkings can also occur *between* features or *between* a feature and syllable/word structure constituent. The features [Labial] and [+continuant], when cooccurring (i.e., linked), result in the feature complex /f/. If [+continuant] is delinked from the feature complex, /f/ will surface as [p] (assuming no other phonological operation). If [Labial] is delinked from [+continuant], the segment is unspecified then for place. For an oral place fricative to be produced, the default place [Coronal] will be then inserted by redundancy rules, /f/ surfacing as [s]. Similarly, if specified features are delinked from a coda (i.e., syllable-final) position, but the coda slot itself is not delinked from syllable structure, a default segment may be inserted to fill the slot. In Fig. 2.2, place features are delinked from coda position, but the Root Node (and [+consonantal] feature) remain. Laryngeal Node can function as a default "place of articulation," when no oral place is specified. Thus, a glottal stop becomes the default coda.

COMBINATORIAL SPECIFICATION AND MARKEDNESS

Combinatorial Specification differs from Radical Underspecification in terms of prediction of underlying features and feature values. According to Radical Underspecification, the default (redundancy) rules correspond to universal markedness considerations (Archangeli, 1988, p. 197). However, examination of vowel data sets from different languages led Archangeli and Pulleyblank (1994) to the

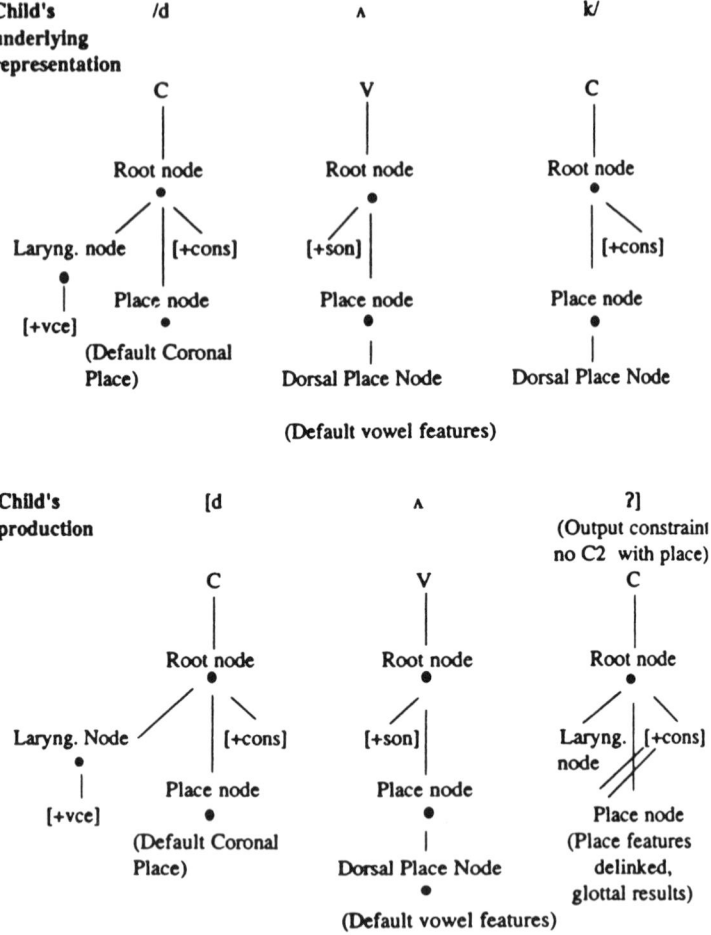

FIG. 2.2. Example of delinking of Place features from coda with insertion of default glottal stop.

paradoxical observation that, universality notwithstanding, underspecified values for features sometimes differed across languages. Thus, *Combinatorial Specification* was proposed, which allows "universally unmarked" (predictable) features or values to be specified in underlying representation in some languages. Competing with this loosening of the strong link between markedness and underspecification, however, is the *Grounding Hypothesis*, which states that combinations of F-elements are restricted by conditions whose content is closely governed by phonetic properties. The stronger a phonetic implication, the greater its role in determining segmental inventories and relative markedness of different inventories. The key difference between Radical and Combinatorial Specification, then, is that Combinatorial Specification makes no direct claims about the relationship between markedness and whether a particular F-element is active or not. In terms of development, Archangeli and Pulleyblank suggested that a learner's initial hypotheses will reflect physically motivated conditions. Given the close link between phonetic grounding and markedness, the link between markedness and specification may thus be stronger in children than in adults whose language deviates from that isomorphic state. However, the general loosening of ties between markedness and underlying representation also allows for different default and specified features, feature values, or structures than those predicted by universal markedness in phonological development. This chapter examines these possibilities for acquisition.

PREDICTION OF SPECIFIED AND UNSPECIFIED PHONOLOGICAL ELEMENTS IN EARLY DEVELOPMENT

In this section, we present predictions for early phonological structure. Predictions and discussion are limited primarily to those aspects of the phonology for which data exist in both the typical and disordered samples (word shapes and general consonant features without respect to word position). We hypothesize that children's word productions will exhibit universally unmarked (and radically underspecified) structures of adult phonologies, if for no other reason than those structures are highly frequent and, in most cases, represent the least complex of phonetic options crosslinguistically. However, based on the Combinatorial Specification proposal we also hypothesize that particular aspects of the specific language being learned, plus factors relating to the acquisition process itself, can result in underspecified and specified structures in children's speech that diverge from the universally unmarked ones. Thus, although Jakobson's hypothesis equated universal unmarkedness in adult phonology with structures in child phonology, we are allowing divergence between child phonology and universal unmarkedness. Factors such as misperception, articulatory immaturity, frequency of input, under- and overgeneration of learned material, and chance occurrence are real-time learning factors that, we submit, can influence how a phonological system is set up in early development. This is in accordance with the Combinatorial Specification perspective, which allows for divergence between markedness and underspecification.

We also hypothesize that the degree of overlap between structures in child phonology and universally unmarked structures will vary across children within and between language groups, because of the relative strength or importance of real-time learning factors in a particular child's case.

Predictions are listed first for word structures, and then for features and segments. In each section, we present universal predictions, language-specific predictions for English that may deviate from universal predictions, and predictions for acquisition that may deviate from universal predictions because of variables particular to the learning process. Evaluating predictions in light of data implies (a) that the predictions themselves are logical hypotheses derived from well-supported theories, and (b) that the data reflect robust developmental trends.

In terms of the predictions, the word structure and feature geometry frameworks utilized necessarily limit the examination of Combinatorial Specification and markedness to those structures and elements included in those frameworks. We have selected commonly utilized frameworks (CV phonology and an extension of McCarthy's, 1988, feature geometry) because of their general applicability and acceptance. We acknowledge that other word structure and feature geometry frameworks might suggest different predictions for some of the phonological elements. The predictions we derive for universals and English are based on literature reports about underspecification and markedness. The predictions for acquisition are based on reports of previous research in child phonology.

We further acknowledge the difficulty of determining when and what kind of developmental data are relevant. In this chapter, we assume that what a child produces is relevant for the enterprise of evaluating predictions. We make no particular claims about underlying representation models in our focus on the children's utterances, but do assume that the surface productions at least inform us about the output constraints and possibilities. Deciding which data are robust is another question regarding data relevance. Regressive and progressive idioms have been reported in studies of phonological development (Ferguson & Farwell, 1975). Thus, patterns that appear in a child's speech at one time may "disappear," only to emerge some time later. Some of our data may be idiomatic in those ways, weakening our claims. Overall, however, the patterns we describe were more consistent than variable for the children involved.

Word Structure

Universal Predictions for Word Structure

Crosslinguistically, the least marked syllable shape is CV, an open syllable with an obligatory onset (Prince & Smolensky, 1993). Combinations of this primary syllable CV result in binary foot structure of the form CVCV, an unmarked and basic word form. Codas are generally restricted across languages. Thus, in earliest child phonology, we expect:

(1) CV syllables, either as single units or binary combinations.

Because codas are generally more restricted crosslinguistically, we expect:

(2) Onset clusters before coda clusters.

Predictions for English and Acquisition

English is a language where consonant codas play a key role in stress assignment (i.e., English is a "Weight by Position" language, Hayes, 1989). Slobin

(1973) proposed that children may have a general learning strategy of paying attention to "endings." Children may, then, focus on the codas when learning a language like English. In this case, predictions for English acquisition would include:

(3) Early marking of singleton codas in child speech, and

(4) Earlier use of word-final clusters than word-onset clusters.

We have no other divergent expectations from universals for English or acquisition in the word shapes studied in this chapter.

Features/Segments

For this section, underlying feature specifications for English are assumed to be as noted in the Appendix. These specifications are explained further in Bernhardt (1992) and Bernhardt and Stoel-Gammon (1994), and are based on McCarthy's (1988) feature geometry. The features are presented by the organizing nodes: Root Node, which comprises major class and manner features [consonantal], [sonorant], [continuant], and [nasal]; Laryngeal Node, which comprises [voice] and [spread glottis] features; and Place Node, which comprises the features Labial (and its dominated feature [round]), Coronal (and its dominated features [anterior] and [distributed]), and Dorsal.

Universal Predictions for Features and Feature Values

Root Node.   Comparable data in the two samples concerns the consonants— stops, nasals, fricatives, glides, and liquids. Thus we limit our discussion to those. The least marked consonants crosslinguistically are assumed to be stops (Maddieson, 1984). Oral stops are considered to be unmarked in comparison with nasals. Thus, for consonants we would expect:

(5) Default features of stops: [−continuant] and [−nasal].

In terms of frequency in world languages, nasals are also very frequent. Thus, we would expect an expansion of the [−continuant] category to include:

(6) Early specification of [+nasal].

Crosslinguistic markedness would predict the less common fricative category to be a later acquisition (specification of [+continuant]). Liquids would be assumed to follow stops, nasals, and fricatives because they are more marked crosslinguistically, and require additional features: specification of both [+consonantal] and [+sonorant] plus [+lateral] for /l/, and Labial-Coronal: [−anterior] for /r/. Thus, for manner categories we would expect:

(7)   (a) Fricatives after stops/nasals, that is, later specification of [+continuant].
      (b) Liquids after fricatives, that is, later specification of above-noted liquid
          features than [+continuant].

Additionally, we would expect:

(8) Appearance of (less complex) [−consonantal], [+sonorant] glides before
    [+consonantal], [+sonorant] liquids.

Laryngeal Node.   Crosslinguistically, unvoiced unaspirated obstruents are
less marked than voiced or aspirated obstruents (Maddieson, 1984). The status of
the glottis is assumed to be [−spread glottis] for consonants. Thus in early
phonology we would expect:

(9) Default features [−voice] and [−spread glottis].

Note, however, that differences in VOT across languages may result in divergent
transcriptions and opinions as to the type of voicing applied to the segments. For
example, in languages where aspirate stops contrast with voiced stops, such as
English, the child's unaspirated production of a stop may be perceived by the
listener as a voiced stop. A similar VOT in stops produced by a French-learning
child might be perceived accurately by French listeners as a voiceless stop
(French having no long-lag aspirate stops).

Specification of [voice] for consonants may proceed gradually, with word
position being relevant. Across world languages, obstruents are less likely to be
voiced word finally (Maddieson, 1984). Hence, for voice contrasts, we might
expect:

(10) Specification of [+voice] in onsets before [+voice] in codas.

Place Node.   Coronal is the most frequent place of articulation across languages, and is considered to be the default place (Paradis & Prunet, 1991). Thus,
in early phonology we would expect:

(11) The default Place feature Coronal [+anterior].

The summation of the aforementioned universal predictions results in our expectation of [t] as a first default consonant.

Predictions for English Features and Feature Values

Laryngeal Node.   We noted earlier that VOT differences across languages
affect adult perception of voiced versus unvoiced stops. English-learning children may initially appear to be "voicing" word-initial voiceless stop targets, until
they learn to aspirate them. Because of the methodological problems in compar-

ing English to other languages without aspiration, we will not make a specific prediction about this, but merely note it.

Place Node.   For place, we do, however, suggest a prediction for English. Labials are more common than Dorsals crosslinguistically (Maddieson, 1984), and English needs both. Thus, for English consonants, we would expect:

(12) Specification of Labial Place before Dorsal Place.

(This prediction derives from Universal Grammar but is a specific prediction for English, which needs both places.)

Acquisition Factors and Predictions for Features and Feature Values

Root Node.   We assume acquisition predictions for Root node features to be equivalent to universal predictions, in accordance with previous phonological acquisition literature. Thus, we expect early appearance of stops, nasals ([−continuant] and [+nasal]), and glides ([−consonantal],[+sonorant]), later appearance of fricatives ([+continuant]), and even later appearance of liquids ([+consonantal],[+sonorant]).

Laryngeal Node.   Crosslinguistic differences and transcription error aside, glottal control difficulties might result in onset stops that had VOT values approximating those of voiced rather than unvoiced unaspirated stops with reference to the adult values for a given language (Macken & Barton, 1980). Therefore, in some children's early phonology, we might expect:

(13) A default value of [+voice] for stops in onset position.

Place Node.   Input frequency, lexical selection, or articulatory difficulty with tongue tip and blade use might lead to:

(14) Defaults for place of articulation that are child-specific.

This might be for the major places of articulation: Labial, Coronal, or Dorsal, or for specific values of one of those major places. For instance, articulatory immaturity or difficulty with tongue tip control might lead to use of coronals that are not [+anterior] (Moskowitz, 1980). Thus, we might find children for whom:

(15) Default coronals are [+distributed] or [−anterior] rather than [+anterior].

METHOD: NORMALLY DEVELOPING SUBJECTS

The 52 subjects (27 girls; 25 boys) were part of a longitudinal study designed to determine the age of onset of particular linguistic milestones for American English and to examine the relationships among these milestones.

Procedures

Parents were asked to track the appearance of their child's first 10 adult-based words by noting the approximate date of appearance and the child's pronunciation of these forms. The age of acquisition of 10 words, according to parental report, ranged from 0;11 to 1;7, with a mean age of 1;3.

Once parents reported that the child had a productive vocabulary of 10 words, the child was recorded in the laboratory in order to confirm the use of adult-based words and verify pronunciation patterns. A speech sample was collected while the subject played with the parent. Sessions were audio and video recorded and were phonetically transcribed in broad transcription. The purpose of the transcription was to verify the presence of consonantal phones and syllable structures of the child's productions.

Analysis

The analyses focused on word shapes and sound classes in the children's words. A list of word shapes for each child was constructed, based on the child's pronunciation of a target form. Thus, if a child said [da] for *dog*, he was credited with a CV word shape. For a sound class to be included as part of the child's repertoire, it had to be used in at least 2 of the 10 words, and it had to match the sound class of the target form. Thus, for example, the child who produced *bottle, no, mommy,* and *doggie* as [babu], [no], [mami], and [dagi], respectively, would be credited with having the sound classes Labial (for [b], [m]), Coronal ([d], [n]), Stop ([b], [d]), and Nasal ([n], [m]) in his repertoire (but not Dorsal, because only one example of a dorsal appeared).

METHOD: SUBJECTS WITH PHONOLOGICAL DISORDERS

The 22 children with moderately severe to severe phonological disorders were participating in nonlinear phonological intervention studies (Bernhardt, 1990, 1993). The children (17 boys, 5 girls) were between the ages of 3 and 6 and had no other major impairments, although some also had delays in language production. The data to be discussed are primarily from initial assessment samples, that is, data uninfluenced by intervention. Any posttreatment data are identified as such, and utilized if relevant to the discussion.

Procedures

For the Bernhardt studies, a 164-item word list was used for a primarily non-imitative elicitation, sampling all English consonants in word-initial position (WI), word-final position (WF), syllable-initial-within-word position (SIWW) and, where possible, syllable-final-within-word position (SFWW). A conversational sample supplemented the single-word list. For the 1990 study, Bernhardt recorded the children's speech with a Nagra IV reel-to-reel tape recorder and Ampex 631 tapes with an AGK D202 microphone, and transcribed the tapes using a Revox taperecorder and Videoconcepts F700 dynamic earphones. The IPA (International Phonetic Association, 1989) symbols and diacritics supplemented by a few extra codings served for the narrow transcriptions performed. For the 1993 study, field speech-language pathologists participating in the study recorded the children's speech using a Marantz PMD 430 audiocassette recorder and a PZM microphone. Tapes were transcribed by research assistants at the university using a Yamaha KX-530 playback recorder and AKG K240 headphones. Transcription agreement over two transcribers was reached on over 95% of the narrowly transcribed randomly selected items for both data sets.

Analysis

Children's words were coded for word shape in terms of consonants and vowels, and features relating to consonants posited in accordance with the Appendix. For this chapter, we have generally limited our discussion to those structures and features that can be compared for the two subject groups (general word structure and consonant features), although we present data for more aspects of the phonology for the children with phonological disorders. As mentioned in the introduction, we are assuming productivity of data for the samples. If any treatment influence is perceived for the disordered data, we have noted that.

RESULTS: NORMALLY DEVELOPING SUBJECTS

Word Structure

Table 2.1 presents a summary of the word structures used in the first 10 words of the normally developing children. A child had to produce the word shape in question twice for it to count acquired (not necessarily as a match with the adult target). In this summary, glides and the glottal [h] are considered consonants. It is assumed that productions of VC started with glottal stops, even though the mothers did not note this in their transcriptions.

Universal Predictions[1]

(1) Predominance of CV syllables: This was strongly confirmed. CV syllables predominate in early word productions. Of the 52 children, 38 (73%) produced at least 2 of the 10 words as a simple CV, and 47 (90%) produced 2 or more CVCV words. No clusters were used.

---

[1]Numbering refers to the prediction numbers given previously.

TABLE 2.1
Expected and Observed Word Shapes for Normal *Ss* and *Ss* with Phonological
Disorders

Syllable/ Word Shape[a]	Expected Word/Syllable Shape by Category[b]		Normal Subjects (n = 52)[b]	Subjects With Phonological Disorders (n = 22)
CV	Univ. = Eng. = Acq.	CV	CV words: 73%	CV words: 100%
	Less expected			[Default C]V[c]: 14%
CVCV	Univ. = Eng. = Acq.	CVCV	CVCV: 90% :90% of those C$_1$ = C$_2$	CVCV: 23%
	Less expected			CV[?]V: 45% CV[Default C]V[c]:59% CVV: 27% CV[s]: 5% [Default C]VCV: 5%
CVC	Univ. Eng. Acq.	CV for CVC CVC early (=Eng.?Univ.?)	CVC words: 31%	CV for CVC: 55% CVC words: 36%
	Less expected			CV[Default C]: 64%
VC[d]	Univ. = Eng. = Acq.	[?]VC[c]	[?]VC words: 4%	[?]V(C): 91%
	Less expected		[?] replacing target C	[Default C]V(C)[c]: 14%

[a]Categories: Expected wordshapes by universals (Univ.), English (Eng.), and acquisition (Acq.). Wordshapes listed in descending order of markedness crosslinguistically (CV least marked).
[b]Data for normals based on two occurrences/10-word sample (whether matches or nonmatches).
[c]Default consonant other than glottal stop, that is, [w], [h], [n], [j], or [t], varying across children.
[d]Although VC words are most marked of the above forms, the glottal stop is expected as a default onset to vowel-initial words.

Predictions for English and Acquisition

(3) Early marking of codas: This was partially confirmed. At least 2 CVC words occurred in the speech of 16 (31%) children, and 2 (4%) children produced at least 2 VC forms. (For several of the VCs, the initial target consonant was missing.)

TABLE 2.2
Expected and Observed Root Node (Manner) Features for Normal *Ss* and *Ss* With
Phonological Disorders

Features/ Sound Classes	Expected Features by Category[a]		Normal Subjects (n = 52)[b]	Subjects With Phonological Disorders (n = 22)
[+son]with [-cons] or [+cons]	Univ.	[-cons],[+son] (glides	[j], [w]: 6%	Glides: 100%
				Glides for liq: 82%
(Liquids and glides)	Eng.	[-cons],[+son]; [+cons],[+son] (glides, liq.)	Word-final /l/: 4%	/l/ onsets: 18% /r/ cosas: 14%
	Acq.	(= Univ.)		
[continuant]	Univ.	[-continuant] (stops)	Oral stops: 100%	Oral stops: 100% Stops for frics: 36%
(Stops and fricatives)	Eng.	[-continuant]; [+continuant] (stops; fric.)	Fric. (no /h/): 27% Fric. (with/h/): 33%	Fric. (no /h/): 72% Fric. (with /h/): 100%
	Acq.	(= Univ.)		
	Less expected			Fric. for stops: 27%
[nasal]	Univ.	[-nasal] unspec. value (oral stop)		Stops for nasals: 9%
(Nasals)	Eng. Acq.	[-nasal], [+nasal] [+nasal] early	Nasals: 65%	Nasals: 91%
	Less expected			Nasals for stops: 5% (occasionally)
Liquids vs. fricatives	Univ. = Eng. = Acq.	Fricatives appear before liquids ([+cont] before [+cons]-[+son])	Fricatives (with /h/) before liquids: 15%	Fric. (with /h/) before liquids: 100%
	Less expected		Liquids before frics. (with /h/): 4%	Liquids before fricatives (no /h/): 9%

[a]Categories: Expected features by universal underspecification (Univ.), English (Eng.), and acquisition (Acq.).

Features/Segments

Analyses of manner and place features of the children's segment productions are presented in Tables 2.2 and 2.3. As noted earlier, in order to be counted as part of a child's repertoire, a segment had to match the target in place or manner

TABLE 2.3

Expected and Observed Place Node Features for Normal Ss and Ss With Phonological Disorders

Features/ Sound Classes	Expected Features by Category[a]		Normal Subjects (n = 52)[b]	Subjects With Phonological Disorders (n = 22)
Labial	Univ.	Specified = later than Coronal	No Labials: 4%	
/p/, /b/, /m/, /f/, /v/, /w/	Eng.	Early (frequent)	Labials: 96%	Labials: 100%
	Acq.	? with respect to Cor; earlier than Dors.	Labials only: 6%	Labials for Coronal, Dorsal: 9%
Coronal ([+ant])	Univ.	Default	Coronals: 90%	Coronals: 100%
	Eng.	Default		
/t/, /d/, /n/, /l/, /s/, /z/	Acq.	? with respect to Labial; earlier than Dorsal	Coronals only: 4%	Coronals for Dorsals: 41%
Dorsal	Univ.	Specified = later; less expected than Labial		
/k/, /g/, /ŋ/	Eng.	Labial before Dorsal	Dorsals: 46%	Dorsals: 59%
	Acq.	(= Univ.)	Dorsal only: 0%	
	Less expected			Dors. for others: 18%
Coronal: [+distrib]	Univ.	[-distrib] (/s/, /z/)	Data not available	
/θ/, /ð/,	Eng.	[-distrib]; [+distrib] /θ/, /ð/, /s/, /z/		
	Acq.	[+distrib]?		[+dist] for [-dist]: 36%
More than one place	Univ.	Labial + Coronal	Labial + Coronal: 78%	Labial + Coronal: 100%
	Eng.	(= Univ.)		
	Acq.	Any two?	Labial + Dorsal: 6% All places: 37%	All places: 59%

[a]Categories: Expected features by universal underspecification (Univ.), English (Eng.), and acquisition (Acq.).

respectively. For the most part, the universal predictions outlined in the introduction are strongly supported by the data.

Universal Predictions

Root Node.   (5) and (6) [−continuant] and [+nasal] as early features: Stops and nasals were frequent in the samples, and thus predictions of default feature [−continuant] and early specification of [+nasal] are confirmed. All subjects produced at least 2 words in which the adult model and the child's form had oral place stops. For 8 (15%) of the children, stops were the only manner class that met the criterion of occurrence (occurring in at least 2 of 10 words). Nasals appeared in the speech of 34 (65%) children. On the other hand, fricatives occurred in the speech of only 17 (33%) children, and liquids (word-final /l/) or glides in the speech of only 5 (10%).

(7) Fricatives–liquid emergence order: Data were indeterminate for this prediction. Fricatives did occur prior to liquids for 8 (15%) children, but 2 (4%) had word-final /l/ prior to fricatives.

(8) Glides versus liquids: Data were also indeterminate for this prediction. Three (6%) children used glides first, and 2 (4%) used liquids first.

Place Node Features.   Of particular interest with respect to the acquisition of place features is the proportion of children who had more than one place of articulation among their early words: 47 (90%) used at least 2 places of articulation, and 19 (37%) all 3 places.

(11) Coronal [+anterior] as an early feature and default: 47 (90%) children had coronal as one place of articulation, suggesting it could have been a default. Coronal was the only place of articulation for 2 (4%). However, 3 (6%) subjects had no coronals.

Predictions for English

Place Node.   (12) Labials earlier than dorsals in English: This was confirmed. Labials were present in the samples of 48 (92%) children, whereas dorsals appeared only when other places of articulation also appeared. Notably, however, 21 (46%) children did use dorsal consonants.

Acquisition Predictions

Place Node.   (14) Child-specific defaults for place of articulation: This appeared to be partially confirmed. Labials were the sole place of articulation for 3 (6%) children.

RESULTS: SUBJECTS WITH
PHONOLOGICAL DISORDERS

Word Structure

Word structure results for children with phonological disorders are presented in Table 2.1.

Universal Predictions

(1) Predominance of CV syllables: This was strongly confirmed for monosyllables. All children produced CV syllables as single units, although 3 (14%) of the children used default onsets instead of true consonants at least some of the time (glottal stop or [h], [h]/[w], or [k]/[g]). Furthermore, 3 (14%) children used default consonants other than glottal stop as onsets to vowel-initial words ([n], [t], [h], [w], or [j]). The CV syllables often replaced more complex syllables in the adult targets. For the CVCV combinations, 5 (23%) subjects had matching consonants only in C_2 position. The rest of the children had primarily default consonants (glottals, glides, or a default coronal fricative) in the C_2 slot. The second consonant of CVCV was missing some of the time for 6 (27%) subjects.

(2) Onset clusters before coda clusters: This was weakly supported. Only one child had this pattern. However, 2 children frequently used onset clusters before they used *any* codas frequently.

Predictions for English and Acquisition

(3) Early marking of codas: This was partially confirmed. About a third (36%, or eight subjects) had productive use of codas. When the other children produced codas (inconsistently), the segments were sometimes matching consonants, particularly nasals, but were usually defaults (glottal stop, [s]).

(4) Coda clusters before onset clusters: This was more strongly supported than the universal prediction of onset clusters before coda clusters. For those children using clusters, 7 used word-final coda clusters before word-initial coda clusters: (C)VCC before CCV(C).

Features/Segments

Tables 2.2 and 2.3 show the results on features and segments for children with phonological disorders.

Universal Predictions

Root Node.   (5) and (6) [−continuant] and [+nasal] as early features: These were frequent in the sample, and thus predictions of default feature [−continuant] and early specification of [+nasal] are confirmed. Most children had stops and nasals, with 2 (9%) using stops for nasals at least some of the time. Stops replaced fricatives for 8 (36%) children. Fricatives (usually coronal fricatives) inconsistently appeared for stops for 6 (27%) children. One unusual pattern was a child's intermittent use of nasals for stops.

(7) Fricatives appearing before liquids: This occurred as predicted. All children used /h/ or oral fricatives before liquids (over the course of the study, even if liquids were therapy targets). If we ignore /h/, and count only supraglottal fricatives, however, 2 (9%) children used the liquid /l/ before fricatives.

(8) Glides before liquids: In the disorder group, all children used glides, and 82% of them replaced liquids with glides, as predicted.

Laryngeal Node.   (9) [−voice] and [−spread glottis] early features: This was partially confirmed. Of the 9 (41%) children who had not yet mastered laryngeal features of English, 4 (18%) fit the predicted universal pattern, and 3 (14%) were inconsistent in their marking of voice.

(10) Voiced obstruents appearing in onsets before appearing in codas: This was confirmed. Only one child contradicted the prediction by having consistent voice contrasts word finally before word initially (the child with the default [k/g] onset). Eight children who did use codas at least some of the time did not use [+voice] codas, in accordance with the prediction.

Place Node Features.   (11) Coronal [+anterior] as an early feature and default: Coronal Place was present in all children's speech. Coronal was a default appearing for Dorsal Place stops for 9 (41%) children. Furthermore, Coronal was the default place for fricatives for 3 (14%).

Predictions for English

(12) Labials before dorsals: This was confirmed. All children had Labial Place at least for some manner category. However, 9 (41%) children produced no Dorsal Place consonants.

Acquisition Predictions

(13) [+voice] the default feature for word-initial stops: This was partially confirmed. This pattern occurred for 2 (9%) children. Furthermore, an additional 3 (14%) had inconsistent voicing patterns word initially.

Place Node.   (14) Child-specific defaults for place of articulation: This was weakly supported. Labial Place stops, nasals and/or fricatives appeared for coronals or dorsals in the words of 2 (9%) children. Dorsal Place stops or nasals were used in place of Coronal or Labial Place stops or nasals for 4 (18%) children.

(15) Default coronals are [+distributed] or [−anterior] rather than [+anterior]: This was partially confirmed. For 8 (36%) children, the [+distributed] feature was the default for coronal fricatives rather than [+anterior] (and for 3 of those children, also for stops).

DISCUSSION: COMPARISON OF THE TWO DATA SETS

Although an exact and complete comparison could not be made, the two groups were similar in many ways. Both sets of children had strong use of CV, stops, nasals, coronals, and labials. In each group, some children used fricatives and dorsals, with liquids being marginal in both groups. In each group, consonant codas were present in the speech of about one-third of the subjects, although not yet uniformly used. For the variables we were able to compare, two differences were noted between the groups. Some of the older children with disorders were advanced in comparison to the younger normally developing children in their use of consonant clusters (either onset or coda). In terms of CVCV production, the younger children were generally advanced in comparison with the older children with disorders. The younger children were able to produce CVCV with supraglottal consonants in C_2 position, whereas only 5 of the children with disorders (45%) used CVCV without default segments in C_2 position. (Only 2 of those subjects used consonant clusters at that point in their development.)

Overall, the data reinforce the notion that children with phonological disorders have phonologies similar to those of younger normally developing children, with some divergence noted with respect to production of consonant sequences. The severity of the disorders comes from the fact that the 52 normally developing children at the 10-word point are as advanced in phonology as the children with disorders aged 3 and above who have vocabularies and other skills commensurate with their chronological ages. For purposes of the theoretical discussion, the similarities allow us to consider the data sets together.

Markedness and Combinatorial Specification

The data for the two groups of children show the value of separating markedness from specification. Although many of the universal predictions are confirmed, divergence reflecting both language-specific and acquisition-specific variables can be seen. Universally unmarked structures that appeared frequently in the children's productions were CV monosyllables, stops, and nasals. Weaker, although probabilistically strong, unmarked structures and orders of acquisition included: (a) coronal as a default place, (b) fricatives appearing before liquids, and (c) [−voice] word-final obstruents appearing before [+voice] word-final obstruents (disorder data only). For English place features, Dorsal followed other places of articulation for many children, an expected language-specific prediction (also a crosslinguistic prediction). No child used Dorsal place to the exclusion of ANY other place. Thus, there were many strong universally unmarked structures present in the children's productions, whether the children were developing at a normal or delayed pace.

As expected, however, not all structures in the children's speech confirmed universal markedness predictions. Conflict of universal predictions and English or acquisition predictions were noted for the following.

1. CVCV: Many of the children with disorders used default segments in C_2 position. Thus, the prosodic structure CVCV itself was robust and in concert with

universal predictions, but feature realization was inhibited. This undoubtedly reflected a particular acquisition factor: the children's articulatory difficulty producing sequences of consonants. Interestingly, consonant sequence constraints are also universal predictions. Yip (1989) designated this as the *Cluster Condition.*

2. Codas: As predicted, we might expect codas to be marked early in a weight-sensitive language such as English. About one-third of each group used codas. However, over half of the group with disorders used default segments in coda position rather than matching consonants, again showing the strength of prosodic structure over feature realization and the strength of consonant sequence constraints. Furthermore, the age difference in the groups is considerable, showing a strong delay for this factor of English acquisition for two-thirds of the disordered group.

3. Clusters and word position: The normally developing subjects were not yet using clusters. Seven of the group with disorders who did use clusters acquired coda clusters before onset clusters, again possibly reflecting the Weight by Position aspect of English.

4. Use of fricatives for stops some of the time by 6 of the children with disorders: Lenition of stops, a weakening process typical of diachronic sound change, may reflect some difficulty with precise articulatory movements.

5. Voicing of obstruents: Five of the children with disorders used voiced, rather than unvoiced obstruent onsets, possibly reflecting general difficulty coordinating timing at the glottis, an acquisition factor relating to physiological immaturity.

6. Coronal [+distributed] as default: Nine of the children with disorders had [+distributed] coronals, usually for sibilants. This again reflects an acquisition factor: general coordination difficulty, in this case for grooving of the tongue tip.

In conclusion, separation of markedness from specification and default predictions as suggested in Archangeli and Pulleyblank (1994) appears useful for describing acquisition data, whether from children with typical or protracted development. It allows us to determine what the strong universals are, and where they have competition from language-specific and acquisition factors. From these two data sets, the strong universals were the basic CV syllable, the two manner classes of stops and nasals, and the two place classes of coronal and labial (also see Lleó et al., chapter 1, this volume, for similar findings in German and Spanish). Weight by Position appeared to be a strong factor of English, affecting early coda marking (see also Lleó et al., this volume, for German). Acquisition factors in the group with disorders were stronger than universals with respect to voicing, tongue grooving, and consonant sequence production in disyllables. These factors all concern motor control, showing the influence of phonetic constraints on phonological output.

For children with disorders, identification of the language-specific and acquisition factors may help us direct our attention to the sources of divergence from universal markedness predictions. Knowing the specifications and defaults of the target language is a necessary prerequisite for planning a theoretically based intervention program. Setting up predictions according to the three components (universals, language-specific variables, and acquisition factors) and comparing a child's data to comparable data from normally developing children can allow a clinician to postulate where a child's system may be influenced by acquisition factors such as articulatory or perceptual difficulties. Thus intervention plans can be tailored more specifically to the child's needs.

ACKNOWLEDGMENT

We are grateful for the support provided for Carol Stoel-Gammon by the National Institute of Health (P01 DC00520) and the Virginia Merrill Bloedel Hearing Research Center at the University of Washington, and for Barbara Bernhardt by the BC Medical Services Foundation.

REFERENCES

Archangeli, D. (1988). Aspects of underspecification theory. *Phonology Yearbook, 5*, 183–207.

Archangeli, D., & Pulleyblank, D. (1994). *Grounded phonology*. Cambridge, MA: MIT Press.

Bernhardt, B. (1990). *Application of nonlinear phonological theory to intervention with six phonologically disordered children*. Unpublished doctoral dissertation, University of British Columbia, Vancouver.

Bernhardt, B. (1992). Developmental implications of nonlinear phonological theory. *Clinical Linguistics and Phonetics, 6*, 259–281.

Bernhardt, B. (1993, November). *A nonlinear phonological intervention field study: Preliminary outcomes*. Paper presented at the American Speech-Language-Hearing Association Convention, Anaheim, CA.

Bernhardt, B., & Stoel-Gammon, C. (1994). Nonlinear phonology: Introduction and clinical application. *Journal of Speech and Hearing Research, 37*, 123–143.

Cairns, H., & Williams, F. (1972). An analysis of the substitution errors of a group of standard English-speaking children. *Journal of Speech and Hearing Research, 15*, 811–820.

Ferguson, C., & Farwell, C. (1975). Words and sounds in early language acquisition. *Language, 51*, 419–439.

Hayes, B. (1989). Compensatory lengthening in moraic phonology. *Linguistic Inquiry, 20*, 253–306.

International Phonetic Association (1947). Report on the Kiel Convention. *Journal of the International Phonetic Association, 19*, 67–80.

Jakobson, R. (1968). *Child language, aphasia and language universals*. (A. R. Keiler, Trans.). The Hague: Mouton. (Original work published 1941)

Leopold, W. (1947). *Speech development of a bilingual child: A linguist's record, Volume II: Sound-learning in the first two years*. Evanston, IL: Northwestern University Press.

McCarthy, J. (1988). Feature geometry and dependency: A review. *Phonetics, 43*, 84–108.

Macken, M. (1980). Aspects of the acquisition of stop systems: A crosslinguistic perspective. In G. Yeni-Komshian, J. F. Kavanagh, & C. A. Ferguson (Eds.), *Child phonology, Volume 1: Production* (pp. 143–168). New York: Academic Press.

Macken, M., & Barton, D. (1980). The acquisition of the voicing contrast in English: A study of voice onset time in word-initial stop consonants. *Journal of Child Language, 7*, 41–74.

Maddieson, I. (1984). *Patterns of sound.* Cambridge, England: Cambridge University Press.

Menyuk, P. (1968). The role of distinctive features in children's acquisition of phonology. *Journal of Speech and Hearing Research, 11*, 138–146.

Moskowitz, B. A. (1980). Idioms in phonology acquisition and phonological change. *Journal of Phonetics, 3*, 141–150.

Paradis, C., & Prunet, J.-F. (1991). *The special status of coronals.* Dordrecht: Foris.

Prince, A., & Smolensky, P. (1993). *Optimality theory: Constraint interaction in generative grammar.* Unpublished manuscript, Rutgers University and University of Colorado, Boulder.

Pye, C., Ingram, D., & List, H. (1987). A comparison of initial consonant acquisition in English and Quiché. In K. Nelson & A. Van Kleeck (Eds.), *Children's language* (Vol. 6, pp. 175–190). Hillsdale, NJ: Lawrence Erlbaum Associates.

Slobin, D. (1973). Cognitive prerequisites for the development of grammar. In C. A. Ferguson & D. I. Slobin (Eds.), *Studies of child language development* (pp. 169–208). New York: Holt, Rinehart & Winston.

Stoel-Gammon, C. (1985). Phonetic inventories, 15–24 months: A longitudinal study. *Journal of Speech and Hearing Research, 53*, 302–315.

White, L. (1989). *Universal grammar and second language acquisition.* Philadelphia, PA: John Benjamins.

Yip, M. (1989). Feature geometry and co-occurrence restrictions. *Phonology, 6*, 349–374.

Consonant Specifications for Adult English[a]

Segment	Root Node	Laryngeal Node	Place Node
/m/	[+consonantal], [+nasal]		Labial
/n/	[+cons], [+nasal]		(Default Coronal: [+anterior])[b]
[ŋ]	[+cons], [+nasal]		Dorsal
/p/	[+cons]		Labial
/b/	[+cons]	[+voice]	Labial
/t/	[+cons]		(Default Coronal)
/d/	[+cons]	[+voice]	(Default Coronal)
/k/	[+cons]		Dorsal
/g/	[+cons]	[+voice]	Dorsal
/f/	[+cons], [+continuant]		Labial
/v/	[+cons], [+cont]	[+voice]	Labial
/θ/	[+cons], [+cont]		Cor: [+distributed]
/ð/	[+cons], [+cont]	[+voice]	Cor: [+distributed]
/s/	[+cons], [+cont]		(Default Coronal)
/z/	[+cons], [+cont]	[+voice]	(Default Coronal)
/ʃ/	[+cons], [+cont]		Cor: [-anterior]
/ʒ/	[+cons], [+cont]	[+voice]	Cor: [-anterior]
/ʧ/[c]	[+cons], [cont] (branching)		Cor: [-anterior]
/ʤ/[c]	[+cons]; [cont] (branching)	[+voice]	Cor: [-anterior]
/w/	[+sonorant]		Labial
/h/	[+cons][+cont]	[+spread glottis]	
/j/	[+sonorant]		(Default Coronal)
/l/	[+cons], [+son]		(Default Coronal)
/r/	[+cons], [+son]		Labial, Coronal

[a]The above encodings and the feature hierarchy diagrams are adapted from McCarthy (1988). See the discussion in Bernhardt and Stoel-Gammon (1994).

[b]Coronal [+anterior] is unspecified; we include it as a reminder that it is the default place.

[c]Affricates are designated with branching structure for the feature [continuant]: [-continuant] [+continuant].

3 The Emergence of Syntax

Margaret Deuchar
University of Wales, Bangor

The main question to be addressed in this chapter is the following: Is Universal Grammar (UG) reflected in the earliest two-word utterances produced by children? In particular, is the categorial component (Chomsky, 1981) available to the child, so that words can be assigned to lexical categories such as nouns, verbs, adjectives, and prepositions? This question is relevant for the current issue of continuity versus maturation: Are UG principles given from the beginning, or do they have to mature? Many theorists (e.g. Hyams, 1992; Pinker, 1984) adopt a continuity approach, according to which UG principles are available to the language learner from the very earliest stage. Those who argue against continuity (e.g., Borer & Wexler, 1987; Radford, 1990), on the other hand, advocate a maturational approach, according to which various principles of UG are made available to the child at various points in her development, rather than all being available at the very beginning.

Much of the debate surrounding the issue of continuity versus maturation has focused on the question of whether lexical categories emerge in child language earlier than functional categories (e.g., determiners, articles, complementizers). In this debate it is assumed by most writers that lexical categories emerge from the very beginning of syntax, thus reflecting the availability from the very beginning of the categorial component. However, in this chapter I challenge that view on the basis of data from the early period of language acquisition which contains lexical items that cannot be assigned to lexical categories, and which, I argue, can only be considered acategorial. This evidence points in the direction of the maturational rather than the continuity hypothesis from an earlier point in child language development than is usually considered.

Radford (1990) exemplifies the position that lexical categories appear from the very beginning of syntax or, specifically, the appearance of the first two-word utterances. Radford suggested that there are three stages in early child syntax: (a) the precategorial stage, (b) the lexical stage, and (c) the functional stage. The first stage is that of one-word utterances and is assumed by Radford to be agrammatical. Radford concluded that the words in this stage are *acategorial*, in that they show no evidence—such as that provided by inflectional morphology—of belonging to grammatical categories. Thus the precategorial stage is characterized by acategorial words: Radford does not make the distinction, as I do, between *precategorial* and *acategorial* words. The second stage is identified by being that of multiword utterances in small clauses, where syntax is assumed to begin. Here, the words are said to belong to lexical categories, that is, NP, VP, AP and PP. According to Radford (1988):

> Small Clauses are . . . *Clauses* in the sense that they are Subject + Predicate structures: more specifically, Small Clauses have the canonical structure [NP XP], where NP is the Subject, and XP is the Predicate: XP here is a category variable which can stand for a phrasal expansion of any of the four major lexical categories (Noun, Verb, Adjective and Preposition), so that XP can be NP, VP, AP, or PP. Thus, Small Clauses can be of the schematic form [NP NP], [NP VP], [NP AP] or [NP PP]. (p. 7)

Examples of small clauses in child speech given by Radford (1988) are:

(1) lady do   [NP VP]   (Jem, 1;9)
     Wayne naughty   [NP AP]   (Daniel, 1;9)
     car away   [NP PP]   (Allison, 1;4)
     bee window   [NP NP]   (Daniel, 1;9). (pp. 18–24)

We may note that, at this "small clause" stage, lexical category membership seems to be assumed on the basis of what we know about the words in the adult language rather than on, for example, the appearance of morphological inflections, which do not seem to emerge until after the beginning of this stage.

EARLY TWO-WORD UTTERANCES

In order to test Radford's position, my own data were examined to determine whether words in the earliest two-word utterances could be assigned exhaustively to lexical categories. My data come from diary records of the speech of my own daughter, Manuela, who acquired English and Spanish simultaneously from birth. The fact that these data are bilingual is not especially relevant in this chapter, and I also examine monolingual English and Spanish data. The data come from two-word utterances produced by Manuela between the ages of 1;7.0 and 1;7.31 and recorded in a daily diary. The utterances in (2) exemplify those that did not pose a problem for Radford's analysis:

(2)   juice gone   [NP VP]   (commenting on an empty cup of juice)
      babero off   [NP PP]   (wanting to take her bib (*babero*) off)

All the words in these two utterances can be assigned to the lexical categories NP, VP, or PP. However, this is not the case with the following utterances:

(3)   more juice   [? NP]   (wanting more juice)
      más juice   [? NP]   (wanting more (*más*) juice)
      juice más   [NP ?]   (wanting some juice)
      oh-dear book   [? NP]   (after dropping book on floor)
      no papá   [? NP]   (commenting on father's absence)

We may note, however, that the question marks in these examples correspond to words that appear to function as predicates in a predicate-argument structure. Thus *more* seems to mean something like *I want*, *oh-dear* indicates something having gone amiss, and *no* here appears to mean nonexistence.

If we now look at some monolingual English data from Braine (1963), we notice a similar division into utterances that appear compatible with Radford's analysis, and utterances that do not. Those that do include:

(4)   Papa away   [NP PP]
      mail car   [NP NP]
      Mama come   [NP VP]

But the examples in (5) do not:

(5)   more car   [? NP]
      more cereal   [? NP]
      more fish   [? NP]
      no water   [? NP]
      no bed   [? NP]
      Calico allgone [NP ?]
      allgone juice   [? NP].

Braine's data were in fact used to argue for *pivot grammar* in the 1960s. Braine and others made an attempt to classify children's early two-word utterances within that framework, which involved making a distinction between two classes of words—a *pivot* and an *open* class. This was supposed to be parallel to the distinction one can make in adult grammar between *open-* and *closed-class* words. Nouns and verbs are examples of open-class words, whereas articles and pronouns are examples of closed-class words. The open class of words characteristically has many members and readily admits new words, whereas the closed class has few members, although these few are used frequently in the language. So-called *pivot* (P) words in child language were proposed as a kind of closed class, whereas other words were known as *open* (O) words. The model was shown not to work for several reasons (see, e.g., Bower-man, 1973, for discussion), mostly distributional, and a semantic approach to early utterances (see Bloom, 1973) was advocated thereafter.

It seems to me, however, that the notion of pivot was an early insight into that which I am calling acategorial, to refer to words used as predicates in early two-word utterances, these words behaving very differently from their counterparts in the adult language and not being assignable to lexical categories. That these predicates are not limited to English can be demonstrated not only by my own bilingual data, but also by some monolingual Spanish acquisition data from Hernández Pina (1990):

(6) botón mamá   'button Mummy'   [NP NP]
     nena cayó   'girl fell'   [NP VP]
     nene grande   'boy big'   [NP AP]

But:

(7) más pan   'more bread'   [? NP]
     no caca   'no poo'   [? NP]

As before, question marks indicate acategorial predicates. For further evidence of the crosslinguistic validity of these categories we can refer to Slobin (1966), who listed pivots that occur in various languages.

Thus far, on the basis of my own and others' data, I hope to have established that some of the words occurring in early two-word utterances cannot in fact be assigned to lexical categories. Those words that function as predicates but that do not belong to lexical categories in the adult language (e.g., *no*, *more*) should be classified as acategorial. On the other hand, those words that do belong to adult lexical categories but that do not yet show appropriate morphology (e.g., *car*, *come*) should be classified as precategorial, on the assumption that forms like *cars* and *coming* will eventually appear to help identify these words as nouns and verbs respectively. (However, we do not expect words like *more* to develop the form *more-ing* or *more-s* later.) Thus I differ in the use of terminology from Radford, in that I draw a distinction between *acategorial* and *precategorial*, which he does not, and where he identifies words in early child language as belonging to lexical categories, I prefer to call them precategorial until clear signs of their lexical category membership have appeared.

It is acategorial, rather than precategorial, words that pose a particular prob-lem for the continuity hypothesis. It can be argued that precategorial items represent underspecified lexical categories, which are nevertheless available to the child from the beginning. However, this cannot be argued for acategorial items, which appear not to reflect UG at all, but rather cognitive and develop-mental factors, as I argue later. In order to explain the disappearance or reanalysis of acategorial items in later child speech, one would have to invoke some kind of *categorial filter*, which would be difficult to reconcile with the continuity approach and easier to account for in *maturational* terms, whereby the child's grammar increasingly approximates the adult one.

We might want to ask where these acategorial predicates came from, given that they are often used in ways somewhat dissimilar from their usage in adult language. Following the intensive work on pivots, Brown (1973) suggested that pivots could be needed to express the semantic operations of *nomination, recurrence,* and *nonexistence,* which seem to be cognitively important notions for 1- to 2-year-olds beginning to use two-word utterances. In my data and that of others, *more* could be said to express recurrence and *no* nonexistence, for example. Brown's observations have more recently been extended to develop the idea that there are specific links between linguistic and cognitive development. Gopnik and Meltzoff (1986) call this the *specificity hypothesis,* and in some of their work (e.g., Gopnik & Meltzoff, 1987) they note similarities between specific Piagetian cognitive developments and linguistic developments. For example, they relate "disappearance" words like *gone* to the understanding of object permanence, "success and failure" words like *uh-oh* (which is presumably equivalent to *oh dear* in my data) to the ability to solve means-ends problems, and the development of naming to the development of categorization abilities. It seems quite plausible to me that the child's early predicates should be words that are available in the input, but which are used to express cognitively salient notions for the child that may be similar, though not identical, to the sense of the words in the adult input.

CONCLUSION

I have argued in this chapter that some data from my own work as well as that of others provides evidence that is not compatible with the continuity hypothesis—if we take the continuity hypothesis to be the assumption that lexical categories of UG are available to the child from the very beginning, and that they are obligatory, as Radford's small clause analysis would suggest. Acategorial predicates that cannot be assigned to lexical categories contradict this assumption. However, these data do seem to be compatible with the maturational hypothesis, not only in the sense that we may assume lexical categories to emerge during the process of acquisition, but also in the sense that this emergence may be related to cognitive maturation.

ACKNOWLEDGMENT

I should like to thank the British Academy for their financial support in the collection of some of the data mentioned in this chapter.

REFERENCES

Bloom, L. (1973). Why not pivot grammar? In C. A. Ferguson & D. I. Slobin (Eds.), *Studies of child language development* (pp. 430–440). New York: Holt, Rinehart & Winston.

Borer, H., & Wexler, K. (1987). The maturation of syntax. In T. Roeper & E. Williams (Eds.), *Parameter setting* (pp. 123–172). Dordrecht: Reidel.

'Bowerman, M. (1973). *Early syntactic development*. Cambridge, England: Cambridge University Press.

Braine, M. (1963). The ontogeny of English phrase structure: The first phase. *Language, 19*, 1–13.

Brown, R. (1973). *A first language: The early stages*. Cambridge, MA: Harvard University Press.

Chomsky, N. (1981). *Lectures on government and binding*. Dordrecht: Foris.

Gopnik, A., & Meltzoff, A. (1986). Relations between semantic and cognitive development in the one-word stage: The specificity hypothesis. *Child Development, 57*, 1040–1053.

Gopnik, A., & Meltzoff, A. (1987). Early semantic developments and their relationship to object permanence, means-ends understanding, and categorization. In K. E. Nelson & A. van Kleeck (Eds.), *Children's language* (Vol. 6, pp. 191–212). Hillsdale, NJ: Lawrence Erlbaum Associates.

Hernández Pina, F. (1990). *Teorías psicosociolingüísticas y su aplicación a la adquisición del español como lengua materna* [Psycholinguistic theories and their application to the acquisition of Spanish as a native language]. Madrid: Siglo XXI.

Hyams, N. (1992). The genesis of clausal structure. In J. Meisel (Ed.), *The acquisition of verb placement* (pp. 371–400). Dordrecht: Kluwer.

Pinker, S. (1984). *Language learnability and language development*. Cambridge, MA: Harvard University Press.

Radford, A. (1988). Small children's small clauses. *Transactions of the Philological Society, 86*, 1–43.

Radford, A. (1990). *Syntactic theory and the acquisition of English syntax*. Oxford, England: Blackwell.

Slobin, D. I. (1966). Early grammatical development in several languages, with special attention to Soviet research (Working Paper No. 11). Berkeley: University of California, Language Behavior Research Laboratory.

4

Early Verbs, Event Types, and Inflections

Eve V. Clark
Stanford University

Verbs are connectors—they link the terms for participants in events. Each verb indicates the roles carried by its associated noun phrases (the agent, location, instrument, and so on). For example, the verb *seize* has agent and theme roles, as in *The dog$_{AGT}$ seized the bone$_{TH}$*; the verb *hear*, an experiencer and theme, as in *The child$_{EXP}$ heard the car$_{TH}$*, and the verb *put*, an agent, theme, and location, as in *The boy$_{AGT}$ put the parcels$_{TH}$ on the table$_{LOC}$*. Verbs also mark grammatical relations. In English, they do this through a combination of word order and inflection. They can be grouped semantically into such event types as activities, accomplishments, achievements, and states. Verbs related in meaning also tend to appear in a similar range of syntactic constructions. These factors suggest that the syntax of a newly encountered verb would be largely predictable from its meaning.

Even if the fit between semantics and syntax is not perfect, it may offer enough of a correlation that children can use semantic information to predict syntactic properties. The question is (a) whether they do this, and (b) what semantic information they need.

Semantic Bootstrapping

One of the first syntactic tasks that faces children is the assignment of words to grammatical categories. It has been proposed that children rely on semantic bootstrapping to do this (e.g., Grimshaw, 1981; Pinker, 1984, 1989). That is, as children map words onto their ontological categories of objects, relations, events, and properties, they can make a preliminary classification of words on the basis of the ontological kinds that they denote. For instance, nouns denote kinds of objects, verbs kinds of relations, and adjectives kinds of properties.

Semantic bootstrapping, then, would allow children a "way in" to the acquisition of not only individual verb meanings, but also to the arrays of argument types that belong with each verb. Subsequently, children must also learn the range of constructions associated with each verb (e.g., Goldberg, 1993; Gropen, Pinker, Hollander, Goldberg, & Wilson, 1989).

A number of linguists have looked at general correlations between semantics and syntax. For example, Gross (1975) argued that systematic study of syntax on a large scale—in his case, the distribution of about 150 syntactic properties for a lexicon of some 6000 French verbs—yields a high correlation with semantics. He showed, for instance, that verbs related in meaning tended to license the same complement types in French and to enter into similar relations otherwise (e.g., the relation between *hurler* 'shout' and *pousser un hurlement* 'give a shout'). To identify such correlations, however, requires the examination of large amounts of empirical data.

Template Verbs

Might children also rely on certain verbs as models or templates for others? That is, do they take the argument structure of one verb as a model for other verbs closely related in meaning to the template? For instance, having learned what *run* means, and having also learned that it takes an agent argument, do children use *run* as a template for subsequent verbs of motion—*walk, race, trot, stroll, slide*—and assign to them the same argument structure as soon as they have identified enough of their meaning? In principle, this would allow children to make inferences about the argument structure and constructional options of verbs closely related in meaning to a verb they already knew.

This would assume that children first identify some of the lexical content of a new verb, and then, from what they have identified, assign a possible argument structure. Furthermore, as they attend to more of the input they hear, they should also begin to associate specific verbs with specific constructions, such as complements introduced by *that* (*say, think, argue*), *to* (*want, ask, begin*), *from* (*stop, prevent*), or constructions such as the dative alternation for verbs like *teach* and *give* (e.g., Goldberg, 1993; Gropen et al., 1989).

In essence, the present proposal is that in learning verbs, children must learn them as parts of constructions, beginning with the appropriate argument arrays and extending to alternation frames and complement structures. A related proposal was put forward by Bybee and Slobin (1982) to account for the patterns observable in children's learning of inflectional morphology. What is being suggested here is that that approach could be extended to look at children's acquisition of verbs in terms of patterns of both associated inflections and associated constructions.

The general hypothesis that provides the starting point for the present research is that the syntax of a new verb is predictable from its meaning. This can be broken down into three subparts: (a) Children identify verb meanings through semantic bootstrapping, by building on their existing conceptual categories of event and state types; (b) children rely on their categories of event types to "classify" the verbs they are learning; and (c) children may treat certain verbs as models that provide templates for the arguments and constructions to be associated with other verbs related in meaning to the models. These hypotheses provide the starting point for questions about what children have to acquire when they acquire a verb—its meaning, its inflections, its argument structure, and the range of syntactic constructions in which it can appear.

EARLY VERBS IN ACQUISITION

This chapter presents some preliminary steps in the testing of these hypotheses. The first goal was to establish just which verbs young children produce, the order in which they produce them, and the knowledge they display, at each stage, about the inflections, arguments, and constructions associated with each one. The first task was therefore to establish a "dictionary" of the verbs produced up to age 3;0.

Three sources of data were used to establish this preliminary dictionary. (a) Diary data from a study of one child, Damon, from which I extracted all the child verb uses from age 1;0 to age 3;0: The diary entries included details of when each episode occurred, the place and occasion, what the child was playing with and/or talking about, who else was there, and (in many cases) what else was said by other participants, as well as notes on the interpretation apparently intended by the child (see further Clark, 1993). (b) Transcript records of a second child, Adam (aged 2;3 to 3;0), from hour-long recordings made every two to three weeks by a visiting observer (transcripts from the Brown corpus in the CHILDES archive; see Brown, 1973; MacWhinney & Snow, 1985): The transcripts are of hour-long recordings made with an observer and the mother, but they contain no contextual information outside whatever is mentioned in the ongoing conversation. (c) Transcript records of a third child, Abe (aged 2;4 to 3;0), from 30-minute recordings made twice a week by one of the child's parents (Kuczaj corpus in the CHILDES archive): These transcripts also lack added contextual information, but the more closely spaced sampling captures details of development not always found in recordings with longer intervals.

Analysis of all the verbs represented in the diary corpus yielded a listing of well over 300 conventional lexical verbs produced by Damon between age 1;3 and 3;0. In the first year (1;3–2;0), he produced 94 lexical verbs, beginning with *do*, *get*, and *go* (the earliest lexical verbs produced).[1] Damon steadily added new verbs to his repertoire at the rate of about 10 a month during his first year of speech production. From 2;1 to 2;6 he added a further 131 verbs, for a cumulative

---

[1]Not counted in the current analysis are any verblike uses of particles like *up*, *down*, *out*, *on*, and *in* or any forms like *uh-oh* or *oops* that were used with verbal force from Damon's earliest words on.

total of 225, and from 2;7 to 3;0 he added a further 96 verbs, for a total of 321 verb types in his repertoire by age 3;0.

Inspection of his early verb uses, however, shows how complex it may be to assess from production alone just what children know about each verb and its argument structure. Consider the earliest verbs Damon produced—the general purpose verbs *do*, *get*, *go*, and *put*, and their typical uses up to 1;7 or so (that is, in his first 4–5 months of verb uses). The utterances in (1) represent the first combinations of main verb *do* with one or more arguments:

(1) (a) 1;2.19   [ə] do that[2]
     (b) 1;3.3   do that
     (c) 1;4.14   me do brush

Do is first used with both an Agent and a Theme argument (1a), but this form could have been based on adult input since none of the particles he used with verbal force at 1;2 appear with any arguments. Later uses of *do* have a Theme only, as in (1b), and then, a month later, *do* reemerges with both Agent and Theme, but this time the Agent takes the form *me* (1c) and thereby provides stronger evidence that Damon was constructing this utterance for himself, and not simply reproducing something heard in the input.

Early uses of *get*, given in (2), reflect the range of early combinations observed:

(2) (a) 1;2.26   get down
     (b) 1;4.7   get that
     (c) 1;4.21   get off
     (d) 1;5.11   get a cracker
     (e) 1;5.11   get me down
     (f) 1;5.18   getget down on floor
     (g) 1;6.25   get on
     (h) 1;7.1   get down floor
     (i) 1;7.1   get down ⟨REPAIR⟩ up, sleep
     (j) 1;7.1   get down cork?
     (k) 1;7.8   get down walk?
     (l) 1;7.15   I get drink
     (m) 1;7.22   get down off
     (n) 1;7.29   get down bottle
     (o) 1;7.29   get down nightnight

Get first emerges in combination with an earlier *down*, and just over a month later, it is produced with a Theme (*that*). It also continues to appear with other

---

²The symbol [ə] represents the neutral, central vowel *schwa*. This *filler* is commonly produced in the pronoun, article, or preposition slot in early language production (see Bernhardt & Johnson, chapter 17, this volume).

particles (*down, on*). Beginning at 1;7, Damon starts to produce this verb in purposive constructions where he would talk about getting down, typically from his high-chair at the table, in order to go somewhere (*walk*) or to fetch some object (*cork, bottle*), or getting up to do something (pretend to *sleep*).

The verb *go*, in the utterances in (3), also exhibited a wide range in early combinations:

(3)	(a)	1;3.3	go down
	(b)	1;4.21	go?
	(c)	1;4.28	this one go bye
	(d)	1;5.4	he go bye
	(e)	1;6.4	go byebye
	(f)	1;6.4	baby go boom
	(g)	1;7.8	go vroom
	(h)	1;7.8	go swimming
	(i)	1;7.15	go watch car

Go starts out being combined with *down* (much like *get*), but then goes on to combine with various pieces of information about manner (*bye, byebye; boom; vroom*). From 1;7 on, it combines with other verbs in the form of the gerundive *swimming* and the proto-complement *watch*.[3]

The fourth general purpose verb, *put*, appears in the range of combinations shown in (4):

(4)	(a)	1;3.10	put back
	(b)	1;3.18	put ball
	(c)	1;4.1	put there
	(d)	1;4.7	put on
	(e)	1;4.14	put them more
	(f)	1;5.4	put the bottle
	(g)	1;6.18	put down floor
	(h)	1;7.1	put it back
	(i)	1;7.1	put it up!
	(j)	1;7.1	put back top. put back ON
	(k)	1;7.15	put it back?
	(l)	1;7.15	[ə] put back
	(m)	1;7.15	all out. put back

Like *get* and *go*, in its earliest uses, *put* occurs in combination with a particle, this time *back*, but within weeks, this verb also appears with a Theme as its sole argument (4b), and with a Locative (4c), again as sole argument. Not until 1;7 do Theme and Locative appear together (*put it back, put it up!*), and subsequent uses

---

[3]Early uses of *gone*, as in (1;4.21) *gone*; (1;5.18) *where's it gone?*; (1;6.4) *juice . . . gone, gone, gone*, or (1;6.4) *gone juice, gone*, are probably unrelated to *go* at this stage.

continue to omit one or other of these arguments on occasion. The first Agent appears at 1;7.15, but only in combination with the Locative (the Theme was omitted).

What is apparent from such uses is that children may know which arguments can appear with a verb—for *put*, the Theme, Locative, and Agent, but they rarely, if ever, produce all the obligatory arguments at once in their early utterances. Moreover, the thematic status of each argument may not always be clear, for example, the indeterminacy of the noun *bottle* as a Locative or an Instrument in the combination with *drink* in (5f):

(5) (a) 1;7.1   drink
     (b) 1;7.1   water, no. drink me milk   [Vb Ag Th]
     (c) 1;7.1   people drinking   [Ag Vb]
     (d) 1;7.1   drink people   [Vb Ag]
     (e) 1;7.1   drink wine   [Vb Th]
     (f) 1;7.15   drink bottle   [Vb Loc/Instr]
     (g) 1;7.15   drink milk?   [Vb Th]

In addition, the relative absence of canonical English word order requires that we be able to call on detailed contextual information in assigning thematic status to nouns in children's utterances.[4] This is apparent both with some of the early instances of *drink*, and with another general purpose verb, *move*, as shown in (6):

(6) (a) 1;7.1   move   [imperative]
     (b) 1;7.8   move feet   [trans: Vb Th]
     (c) 1;7.8   plane move   [trans: Th Vb]
     (d) 1;7.8   move plane   [trans: Vb Th]
     (e) 1;7.15   more move   [imperative]
     (f) 1;7.15   plane move   [trans: Th Vb]
     (g) 1;7.15   me move book   [trans: Ag Vb Th]
     (h) 1;7.22   move plane, ball   [trans: Vb Th Instr]

For example, in (6c) and (6d) *plane* was assigned the role of Theme because, in context, Damon was first watching someone else make a plane on his mobile move, and then moving one of them himself. But it was not until 1;7.17 that he also mentioned the Agent of the action (*me*).

In summary, early verb uses are difficult to classify: The verbs themselves typically lack all inflections; they often lack one or more arguments; and the word order in the utterances produced offers at best an unreliable guide to grammatical relations.

Event Types

Philosophers and linguists have made a number of converging proposals about major verb types, from Vendler (1967), to elaborations of Vendler's scheme by

---

[4]In fact, Damon's word order at this stage appeared to be dictated largely by the order in the preceding speaker's most recent utterance, such that the entity or event mentioned last often became the first thing mentioned in his subsequent utterance.

Dowty (1979) and Van Valin (1990). But the syntactic tests for distinguishing one type of verb from another cannot be applied properly where the data consist, often, of a bare verb with only one argument. One- and 2-year-olds do not use temporal adverbs and initially they omit most verb inflections.

To assign verbs to semantic classes, I therefore relied on contextual information in the diary entries to distinguish event types. The context provided details of what the child was doing before and after the utterance, typically along with any preceding or following adult utterance, and other notes relevant to the child's apparent intention. Early verb uses in the diary data were quite readily assigned to one of four major classes of events—activities, accomplishments, achievements, and states. These four classes correspond to the classes established by Vendler (1967) and Dowty (1979) on the basis of syntactic tests. However, because such tests were not applicable to the present data, I instead relied on contextual information to classify each event type and, hence, the verb used. *Activities* were events where the child was engaged in or watching some ongoing action (such as someone running along a path or someone splashing water at someone else in a swimming pool). *Accomplishments* were events where an agent produced some change of state in something through an action or series of actions (as when the child knocked down a pile of blocks, all at once or one by one, so the pieces were scattered, or when he watched someone tear a piece out of the newspaper). *Achievements* were events where the child engaged in some activity, often with effort, to achieve some goal (as when he climbed up the ladder of a slide and announced his arrival at the top). Finally, *states* were instances where he talked about someone being in some state (e.g., asleep, tired). Notice that the same verb does not necessarily belong to the same event class on all occasions of its use. A verb like *walk*, for example, could designate an activity on one occasion but an accomplishment on another. Compare "The boy walked" with "The boy walked the dog."

The proportions of verbs in each of these classes, in each of the 6-month slices of data examined, are given in Table 4.1. The largest category of verbs used throughout by Damon was that of *Activity* verbs. These made up 55% of all lexical verb types up to age 2;0 and remained stable at nearly 58% through the next year. The next largest category was made up of *Accomplishment* verbs, with 32% up to age 2;0, rising to 39% in the second half of the next year. The two remaining categories, *Achievement* and *State* verbs, accounted for a much smaller proportion of all the verb types produced, with Achievement verbs averaging close to 6% overall, and State verbs averaging a little over 8%.

Early Inflections

Further validation of this context-based verb classification comes from Damon's acquisition of verb inflections. One hypothesis that follows from children's distinguishing verb types on the basis of their inherent aspect or Aktionsart (consistent with the event types just described) is that when children first begin to produce

TABLE 4.1
Percentage of Verbs by SemanticType: Damon

Age	Activ.	Accompl.	Achiev.	State
1;7 - 2;0	55	32	5	7
2;1 - 2;6	48	36	7	9
2;7 - 3;0	47	39	5	9

Note. From Clark, unpublished diary data.

inflections, they should add each inflection first to just those verbs whose inherent semantics appears most compatible with the meaning of that inflection.

This hypothesis makes two predictions: (a) Children should add -ing, used to mark the duration of an action, first to Activity verbs, and only later to Accomplishment verbs; and they should not use -ing with either Achievement or State verbs since their inherent aspect is incompatible with the durational meaning of -ing. And (b) they should add -ed, used to mark past time and hence completion, first to Accomplishment verbs, and only later to other verb types. These two predictions, if supported, would offer further evidence that children distinguish the semantic types identified up to this point on contextual grounds.

Damon produced his first verb inflections at around 1;8. As predicted, most uses of -ing appeared first on activity verbs. Up to age 2;0, activity verbs accounted for 90% of his -ing uses and the percentage of -ing uses on activity verbs remained very similar over the course of the next year. At the same time, also as predicted, there were essentially no uses of -ing on either accomplishment or state verbs. These data are shown in Table 4.2.

TABLE 4.2
Verbs, Semantic Types, and Inflections: Damon

Age	Type	-ING	-ED	-S
1;7 - 2;0	Activity	90	30	0
	Accomplish.	5	60	0
	Achievement	0	0	0
	State	5	10	100
2;1 - 2;6	Activity	88	22	37
	Accomplish.	5	52	37
	Achievement	3	15	10
	State	5	10	16
2;7 - 3;0	Activity	94	16	38
	Accomplish.	1	63	42
	Achievement	1	12	0
	State	4	10	20

Note. From Clark, unpublished diary data.

Also as predicted, most of Damon's -*ed* uses, prior to age 2, appeared first on accomplishment verbs (60%), with another 30% on activity verbs. In the next 12 months, he extended his uses of past tense -*ed* to the other verb types as well.

This general pattern of emergence for the past-tense marker, -*ed*, is consistent with the findings in other languages on early uses of past-tense forms (e.g., Aksu-Koç, 1988; Antinucci & Miller, 1976; Bloom, Lifter, & Hafitz, 1980; Volterra, 1976). Antinucci and Miller (1976), for example, noted that the first uses of past tense -*ed* in English appeared on accomplishment verbs—causative verbs that marked a change of state. They documented a similar pattern in Italian acquisition, but with added evidence that the change of state itself was critical to children's uses of the past participle: 2-year-olds acquiring Italian made the past participle agree in gender and number with the direct object (the noun that designated the entity affected or changed by the action), as shown in (7):[5]

(7) (a) 1;8 *prese io (calze)*
                = *Ho preso le calze*
                'I took the shoes'
      (b) 1;10 *la signora ha chiusa la porta*
                = *La signora ha chiuso la porta*
                'The woman closed the door'
      (c) 2;0 *hai persi due (animaletti)*
                = *Hai perso due animaletti*
                'You've lost two animals'
      (d) 2;4 *ho sbagliata strada*
                = *Ho sbagliato strada*
                'I took the wrong street'

Finally, up to age 2;0, Damon's only uses of the simple present -*s*, typically used for habitual or generic actions in English, were all on state verbs. In the next year, his uses extended to both activity and accomplishment verbs, but they remained very rare on achievement verbs. Again, the latter observation is consistent with the inherent point-in-time meaning associated with achievement verb meanings.

Overall, then, analysis of the emergence of verb inflections supports the context-based assignment of verbs to the event categories of Activity, Accomplishment, Achievement, and State.

Verb Types for Adam and Abe

The repertoire of verbs in Damon's diary data is closely paralleled in number and types by the repertoires represented in the transcripts for Adam and Abe in the CHILDES archive (MacWhinney & Snow, 1985).

---

[5]In adult Italian, the past participle is invariable when the auxiliary is *avere* (to have), and agrees with the Subject in number and gender when the auxiliary is *essere* (to be). Agreement with the direct object, with *avere*, occurs only when the object precedes the verb.

TABLE 4.3
Cumulative Number of Verbs Produced by Three Children

	Damon		Adam		Abe
1;7 - 2;0	94				
2;1 - 2;6	225	2;3 - 2;6	91	2;4 - 2;6	100
2;7 - 3;0	321	2;7 - 3;0	172	2;7 - 3;0	219

Sources. Clark, diary data; CHILDES Archive data (MacWhinney & Snow, 1985).

From the first transcript on, beginning at 2;3 for Adam and 2;4 for Abe, both children steadily added verbs to their repertoires, and many of their verb uses overlapped directly with uses observed in the diary data. The relative numbers for all three children can be seen in Table 4.3. By age 3;0, Adam had produced 172 different verbs and Abe 219.

When the inventories from these two children were assigned to event-type categories, using the linguistic record to assess the intended meaning (as far as

TABLE 4.4
Percentage of Verbs by Semantic Type: Adam

Age	Activity	Accomplish.	Achievement	State
2;3 - 2;6	42	38	5	14
2;7 - 3;0	47	38	5	9

Source. CHILDES Archive data (MacWhinney & Snow, 1985).

TABLE 4.5
Percentage of Verbs by Semantic Type: Abe

Age	Activity	Accomplish.	Achievement	State
2;4 - 2;6	49	3	5	13
2;7 - 3;0	44	42	5	9

Source. CHILDES Archive data (MacWhinney & Snow, 1985).

was possible),[6] the proportions of verbs in each category, shown in Tables 4.4 and 4.5, appear to be very similar to those found in the diary data.

CONCLUSIONS

The general conclusions here pertain only to verb uses from about age 1;6 to age 3—a period during which children use few of the temporal and inflectional elements generally relied on in testing for semantic distinctions among verbs. I have therefore relied on contextual and linguistic evidence that children do attend to certain semantic differences, differences relevant to inherent verb meanings at this early a stage in acquisition. Evidence that they do so provides some general support for the view that children move from the lexical meaning of the verb itself to acquisition of the structures, including argument array and constructions, that are conventionally associated with each verb.

The preliminary findings reported here are, first, that children distinguish the general verb types that have been identified as denoting the event types activity, accomplishment, achievement, and state, presumably on the basis of conceptual distinctions in their representations of different event types. Second, additional evidence supporting the distinctions among verb types comes from the earliest production of verb inflections in English: -ing is used first on activity and later on accomplishment verbs; it appears only rarely on achievement or state verbs. In addition,-ed appears at first mainly on accomplishment verbs, but extends to the other verb types between the ages of 2 and 3. (These data were available only for one of the three children.)

These findings also raise a number of issues. First, early uses of lexical verbs may involve just the verb on its own, and so offer no real evidence for the (adult) part-of-speech categorization of the specific lexeme as a member of the grammatical category *Verb*. Second, early verb uses often appear with only one or two arguments instead of the full array. It is unclear whether children's omissions reflect incomplete knowledge about the array of arguments for specific verbs, or whether they are simply depending on the nonlinguistic and linguistic context to fill in as given whatever is missing from each utterance.[7] Third, below age 3;0 children often fail to produce all the conventional clues to the grammatical relations intended in their utterances. At age 2;0, they are just beginning to use verb inflections and so do not yet rely on them consistently; and in English, verb

---

[6]The transcripts did not contain the contextual information available in the diary record, and the nature of the utterances again precluded using standard linguistic tests to assign verbs to the categories of activity, accomplishment, achievement, or state. By way of compromise, we used the linguistic record plus comparisons with instances of the same verbs in the diary data, to make assignments to event types.

[7]Some support for the latter comes from the fact that different arguments of the same verb are missing on different occasions; see, for instance, the examples cited of *put, hit,* and *drink.*

inflections offer minimal information about person and number (compared to Italian, say), or about tense. Word order is often ignored at this stage and so cannot be treated as criterial for identifying grammatical relations prior to, or even after, the emergence of inflections. Contextual information therefore becomes critical in the interpretation and analysis of such utterances as "turtle bite" (meaning "[I] bite [a/the] turtle," age 1;7) or "plane move" (meaning "[you] move [the] plane," age 1;7.8).

In short, the findings so far are consistent with the hypothesis that children do make use of verb meanings and their inherent aspects from an early stage. This in turn suggests that they should be able to use semantic information to make inferences about argument arrays and constructions. This study is just a first step in showing how children exploit the semantic information they have about verbs as they begin to use them. The extent to which this affects their acquisition of argument structure and of the syntactic constructions associated with each verb is the next thing to assess.

ACKNOWLEDGMENTS

This research was supported in part by the Center for the Study of Language and Information, Stanford University. I would like to thank Ephraim Swanson-Dusenbury for help in coding and analyzing data.

REFERENCES

Aksu-Koç, A. (1988). *The acquisition of aspect and modality: The case of past reference in Turkish.* Cambridge, England: Cambridge University Press.

Antinucci, F., & Miller, R. (1976). How children talk about what happened. *Journal of Child Language, 3*, 167–189.

Bloom, L., Lifter, K., & Hafitz, J. (1980). Semantics of verbs and the development of verb inflection in child language. *Language, 56*, 386–412.

Brown, R. (1973) *A first language: The early stages.* Cambridge, MA: Harvard University Press.

Bybee, J. H., & Slobin, D. I. (1982). Rules and schemas in the development and use of the English past tense. *Language, 58*, 265–289.

Clark, E. V. (1993). *The lexicon in acquisition.* Cambridge, England: Cambridge University Press.

Dowty, D. (1979). *Word meaning and Montague grammar.* Dordrecht: Reidel.

Goldberg, A. E. (1993). Another look at some learnability paradoxes. In E. V. Clark (Ed.), *The proceedings of the 25th annual Child Language Research Forum* (pp. 60–75). Stanford, CA: Center for the Study of Language & Information (distributed by Cambridge University Press).

Grimshaw, J. (1981). Form, function, and the language acquisition device. In C. L. Baker & J. J. McCarthy (Eds.), *The logical problem of language acquisition* (pp. 183–210). Cambridge, MA: MIT Press.

Gropen, J., Pinker, S., Hollander, M., Goldberg, R., & Wilson, R. (1989). The learnability and acquisition of the dative alternation in English. *Language, 65*, 203–257.

Gross, M. (1975). On the relations between syntax and semantics. In E. L. Keenan (Ed.), *Formal semantics of natural language* (pp. 389–405). Cambridge, England: Cambridge University Press.

MacWhinney, B., & Snow, C. E. (1985). The child language data exchange system (CHILDES). *Journal of Child Language, 12*, 271–294.

Pinker, S. (1984). *Language learnability and language development.* Cambridge, MA: Harvard University Press.

Pinker, S. (1989). *Learnability and cognition.* Cambridge, MA: MIT Press.

Van Valin, R. D. (1990). Semantic parameters of split intransitivity. *Language 66,* 221–260.

Vendler, Z. (1967). *Linguistics in philosophy.* Ithaca, NY: Cornell University Press.

Volterra, V. (1976). A few remarks on the use of the past participle in child language. *Italian Linguistics, 12,* 149–157.

5 Why Are Formal Systems Early to Emerge?

Yonata Levy
The Hebrew University, Jerusalem, Israel

This chapter has two parts: the first sets the discussion concerning the development of formal linguistic systems within current theoretical debates and reviews findings that demonstrate early acquisition of such systems. The second proposes an answer to the question that the title of the chapter poses. It is a tentative proposal, which calls for further discussion and more empirical work.

FUNCTIONAL AND FORMAL LINGUISTIC APPROACHES

Central among the debates that have dominated the field of language acquisition is the controversy between the functionalist and the linguistic approaches to language development. Within the context of this debate, the question concerning the early emergence of formal systems is crucial.

Although there are various formulations of functionalism, central to this approach is the view that the learning of grammar is parasitic on other, developmentally prior systems (e.g., Bates & MacWhinney, 1989; Ninio & Snow, 1988; Schlesinger, 1994; Van Valin, 1993). Cognitive and social-functional systems are considered to be the main pacesetters for development, while linguistic structures are expected to follow rather than lead the process, precisely because of their specificity.

This is a rather attractive view since, clearly, there are developmental events that precede language. Auditory, visual, and tactile perception, as well as elements of spatial cognition, are used by the infant before the first words occur. Certain social skills and various acts of communication are not dependent on the emergence of language and, in fact, predate it. All of these could be deployed to bootstrap language. It is, therefore, an a priori plausible assumption to consider early grammars as derivatives of such more basic systems, if indeed those can be shown to account for the facts of acquisition.

The linguistic approach argues that language cannot be explained away by reference to other, supposedly more elementary, systems. This approach presupposes a language-specific module, in which categories and processes are specifically linguistic and do not derive from any other preexisting, or coexisting, cognitive or social-functional structures. The linguistic approach views human languages as sharing certain structural characteristics, that is, a Universal Grammar (UG) of a fixed and unique form, which is a major determinant in acquisition. Reference is often made to *maturation* processes as determining order of development (e.g., Borer & Wexler, 1987) and to the *emergence* of structures rather than to learning, which, for the most part, is expected to take place under the constraints imposed by UG (Gleitman, 1990).

Clear empirical predictions follow from these theoretical orientations with regard to order of development: Assuming that order of development reflects basic operations, the prediction of the functionalist approach is that formal linguistic subsystems that do not map onto cognitive-semantic or social-pragmatic distinctions will be acquired by children later than systems for which such mappings are relevant, other things being equal.

The linguistic approach holds that the child acquires a set of structures—that is, grammar—that are specifically linguistic and that may or may not map onto other systems. From the linguistic standpoint, the prediction is that language-specific structures will be acquired by the child from the earliest phases. There will be no obligatory correlation between the time of emergence and the nature of the linguistic categories and paradigms and that of other cognitive systems. Order of development will be set by Universal Grammar and by learning mechanisms that are predisposed toward learning systems such as are exploited by language.

The development of formal linguistic systems, typically morphological or syntactic, can serve as a test case for these opposing developmental predictions. However, whereas this is a rather direct test of the predictions of the functionalist approach, it is only indirectly so with regard to the linguistic approach. Although the learning of morphological paradigms indeed speaks to the issue of the child's ability to master formal, language-specific systems, it does not address the issues related to Universal Grammar in any direct way. However, if it can be shown that such formal paradigms are readily acquired by the young child in the beginning phases of language development, the plausibility of the linguistic approach and the claims it makes concerning the types of systems young children can and do work with will be enhanced.

In the sections to follow, studies of the acquisition of morphology in various languages, in both normal and pathological populations of children, are reviewed. The picture that emerges from these studies is a uniform one and it speaks to the issue of the early learning of morphology.

Crosslinguistic Studies

A relatively well-studied area in morphology concerns the acquisition of gender systems. Data from the development of gender in languages as unrelated as Hebrew, English, German, Polish, French, and Russian, all of which mark linguistic gender on animate and on inanimate nouns and exercise gender agreement, suggest that children take advantage of the systematicity that is manifested in the morphophonological patterning and acquire linguistic gender marking on inanimate nouns rather early, provided the distributional facts are accessible (Levy, 1983). Errors continue to occur in the choice of pronouns, namely, in places in which the clue to linguistic gender is not some formal property of the noun, but rather the gender of the reference of the pronoun in the real world.

However, studies concerning gender acquisition in Icelandic (Mulford, 1983, 1985) and German (Mills, 1986) have suggested that a semantic notion of gender might be at play during these early phases, which is in direct contradiction with the findings reported by Levy (1983). But once the theoretical question is restated contradictions disappear and the data all point to the same conclusion (Levy, 1988).

Consider the studies by Mulford (1983, 1985), which are concerned with the development of gender by Icelandic children, aged 4 to 8 years. In Icelandic, neither natural gender nor formal properties of nouns are very good predictors of linguistic gender. There is, however, some regularity in both the noun endings and in the correspondence between linguistic and natural gender. Assuming that the availability of the cognitive notion of gender is independent of language, the prediction of the early-formal-learning thesis is that differences in the time and rate at which gender is acquired should be the result of the predictability of the formal aspects of the system. Mulford's data fit with this prediction, because her youngest subjects (aged 4 years) handled syntactic gender of familiar and nonce words at the level of around 34%, which is chance level, given that there are three linguistic genders in Icelandic. The children were 51% correct for natural gender, which is chance level when the relevant distinction is that of the sex of the referent in the real world. Notice that the fact of recognizing animacy or sex distinctions in a particular situation is not the issue; rather, it is the use of extralinguistic information for the assignment of the right morphological form— that is, the grammaticization of gender (Slobin, 1985).

Mulford (1985) cited naturalistic observations from a younger child learning Icelandic in corroboration of the data from her experiments. This child made errors in the assignment of natural gender to nouns until she was almost 3. It was only then that she started to use natural gender as a linguistic organizer of word morphology. This description fits well with observational data from other languages (see Slobin, 1985).

A comparison of these findings with studies of the development of the notion of natural gender enhances their validity. This literature suggests that notions of gender identity and gender constancy emerge between the ages of 2 and 3 (Bem, 1981). Natural gender becomes particularly salient in classificatory tasks in the 4th year of life (Serbin & Sprafkin, 1986). The language data is in accordance with this timetable.

Mulford's (1985) data supports the claim that the differences between Icelandic children and children learning some of the other languages reported in the literature lie in the nature of the morphological systems that they were attempting to master. A highly transparent system like Hebrew is captured quickly and early. For the most part, it is learned *before* the emergence of natural gender as a linguistically salient feature. A complex, nonsystematic, plurifunctional system like Icelandic is acquired slowly and painstakingly, as Mulford's data suggest. It requires a process that stretches into the period in the children's development in which the cognitive notion of gender becomes salient.

Mills (1986) set out to investigate gender marking on pronouns by English and German children. The children were asked to select proper names, which were then used to elicit referential pronouns. The findings in Mills's study show near-ceiling performance by her youngest German group (age 3;8), which was not found for the English children. Mills chose to interpret these findings by reference to the cognitive notion of gender. However, it is not clear that these findings indeed require such an explanation. Because proper names in German share phonological markings that are characteristic of feminine and masculine nouns, the German children, but not the English children, might have been cued by the phonological features of the proper names of their choice.

Another linguistic subsystem that may be studied using the same methodological approach as gender is countability. The developmental question concerns the nature of the subcategorization of count and mass nouns, for which both semantic and syntactic support is available in the input. Two different predictions arise: Whereas semantic correlations should predispose the child to acquire the count-mass subcategories as a distinction between names for objects versus names for substances, the linguistic approach predicts that syntactic cues will be most effective in the early learning of the use of determiners and plurals.

Gordon (1985) tested 3- to 5-year-olds in a word-learning paradigm. The results suggest that when the children were able to consistently respond on the basis of either semantic or syntactic cues, they overwhelmingly categorized on the basis of the syntactic context. Of interest to the present discussion is the observation that for the older groups both syntactic and semantic clues served as systematic bases for categorization. However, the younger group consistently preferred the syntactic clues to the semantic ones.

These experimental findings were further supported by longitudinal data from two children, aged 1;9–3;6 and 2;3–3;5. The data showed no evidence of noun miscategorization on the basis of semantic properties. On the other hand, both subjects used nonprototypical count nouns in the appropriate syntactic context, that is, with the correct determiner.

Gathercole (1985) addressed the same theoretical issues through the study of children's use of *much* and *many*. The results suggest that children begin by learning the count/mass distinction as a morphosyntactic distributional distinction. They appear to learn first the appropriate forms of nouns and then to couple the quantifiers with the already established forms of the nouns, associating *many* with plurals long before they restrict *much* in direct noun modification to use with the singular. Children recognize errors in the use of *many* before they recognize errors in the use of *much*—in particular, those errors involving correct plural forms of count nouns. Gathercole's findings suggest that young children treat *much* and *many* as almost synonymous ways of indicating quantity. In addition to the linguistic tasks, each child was tested for the conservation of number and substance on a judgment and correction task. No correlation was found between performance on the conservation and on the linguistic tasks.

Bloom (1990, 1994) recently criticized Gordon (1985) and Gathercole's (1985) work and suggested that semantic factors are accountable for the acquisition of the count/mass distinction in English. Bloom argues, convincingly I think, that there is a bidirectional syntax-semantics mapping between count nouns and kinds of individuals and mass nouns and kinds of portions, and that such mappings take place under the impact of strong cognitive biases to encode discrete physical objects as individuals and substances or collections of particles as portions. Although this seems a likely procedure for "bootstrapping" the count/mass distinction and possibly also nouns in general, Bloom also resorts to paradigm building and to children's sensitivity to the syntax of the count/mass distinctions for development beyond the very initial stages. It does seem, however, that Bloom (1994) is offering a convincing way of viewing the mapping relationships that exist between the cognitive notion of individuals and portions and the syntax of the count/mass nouns, yet one that does not necessarily engage the acquisition process.

Consider next those studies that compared the developmental evidence for the use of word order with evidence concerning the development of morphological marking. Mervis and Johnson (1991) studied the acquisition of the plural morpheme in English. The claim that word order is more accessible to the young English speaker than morphological markings (e.g., Brown, 1973; Pinker, 1984), which has been an enduring myth in the acquisition literature, is being shaken by the findings from this longitudinal case study. The authors presented evidence for the precedence of morphology over syntax for their young subject. Such is the case with the plural marking, the progressive, the diminutive, the possessive, and the past tense, which the child used before producing two-word combinations, that is, before syntax. A separation of meaning from form was only possible with regard to -*ing* and past tense -*ed*, hence witnessing good performance, indeed tells us that the child has mastered morphology, but it does not allow us to decide whether this was done through the use of meaning or on the basis of formal features exclusively.

Weist and Wilkowska-Stadnik (1986) were likewise concerned with the claim that the child's capacity to use word order—namely, syntax—as a grammatical device is particularly primitive. In Polish, it is possible to contrast word order, inflectional information, and pragmatic information within the sentence. Naturalistic speech samples from children aged 1;7 to 2;5 were analyzed along with test data from 2- and 3-year-olds.

The authors argued for the existence of syntactic functions that are not reducible to semantic distinctions from as early as age 1;6. They suggested that those might be observed through the children's use of inflectional morphology. An effective utilization of inflectional strategies was observed even in the youngest subjects in the study, who were under 2 years and already using a variety of inflected forms. A similar finding held for the marking of inflectional features such as tense and aspect. Weist and Wilkowska-Stadnik argued that in no period in their linguistic development do Polish children use bare stems. This is not surprising and has been reported for other languages as well (Levy, 1988), for to use bare stems in a language where words are obligatorily inflected would require considerable abstraction and result in the production of forms the like of which are never attested in the input.

Tracy (1986) studied the acquisition of case morphology in German. A fully developed German case system involves several levels of linguistic organization with differing contributions from syntax, semantics, morphology, phonology and pragmatics. Tracy's claim is that the learner constructs the morphological case system by searching for correlations across these various linguistic subsystems. Tracy noted that 2- and 3-year-old German children use inflections productively, yet they may rely on word-order strategies in comprehension. The acquisitional facts, as she observed them, suggest that although inflections may be used productively, they are not seen at first as cues to meanings in comprehension. In other words, at a period in which the formal system has been mastered, its semantic underpinning may still be little understood.

The findings concerning the Hebrew verb system, the *binyanim,* reveal a similar trend. The binyanim present a conjunction of semantic, syntactic, and morphophonological features that is typical of Semitic languages. The acquisition of the binyan system has been extensively studied (e.g., Berman, 1982, 1985; Levy, 1988). Berman argued that children start out with unanalyzed forms of verbs and continue to use a rich variety of verb forms, not knowing that the formal manipulations between these various verb patterns may be systematically used to achieve modulations of meaning. It is only around age 4, a long time after they have been using most verb patterns productively, that children make errors that suggest they are mastering the semantics of the binyanim.

Data from young 2-year-olds (Levy, 1988) show that they treat differentially the consonantal roots of words, which in Hebrew are stable across word categories, and the vocalic patterns, which serve to distinguish between nouns and verbs, as well as among words within classes. Without going into details of Hebrew word structure, the conclusion from this work is that the formal properties of Hebrew word structure are learned early, prior to the understanding of the various semantic distinctions that these formal manipulations may serve to convey. Furthermore, these data suggest that even at this early stage there may be a rudimentary notion of formally defined word classes. These findings are very similar to those reported for English by Mervis and Johnson (1991, see earlier discussion), who argued that the child has a formally defined Noun category prior to any real syntax.

Yet a different perspective on the issue of early-formal-learning is offered by Meisel (1986), who studied the development of word order and case marking in bilingual German-French children. Based on the differential use of grammatical devices for the two languages, Meisel argued that as soon as multiword utterances appear in bilinguals, there is evidence for a separation of the grammatical systems. His findings reveal a simultaneous emergence in both languages of case markings, pronominal subjects and verb inflections. He considered it to be an indication that the children are using morphological means to encode syntactic functions. Meisel rejected the claim that new formal devices are acquired to satisfy functional needs and argues that new forms are acquired just because they are part of the linguistic system to which the child is exposed. Grammar is seen as autonomous with respect to other areas of mental development, including the linguistic-functional.

Children With Neurological Deficit

What is the developmental picture in children with neurological deficit? Curtiss (1988) and Curtiss and Yamada (1981) studied the language performance of Antony—a retarded 7-year-old, with a Leiter IQ of 50 and a mental age of 2;9. Antony scored below all norms on all cognitive tests and was below the 2-year-old level. However, he was well within the norms for his age in his use of formal syntactic structures in spontaneous speech. He scored poorly on comprehension of locative prepositions, time adverbs, and disjunctions. His production of inflectional morphology was also poor, which might be explained by the fact that in English, inflectional morphology serves almost exclusively to introduce meaning distinctions such as tense, aspect, gender in the 3rd person, and plural, whereas there are no arbitrary morphological systems such as gender marking of inanimate nouns.

Syntax seemed well preserved in comprehension and Antony scored well on wh-questions, relativization, and auxiliaries. Furthermore, Curtiss (1988) and Curtiss and Yamada (1981) pointed out that Antony never made errors such as placing verb markers on nouns, or using affixes as suffixes. This is similar to the findings for normal 2-year-olds that led to the postulation of rudimentary word classes in very young children (Levy, 1988; Maratsos, 1981). The authors argued that Antony has extracted the syntactic and morphological constraints, without the semantics they serve to encode.

Cromer (1988, 1991) maintained that such a profile is, in fact, characteristic of the language of retarded individuals. Summarizing what is known about language and cognition in retarded children, Cromer concluded that deficits are primarily found in linguistic components that are dependent on the conceptual system. Laura, a retarded adolescent studied extensively by Yamada (1990), presents a linguistic profile that supports these claims.

Leonard, Sabbadini, Leonard, and Volterra (1987) studied morphology in the speech of specifically language impaired Italian and English-speaking children. The different status of morphology in the two languages allowed for some interesting comparisons. Contrary to expectations, it was found that deficits were related to the opacity of the rules involved, to homonymy between morphemes and to phonological difficulties. Deficits did not correlate with grammatical properties within the verb system nor in any other place in the grammar.

Levy, Amir and Shalev (1992) studied the language of a child with a congenital, left-hemisphere brain infarct learning Hebrew as his first language. Although this child's neurological history was very different from that of the children reported earlier in this section, his linguistic profile was very similar to theirs. This child had a relatively unimpaired morphology with pronounced deficiencies in semantics and pragmatics, which far exceeded his error rate in either morphology or syntax. The data showed better mastery of formal aspects of the morphological system, wherever those could be separated from the meanings they serve to convey. In view of the complexity of Hebrew morphological system, this was a considerable feat.

The aforementioned findings can be summarized as follows. In cases in which the structure of the language allows for a separation of various facets of a given subsystem, such as gender and verb patterns in Hebrew, countability and word classes in English, and word order and case marking in Polish and German, young normal children, as well as children with various types of congenital brain pathologies, mastered the formal system relatively early. It was shown that the degree to which form mapped onto function was not the main predictor of order of acquisition. These findings therefore do not support the predictions of functionalist theories, yet they increase the plausibility of the linguistic approach in that they demonstrate children's ability to attend to purely formal, distributionally based systems.

ON THE PROPERTIES OF FORMAL
LINGUISTIC SYSTEMS

What properties of these formal systems are accountable for the ease with which children seem to acquire them? The prototypical response of mainstream proponents of the linguistic approach to this question would be that order of acquisition is determined by Universal Grammar and by the input data that decides between possible alternatives. In current terminology one talks about the setting of parameters (Chomsky, 1986). Within this framework, structures in children's language are seen to *emerge* or *mature*.

However, the response that is offered in this chapter is a learning-theoretic one, which focuses on the structural commonalties among the various systems referred to above, for which the acquisitional facts seem to be depicting a surprisingly consistent picture. From the perspective of learning, ease of acquisition must be affected by the degree of opacity of the paradigms. Opacity is a function of the presence of homonymity, fusion of forms and number of exceptions, and is a major determinant of complexity. But are there other factors, besides opacity, that contribute to complexity?

I suggest that another factor that may account for the degree of complexity of a linguistic subsystem for the young learner is its autonomy, or *closedness*. A system is considered "closed" when its rules and primitives are defined in a way that is internal to the system, with no necessary input from other systems or domains. Chess is an example of a closed system: The pieces that are involved in the game are defined in relation to the board and to each other, that is, by game-internal definitions. The rules according to which the pieces move, as well as the definition of winning are, likewise, game-internal. It is only via labels such as King, Queen, and Knight, which carry meaning, that the game "makes contact" with other paradigms. Within morphology, the notion of a closed system is analogous to that of an unlabeled paradigm. Unlike Fodorian modularity, being *closed*, as it is used here, refers to the structure of the data and is neutral with regard to the ways that this structure might be represented in the mind.

The morphological systems that were reviewed earlier constitute relatively closed systems, in the sense described here. For example, Hebrew gender is a classificatory system of nouns. With respect to inanimates, it is entirely determined by the phonological properties of the final syllable of the noun, which, in turn, determines the choice of the correct plural ending from a number of available allomorphs.

There is an inherent circularity in the logical notion of a closed system, for certain things must be given or else the system cannot be bootstrapped. Thus, unless the child had the notion of a syllable and knew about the phonology of Hebrew, he could not construct the gender paradigm. The same requirement exists for learning cases in German or Polish. Similarly, prior to the learning of the formal properties of the binyan system in Hebrew, there must be a classification of words into two classes, roughly synonymous with nouns and verbs, while for the acquisition of word order, the child must know about words as units in the sentence. All of these requirements are external to the systems involved.

Consequently, rather then viewing linguistic systems as closed systems, we should think of them as varying in their degree of autonomy. For example, morphophonological systems are closed relative to morphosyntactic systems, while the later are more autonomous than other syntactic operations. Syntactic constraints on binding and the movement of constituents, by their very nature, are more autonomous in the sense used here than subcategorization frames. The least autonomous of all are systems within semantics and pragmatics.

It might therefore be hypothesized that dependencies among systems *increase* the complexity of the learning task for the young child. Arriving at a systematization of a closed system is simpler than learning an open paradigm. If indeed closed systems are less of a problem for the developing child, while systems for which form-function correspondence is the key feature constitute more difficult problems, then systems such as gender in inanimates, progressive *-ing,* and form classes are indeed expected to develop early. They are, likewise, expected to constitute less complex problems for children who acquire language with less than an intact brain, as was the case with the children studied by Cromer (1988, 1990), Curtiss (1988, Curtiss & Yamada, 1981), Yamada (1990), and Levy et al. (1992).

Summarizing, I suggest that the degree of closedness of a linguistic system affects the ease with which it is acquired. The more closed a system is, the less complicated a learning problem it presents. This then, argues against the view point of functionalism, since it predicts that being relevant—that is, relating to more than one closed level of analysis—will result in further complexity and, hence, such structures will not be acquired early. However, being relevant is of course crucial for language knowledge, so, eventually, systems have to be opened and types of knowledge have to be integrated. From a developmental perspective this will constitute a more advanced stage.

Returning to the question that the title of this chapter poses, I suggest the following: Formal systems appear early in children's language because, given their nature, they constitute intrinsically easier problems. Finally, and most tentatively, it seems that having the properties of a closed system is not specific to linguistic systems. It is expected that this parameter will predict ease of mastery in other cognitive domains as well.

REFERENCES

Bates, E., & MacWhinney, B. (1989). Functionalism and the competition model. In B. MacWhinney & E. Bates (Eds.), *The crosslinguistic study of sentence processing* (pp. 3–73). Cambridge, England: Cambridge University Press.

Bem, S. (1981). Gender schema theory: A cognitive account of sex typing. *Psychological Review, 88,* 354–364.

Berman, R. A. (1982). Verb-pattern alternation: The interface of morphology, syntax and semantics in Hebrew child language. *Journal of Child Language, 9,* 169–191.

Berman, R. A. (1985). Acquisition of Hebrew. In D. I. Slobin (Ed.), *The crosslinguistic study of language acquisition, Vol. I: The data* (pp. 255-371). Hillsdale, NJ: Lawrence Erlbaum Associates.

Bloom, P. (1990). Syntactic distinctions in child language. *Journal of Child Language, 17,* 343–355.

Bloom, P. (1994). Syntax-semantics mappings as an explanation for some transitions in language development. In Y. Levy, (Ed.), *Other children, other languages* (pp. 41–75). Hillsdale, NJ: Lawrence Erlbaum Associates.

Borer, H., & Wexler, K. (1987). The maturation of syntax. In T. Roeper & E. Williams (Eds.), *Parameter setting* (pp. 123–172). Dordrecht: Reidel.

Brown, R. (1973). *A first language: The early stages.* Cambridge, MA: Harvard University Press.

Chomsky, N. (1986). *Barriers.* Cambridge, MA: MIT Press.

Cromer, R. (1988). Differentiating language and cognition. In R. Schiefelbusch & L. Lloyd (Eds.), *Language perspectives: Acquisition, retardation, and intervention* (2nd ed., pp. 69–87). Baltimore, MD: University Park Press.

Cromer, R. (1991). *Language and thought in normal and handicapped children.* Cambridge, MA: Basil Blackwell.

Curtiss, S. (1988). Abnormal language acquisition and the modularity of language. In F. J. Newmeyer (Ed.), *Linguistics: The Cambridge Survey* (Vol. 2, pp. 96–116). Cambridge, England: Cambridge University Press.

Curtiss, S., & Yamada, J. (1981). Selectively intact grammatical development in a retarded child. *UCLA Working Papers in Cognitive Linguistics, 3,* 61–91.

Gathercole, V. (1985). 'He has too much hard questions': The acquisition of the linguistic count-mass distinction in *much* and *many. Journal of Child Language, 12,* 395–415.

Gleitman, L. R. (1990). The structural sources of word meaning. *Language Acquisition, 1,* 3–55.

Gordon, P. (1985). Evaluating the semantic category hypothesis: The case of the count-mass distinction. *Cognition, 20,* 209–242.

Leonard, L., Sabbadini, L., Leonard, J., & Volterra, V. (1987). Specific language impairment in children: A cross-linguistic study. *Brain and Language, 32,* 233–252.

Levy, Y. (1983). It's frogs all the way down. *Cognition, 15,* 75–93.

Levy, Y. (1988). The nature of early language—Evidence from the development of Hebrew morphology. In Y. Levy, I. M. Schlesinger, & M. D. S. Braine (Eds.), *Categories and processes in language acquisition* (pp. 73–98). Hillsdale, NJ: Lawrence Erlbaum Associates.

Levy, Y., Amir, N., & Shalev, R. (1992). Language development in a child with a congenital LH lesion. *Cognitive Neuropsychology, 9,* 1–32.

Maratsos, M. (1981). Problems in categorial evolution: Can formal categories arise from semantic ones? In W. Deutsch (Ed.), *The child's construction of language* (pp. 245–261). New York: Academic Press.

Meisel, J. (1986). Word order and case marking in early child language. Evidence from simultaneous acquisition of two first languages: French and German. *Linguistics, 24,* 123–186.

Mervis, C., & Johnson, K. E. (1991). Acquisition of the plural morpheme: A case study. *Developmental Psychology, 27,* 222–235.

Mills, A. E. (1986). Acquisition of the natural-gender rule in English and German. *Linguistics, 24,* 31–45.

Mulford, R. (1983). Semantic and formal factors in the comprehension of Icelandic pronoun gender. *Papers and Reports on Child Language Development, 22,* 83–91.

Mulford, R. (1985). Comprehension of Icelandic pronoun gender: Semantic versus formal factors. *Journal of Child Language, 12,* 443–454.

Ninio, A., & Snow, C. E. (1988). Language acquisition through language use: The functional sources of children's early utterances. In Y. Levy, I. M. Schlesinger, & M. D. S. Braine (Eds.), *Strate-*

gies and processes in language acquisition (pp. 11–30). Hillsdale, NJ: Lawrence Erlbaum Associates.

Pinker, S. (1984). *Language learnability and language development.* Cambridge, MA: Harvard University Press.

Schlesinger, I. M. (1994). Two approaches to the acquisition of grammar. In Y. Levy (Ed.), *Other children, other languages* (pp. 77–112). Hillsdale, NJ: Lawrence Erlbaum Associates.

Serbin, L. A., & Sprafkin, C. (1986). The salience of gender and the process of sex typing in three-to-seven year old children. *Child Development, 57,* 1188–1199.

Slobin, D. I. (Ed.). (1985). *The crosslinguistic study of language acquisition, Vol. 1: The data.* Hillsdale, NJ: Lawrence Erlbaum Associates.

Tracy, R. (1986). The acquisition of case morphology in German. *Linguistics, 24,* 47–78.

Van Valin, R. (1993). A synopsis of role and reference grammar. In R. Van Valin (Ed.), *Advances in role and reference grammar* (pp. 1–164). Amsterdam: Benjamins.

Weist, R., & Wilkowska-Stadnik, K. (1986). Basic relations in child language and the word-order myth. *International Journal of Psychology, 21,* 1–19.

Yamada, J. (1990). *Laura—A case for the modularity of language.* Cambridge, MA: MIT Press.

6 Acquisition of Noun Class Systems in Related Bantu Languages

Susan M. Suzman
University of the Witwatersrand
Johannesburg, South Africa

Crosslinguistic studies of related languages indicate that small differences in the realization of morphological systems may cause variation in the process and timetable of acquisition. For example, Slobin (1966) and Smoczynska (1985) found that small phonetic differences in the pronunciation of gender suffixes in Polish and Russian significantly affected the timetable of acquisition of gender. Peters (in press) called these studies *minimal pair* studies, involving minimal pair sets of languages—closely related languages with similar morphological systems.

In this chapter, I examine the range of variation in another type of gender phenomenon, the noun class (NC) prefix system found in the Bantu languages of Africa. For a discussion of different types of gender systems, the reader is referred to Corbett (1991). The Bantu language family consists of more than 350 languages characterized by a particular type of noun class and agreement system. In many Bantu languages, nouns are classified according to grammatical gender or noun class, which is indicated by a prefix on the noun stem. The number of gender classes in these languages ranges between 10 and 20. Most other sentence constituents are brought into agreement with the head noun by means of agreement prefixes. The extent of the morphosyntactic systems in Bantu languages results in early use of parts of these systems, a factor that provides a rich source of data for investigating the acquisition of noun class prefixes.

As in this study, most developmental work in Bantu languages has to date

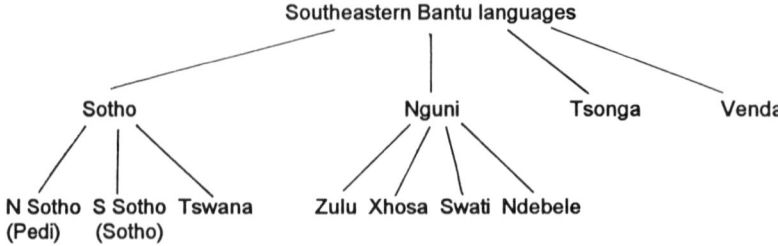

FIG. 6.1. The southeastern (SE) branch of the Bantu languages

been done in the languages of Southern Africa. Here, I draw on naturalistic data in the four languages of the Southeastern branch of the Bantu family shown in Fig. 6.1: Sotho, Tswana, Swati and Zulu.

As indicated in Fig. 6.1, Zulu and Swati are closely related languages within the Nguni subgroup and, similarly, Sotho and Tswana are related Sotho languages. Within the Sotho and Nguni groups, the languages are generally mutually intelligible. Overall, the languages in the Southeastern group are structurally quite similar, as indicated by the cognates given in Table 6.1.

Differences among the prefixes above are seen in the prefix vowels, which have, however, similar phonetic values, length (disyllabic and monosyllabic), syllable structure (VCV, CV, V, C), segment identification, suprasegmental features and whether they begin with vowels or consonants.

Noun class prefixes are regularly associated in singular and plural pairs in

TABLE 6.1
Cognates in Zulu, Swati, Sotho, and Tswana

Noun Class	Zulu	Swati	Sotho	Tswana	Gloss
1	umu-ntu	umu-ntu	mo-tho	mo-tho	'person'
5	i-sela	li-sela	le-sela	le-sela	'thief'
7	is-andla	s-andla	se-atla	se-atla	'hand'
9	in-komo	in-khomo	khomo	kgomo	'cow

TABLE 6.2
Zulu Prefixes (Classes 1-10)

Noun Class	Singular		Noun Class	Plural	
1	umu-ntu	'person'	2	aba-ntu	'people'
1a	u:-mama	'mother'	2a	o:-mama	'mothers'
3	umu-thi	'tree'	4	imi-thi	'trees'
5	i:-sela	'thief'	6	ama-sela	'thieves'
7	isi-cathulo	'shoe'	8	isi-cathulo	'shoes'
9	iN-komo	'cow'	10	iziN-komo	'cows'

many but not all of the noun stems, as illustrated in Table 6.2 for Zulu nouns.[1]

Traditionally, it has often been assumed that the large number of morphological classes in Bantu languages derives from the classification of semantically similar objects into morphological classes (Denny & Creider, 1986; Welmers, 1973). Doke (1954) observed that nouns referring to people, living inanimates (trees and plants), animals, and natural semantic groups occur in distinct morphological classes in Zulu. However, Herbert noted that "there is little agreement on the exact nature of the Proto-Bantu system" (1991, p.105), although semantic associations are perpetuated in traditional descriptions such as Doke's. If there were a semantic basis historically, it is severely attenuated in contemporary Bantu languages, in which most noun classes are semantically heterogeneous and primarily morphological in nature. However, there remains a partial but arguably important form-meaning correlation between nouns denoting human beings and noun classes (NC) 1, 1a, 2, and 2a.[2]

Although noun class systems characterize all Bantu languages, they vary crosslinguistically in phonological and morphological properties, as noted earlier. Table 6.3 presents the comparative prefixes for the languages investigated in this chapter.

---

[1]In this chapter, we use language names without noun class prefixes, following the general tradition of scholarship on African languages, such as is illustrated in Welmers (1973). The use of the prefix in Southeastern Bantu languages is a local political development, but even in the region it is inconsistently applied, as seen in Se-sotho, Si-swati, Se-tswana, and Zulu. Readers should be aware that Sesotho and Sotho are the same language.

[2]In Zulu, for example, most nouns in the "human" classes refer to people as members of classes (NCs 1 and 2), such as boy, father, teacher, and preacher, or as individuals (NCs 1a and 2a), names like Unqoba, father, and mother.

TABLE 6.3
Comparative Noun Class Systems (Classes 1-10)

	Nguni		Sotho	
Noun Class	Zulu	Swati	Sotho	Tswana
1	um(u)	um(u)	mo	mo
2	aba	ba	ba	ba
1a	u:	Ø	Ø	Ø
2a	o:	bo	bo	bo
3	um(u)	um(u)	mo	mo
4	imi	imi	me	me
5	I: (<ili)	li	le	le
6	ama	ema	ma	ma
7	isi	si	se	se
8	izi	ti	li	di
9	iN	iN	Ø	Ø
10	iziN	tiN	li	di

Several differences in these prefix systems are apparent. First is the ostensible difference between the vowels in Nguni and Sotho. Sotho and Tswana vowels /e/ and /o/ find their counterparts in Zulu and Swati /i/ and /u/. Although they are written differently, the phonetic value of the vowels is similar, Sotho and Tswana /e/ and /o/ being described as lax rather than tense high front and back vowels.

More importantly, the prefixes differ in composition, depending on whether there is a vocalic pre-prefix preceding the prefix. The Sotho languages have a monosyllabic prefix, illustrated in NC1 /mo/, whereas Zulu has a disyllabic pre-prefix and prefix, i.e. /u-mu/ for NC1. (See Table 6.1.) In terms of morphology, the pre-prefix in Zulu has a predictable identity, being the same as the prefix vowel, as the example illustrates. Swati has both monosyllabic and disyllabic prefixes and presents a midway point between Sotho and Zulu, a factor that may be anticipated to influence patterns of acquisition.

Because of the pre-prefix, Zulu nouns usually commence with a vowel. Due to a majority of singular nouns in young children's speech (Connelly, 1984; Suzman, 1991), this means a preponderance of high front /i/ and high back vowels /u/, vowels that closely approximate maximal phonetic oppositions. Prefixes in the Sotho languages are, by contrast, consonant-commencing, with a range of different consonants introducing prefixes, as in /mo/, /le/ and /se/.

The pre-prefix in Bantu languages is hightoned whereas the Bantu prefix is lowtoned. In languages with a pre-prefix like Zulu, nouns have a high tone initially associated with that segment; in the Sotho languages, nouns generally commence with lowtoned prefixes.

Zulu prefixes interact with syllable structure rules. Bantu languages strongly favor CV sequences within word and utterance. The CV structure of the prefixes of the Sotho languages preserves this syllable structure, whereas Zulu prefixes would appear to violate it because they often have VCV structure. However, there is optional syntactic elision of the final vowel of a word in a sequence of two vowels (V# #V) across a morpheme boundary in rapid or colloquial speech; for example, *thatha isicathulo* becomes *thath' isicathulo* 'take the shoe' with the elision of the verb vowel. Verb-noun sequences are among the environments in which elision takes place in Zulu (Ziervogel, 1967) and they provide an important context for the use of the pre-prefix.

Finally, the comparative chart in Table 6.1 shows that the Sotho languages and Swati have zero morphemes, or "holes" (Demuth, 1992) in the paradigm, unlike Zulu, which has overt prefixes throughout the system. Although only a few classes have a zero morpheme in the Sotho languages, they include the *human* class, NC1a, consisting of personal names and kinship terms—empirically important in young children's speech.

In colloquial or fast speech, other Tswana and Sotho prefixes may be optionally omitted when there is an accompanying agreeing constituent with an agreement marker on it, i.e. *kolo sa-ne* 'that school' (literally, "school that") rather than *se-kolo sa-ne,* which has the full prefix. In this example, the NC7 marker is found on the modifier "that" and may therefore be omitted on the noun itself. Tsonope (1987) proposed that optional prefixes in casual speech may account for the lack of prefixes on children's nouns in the earliest stages. The noun class prefix is generally included in all speech styles in Zulu.

Structurally and pragmatically, then, prefixes in these languages differ according to a number of criteria: morphological content, syllable structure, tone, overt manifestation within the system, and obligatory use. The differences among the prefix systems combine to provide a profile of contrastive values, as summarized in Table 6.4.

TABLE 6.4
Crosslinguistic Comparison of Features of Noun Classes

Factor	Zulu	Swati	Sotho	Tswana
Pre-prefix	+	+/-	-	-
Vowel-commencing	+	+/-	-	-
VCV	+	+/-	-	-
High tone	+	+	-	-
Consistency	+	-	-	-
Maximal phonetic oppositions	+	+/-	-	-
Obligatory use	+	+	-	-

The positive values for the Zulu prefixes suggest that they are transparent in a number of ways that the Sotho language prefixes and, to a lesser degree, the Swati prefixes are not. Zulu prefixes are longer and have hightoned vocalic pre-prefixes with predictable phonetic values. Such features are interpreted as contributing to perceptual salience, a concept that is discussed here in terms of Brown's (1973) sense of length and number of syllables as well as in terms of segment identification and suprasegmental factors as discussed in Peters (1983). Because Zulu prefixes are both perceptually salient and obligatory in input, it is predicted they would be accessible to children before prefixes in the Sotho languages and, to lesser extent, prefixes in Swati, which shares features with both of the other groups.

Despite the differences presented earlier, the morphosyntactic systems of all of these languages share basic similarities. The noun class prefix is not an isolated noun classification marker, but determines agreement elsewhere in the sentence. Phrasal constituents and the verb are marked to agree with the head noun, as illustrated in (1) for Zulu. Agreement is variably alliterative in Bantu languages, as seen in the examples in (1), where prefixes in class 1 are less alliterative than they are in class 2.

(1)   Noun classes as determinants of sentential agreement
       (SM = Subject marker, AM = Adjective marker, RM = Relative marker)
       Umu-ntu   *omu-de*   *o-sebenzayo*   *u-khathele*
       NC1-person   AM1-tall   RM1-working   SM1-tired
       'The tall person who is working is tired'

       Aba-ntu   *aba-de*   *aba-sebenzayo*   *ba-khathele*
       NC2-people   AM2-tall   RM2-working   SM2-tired
       'The tall people who are working are tired'

The pervasiveness of noun class and agreement in these languages arguably contributes to their perceptual salience, a factor that may neutralize crosslinguistic differences and make the child's language acquisition task quite comparable across different languages. Certainly, an overview of the comparative morphosyntactic systems suggests that they present children with similar acquisition tasks, with language-specific morphophonological properties of prefixes raising questions about how, if at all, variation in presentation of these systems affects acquisition.

RESEARCH BASE FOR
CROSSLINGUISTIC COMPARISON

This chapter follows the work of Connelly (1984), Demuth (1988, 1992), Kunene (1979), Suzman (1980, 1991), and Tsonope (1987). All of these researchers have investigated to some extent the acquisition of the noun class system and its role in

TABLE 6.5
Researchers, Subjects, and Type of Study

Researcher	Subjects and Age	Type of Study	Language
Connelly	4 (2) 1;6 - 2;9 (2) 3 - 4	Q	Sotho

Demuth	4 (2) 2 - 3
	    2;4 - 2;9
	    2;8 - 4;1
		Q	Sotho

Kunene	2 2;3 - 3	Q	Swati
Tsonope	2 1;11 - 2;6 2;5 - 3	Q	Tswana

Suzman	3 1;10 - 3;2
	    1;10 - 2;9
	    2;2 - 3;6
		L	Zulu

Note. Q = quasilongitudinal, L = longitudinal

agreement assignment. In particular, Connelly (1984) has investigated the acquisition of the nominal morphology of Sotho noun classes, while Kunene (1979) Demuth (1984), Tsonope (1987) and Suzman (1991) dealt with noun class markers and aspects of agreement in Swati, Sotho, Tswana, and Zulu respectively. Researchers, their subjects and studies are summarized in Table 6.5.

Although the studies are quite similar in their approach to the study of child speech development, differences in focus and consideration of input affect the comparability of the data. The results are discussed as closely as the data from the respective studies allow.

RESULTS

A consensus on the general timeline of acquisition of a subset of noun class prefixes emerges from the study of nominal morphology in these languages. Children initially acquire a reduced version of the adult system due to predominance of singular forms and uneven productivity of the noun classes in usage (Suzman, 1991). Regarding nouns, Connelly (1984) and Tsonope (1987) found approximately 80% of singular nouns in child speech. The prevalence of singular nouns effectively halves the number of prefixes to be learned from the adult system. Further reduction in the subset of singular prefixes to be learned was reported by Connelly (1984), Tsonope (1987) and Demuth (1988), due to the widespread use of nouns in NC9, the default class in Sotho and Tswana. In urban Zulu, I have reported elsewhere that children predominantly used noun classes

1a, 5, and 9.[3] This dramatic reduction of the prefix system focuses the child's attention on a subset of singular noun classes and arguably makes the child's initial acquisition task in Bantu languages comparable to learning a European gender language with three gender classes.

All researchers found morphological strategies in the acquisition of noun structure. Children make few segmentation errors between prefix and stem and appear to have access to the internal structure of nouns at an early age. There is little or no evidence of learning nominal forms as unanalyzed wholes.

Likewise, there is consensus about children using variable forms of nouns, especially in the early stages. Suzman (1991) reported that the major contrast was between nouns with and without prefixes, whereas Kunene (1979), Connelly (1984), Demuth (1988), and Tsonope (1987) found stems only, partial or shadow prefixes, and full prefixes occurring concurrently.

Although similar lines of development are found crosslinguistically, close analysis of the timetable and process of acquisition reveals interesting differences in the interpretation of the data and in the detail of acquisition.

Early Onset of Prefixes in Zulu

Suzman (1991) reported early acquisition of prefixes in Zulu, with approximately one half of 2-year-old children's nouns occurring with prefixes, although not necessarily the appropriate adult forms. It was found that the inclusion of a prefix on the noun was often contextually determined, with prefixes being omitted in subject position—as in (2a) and (2c)—and in citation form but included in object and final position, as in (2b) and (2d).

(2) Positionally determined prefix use: Lindi (1;11)

Child Utterance	Adult Zulu
(a) **nan'***uzumoya*	*U-nana u-zw'umoya*
	'The baby feels the wind'
(b) *kis'***u-nana**	*Gqokis'u-nana*
	'Dress the baby'
(c) **mama** *gokis'u-nan*	*U-mama ugqokis'u-nana*
	'Mother dresses the baby'
(d) *su'mehl'Li* **u-mama**	*U-sul'amehlo ka-Lindi, umama*
	'Mother wipes Lindi's eyes'

In these examples, the presence or absence of a prefix depends on its position in the sentence and the operation of elision rules. The nouns for 'baby' and 'Mother' occur with prefixes when following the verb, but without them when preceding the verb. The omission or reduction of linguistic elements in utterance-

---

[3]Herbert (1978, 1991) argued that this contrast may effectively be NC1a and NC 5/9 in contemporary Zulu, due to the reanalysis of the prefix nasal as part of the stem in NC9 nouns, resulting in the merging of the two /i/-commencing classes.

initial position and their retention following the verb are not unique to Zulu, being commonly observed in young children's speech (Limber, 1973). Some of the variation in noun forms (discussed as "concurrent stages of acquisition" by Demuth, 1992) might be accounted for in terms of predictable alternations due to utterance position, as discussed earlier for Zulu. Omissions are at least partly contextually determined, suggesting that children's use of prefixes underestimates their knowledge of them in the early stages. If this is the case, children learning Zulu have access to the internal structure of nouns at a very early age indeed.

Prosodic Factors

In the preceding discussion, object position was seen to encourage use of full nominal form. In addition, prosodic features in Zulu highlight the prefix in this position. In careful speech (3a), the final vowel of the verb (underlined italics) is not elided preceding the prefix vowel on the following noun. However, in informal registers such as are found in adult-child speech, elision rules (3b) delete the first of two vowels across morpheme boundary (3c), preserving CV structure. In child speech, the Zulu pre-prefix and prefix may be reduced to the pre-prefix, as in (3d), but the pre-prefix is rarely omitted, presumably because it would result in C'CV sequences, which would violate syllable structure rules:

(3) Speech registers and elision rules in Zulu
    (a)   Careful standard register
           (no elision):   *thatha isi-cathulo*
                                        (CV VCV)
    (b)   Zulu elision rule: V# - #V > #V
    (c)   Colloquial register (elision):   *thath'isi-cathulo*
                                          (C'VCV)
    (d)   Typical child speech: *thath'i-kathulo*
                                          (C'V-CV)
                                        'take the shoe'

Elision rules force the use of the pre-prefix plus prefix in object nouns as illustrated, a fact that arguably brings the pre-prefix to the child's attention.[4] The Zulu data support Peters's proposal that "prosody may serve the learner, not only

---

[4]Prosodic factors do not operate in this context in Bantu languages with monosyllabic prefixes because omission or retention of the prefix maintains CV syllable structure. In Swati, retention (a) or omission (b) of prefix leaves syllable structure unaffected.
    Swati
    (a)   Adult speech: *Tshatsha si-cathulo*
                               (CV CV-CV)
    (b)   Child speech: *Tshatsha cathulo*
                               (CV CV)
                               'Take the shoe'

as an aid in segmentation, i.e. in finding boundaries, but also to highlight aspects of morphological structure on which to focus" (1994, p. 16). The literature provides other examples of prosodic features that appear to play a role in determining the early form of nouns. Demuth proposed that the strong bias in Bantu toward disyllabic stems with "penultimate lengthening, a feature sometimes called penultimate 'stress' " (1992, p. 592), would lead children learning these languages to notice trochaic feet in linguistic structures. In nouns like *se-fate* 'tree' and *di-fate* 'trees', the children would be predicted to use the stem *fate* rather than the full form, as they apparently do. The observation can be extended to Zulu nouns since most of the early prefixes—that is, noun classes 1a, 5 and 9—are monosyllabic. Although this predicts that both Sotho and Zulu children would use prefixless nouns, the elision rules in Zulu maintaining CV syllable structure may provide an additional prosodic motivation for the earlier acquisition of the internal structure of Zulu nouns over those of Sotho.

Crosslinguistic Age of Acquisition

Unfortunately, there is no direct comparison of early prefix use crosslinguistically, due to differing research foci. In all the developmental studies except Suzman (1991), the emphasis is on error analysis, and there are no quantified data to compare with Suzman's finding of 50% use of a subset of singular prefixes at age 2. However, analyzing the data as closely as possible allows for some indirect conclusions about onset and development of prefixes. First, more variability in prefix form is reported in Sotho and Tswana than in Zulu. Demuth reported that before 2 years of age "nouns of all classes frequently occur with Ø prefix," and, until 2;6, nouns "continue to be used with Ø or a 'partial prefix' " (1988, p. 309). However, she also noted the frequent use of zero, partial, and full prefixes in consecutive utterances at age 2;1. Tsonope also found "co-occurrence" of varied noun forms "even in consecutive utterances" in Tswana (1984, p. 52). In Sotho, Connelly (1984) found a high proportion of phonological and morphological errors in nouns at 1;6 and rapid development to "almost no errors at 27 months" (p. 66). He noted that "It is important to stress that during any recording session there was a greater or smaller number of nouns which were not 'errors': nothing will be said about these" (p. 68). He further stressed: "The first [point] is that the children are using the great majority of nouns in the adult form at *all* stages represented by this study but that such usage is not insightful for the hypotheses we are entertaining" (p. 75). Variable nominal forms appear to exist within a framework of appropriate prefix use in Connelly's data and suggest that acquisition occurs earlier than has been discussed in the literature on Sotho acquisition, due to the emphasis on error analysis as a means of deciphering the process of acquisition.

Certainly, with the exception of Kunene (1979), where individual variation cannot be discounted, generally early acquisition (but not necessarily accurate

TABLE 6.6
Age of Acquisition of Noun Class Prefixes

	Sotho		Tswana	Swati	Zulu
Connellly		Demuth	Tsonope	Kunene	Suzman
2;3 (100%)		2;6	2;6	3;8	1;11 (50%) 2;4 (85%)

use) of prefixes has been observed, as summarized for the different acquisition studies in Table 6.6. The early acquisition of noun class prefixes supports the general finding that integral features of a language are accessible to children learning language, as observed by Berman (1986). Although Connelly (1984) raises the complexity of the noun class system as a learning problem for children, it seems that nouns with prefixes are as easy to learn as noun stems alone.

Patterns of Acquisition

It is important to note that noun class prefixes are learned in a gradual and mainly accurate way. Setting the accuracy of acquisition of noun class prefixes within a larger morphological context, there was less overgeneralization with noun class prefixes than with agreement prefixes less closely associated with the head noun.

Prefix systems, crosslinguistically, are accessible to children at an early age and children seem to use similar strategies in simplifying them, as seen in an analysis of the major "errors" found in the data.

The finding of stems only or prefixless forms, observed in the Sotho languages and in Swati (Kunene, 1979), in the early stages indicates a development from noun stems to adult prefixes on nouns. In this process, Zulu children seem to take an early lead, with 50% use of prefixes at age 2. Sotho children at this point use more variable noun forms, including *shadow* prefixes. However, Zulu children appear to lose their lead. Connelly (1984) found nearly 100% accurate prefix production by 2;3, compared to Suzman's (1991) breakdown of prefixes used by her subjects at age 2;4, shown in Table 6.7.

A surprising degree of overgeneralization was observed in Zulu at a time when Connelly (1984) reported errorless acquisition in Sotho after a period of protracted use of a shadow prefix. Suzman (1991) found evidence of overgeneralization of what appeared to be the NC9 prefix (or possibly simply the preprefix /i/ that was associated with NC9 agreement) that persisted through age 3. She found occasional use of reduced or shadow prefixes, but no significant trends

TABLE 6.7
Zulu Children's Prefix Use, Age 2;4

Child's Name	Prefixes (correct)		Prefixes (overgeneralized)		Omissions	
Nqoba	47	(67%)	20	(29%)	3	(4%)
Thulani	38	(54%)	16	(23%)	16	(23%)
Busanathi	48	(69%)	9	(13%)	13	(19%)
Tokens: 70						

in this direction. On the other hand, Connelly (1984), Demuth (1988), and Tsonope (1987) found evidence of significant use of a "partial" (Demuth, 1988) or "shadow" (Demuth, 1992) prefix, with Tsonope quantifying its use at 3.6% of all nouns used. These researchers report only a slight tendency to overgeneralize the default NC9 prefixes in Sotho and Tswana.

Overgeneralization in Zulu and shadow prefixes in Sotho appeared to be language specific manifestations of strategies to simplify the morphological systems being learned. They are discussed in more detail below.

Shadow Prefixes. Researchers in Sotho and Tswana report a range of placeholder morphemes—in Sotho /a/ (Demuth, 1988), /ʌ/, [ə], or /e/ (Connelly, 1984); in Tswana /e/ (Tsonope, 1987)—preceding the noun stem. The strongest statement about the status of this morpheme comes from Tsonope; he found a prefixal /e/, which he observed is not a "prefix qua adult prefix" and does not "imply any necessary relationship between /e/ and a particular adult prefix" (1987, p. 62). Connelly, on the other hand, noted two forms "where the progression is (a) placeholders, then (b) prefixes converging morphophonemically onto the correct prefix" (1984, p. 79).

Although the interpretation of these shadow forms at this stage may be undecided, Tsonope (1987) noted that they overgeneralize to nouns with zero morphemes in adult speech, as shown in Table 6.8 on page 99, and are identical to the NC9 subject marker which he proposes is their source.

The data suggest a placeholder strategy for marking a structural element that is not phonologically perceived in terms of the adult prefix, due, as noted earlier, to the variable nature of the form and use of the Sotho and Tswana prefixes.

Overgeneralization. Children learning Zulu generally alternate between using correct and overgeneralized NC9 prefixes for nouns, as is illustrated in the following typical conversation between Nqoba (N), age 2;3, and her cousin Mpiyakhe (M).

TABLE 6.8
Prefixal /e/ in Tswana Nouns

Child Prefixal /e/ Form	Adult Form	Gloss
ekatse	Økatse	'cat'
ekoloi	Økoloi	'vehicle'
etogo	no-togo	'soft-porridge'
etonki	Øtonki	'donkey'
enonane	Ønonyane	'bird'
emakhoba	Øma-kqowa	'white people'
esekele	Øbaesekele	'bicycle'

(4) Overgeneralized and correct forms

	Zulu	NC	Gloss
N:	i-tulo	9	'stool'
	(isi-tulo)	(7)	
N:	na-y' i-tulo	9	'here is the stool'
	(na-si isi-tulo)	(7)	
M:	si-phi?	7	'where is it?'
N:	na-si	7	'here it is'

Later, the child asked:

N:	si-ph' is'tulo?	7	'where is the stool?'

But a few minutes later, she commented:

N:	na-yi, i-tulo	9	'here is the stool'
	(nasi isitulo)	(7)	

Following this, she queried again:

N:	si-ph' i-tulo	7,9	'where is the stool?'

In this conversation, Nqoba switches back and forth between overgeneralized NC9[5] and adult NC7, tending to use overgeneralized forms in her self-initiated utterances and correct forms in response to a previous utterance. Overgeneralized forms are frequent and persistent in children's self-initiated utterances, especially in general questions and responses, such as "Where is it?" and "Here it is." Although children gradually and accurately acquired new noun classes, overgeneralized NC9 forms continued to be used by some children until age 3.

In addition, there is a certain slippage among the /i/-commencing classes 5, 7, and 9 in urban Zulu, supporting Herbert's (1978) analysis of the nasal of NC9 being reanalysed as part of the stem. Fluctuating noun class membership is found in nominal forms of all children, as illustrated in Table 6.9. Direction of overgeneralization is toward NC9.

---

[5]Forms like itulo are ambiguous in terms of noun class membership.

TABLE 6.9
Overgeneralized or Fluctuating Noun Classes in Child Speech

Child	Adult	Gloss
(Class 9)	*(Class 7)*	
i-kwama	*isi-khwama*	'purse'
i-kathulo	*isi-cathulo*	'shoe'
i-tulo	*isi-tulo*	'stool'
i-puni	*isi-puni*	'spoon'
i-timela	*isi-timela*	'train'
(Class 5)	*(Class 9)*	
i-moto	*i-moto*	'car'
i-komishi	*in-komishi*	'cup'

Nouns of NC7 tended to occur in NC9 in children's speech, as seen in the first examples in Table 6.9. The last two examples represent fluctuations between noun classes that also occur in adult urban Zulu and support a merging of noun classes 5 and 9, as mentioned earlier.

DISCUSSION

Following on Peter's metaphor of 'minimal pair' studies, I suggest that shadow prefixes and overgeneralized prefixes are in complementary distribution in languages whose noun class systems have different phonological and morphological properties. Due to the fact that all singular prefixes are either /i/- or /u/-commencing, Zulu children learn a system that is, superficially, more transparent than that encountered by Sotho children (see Table 6.4). Confronted with a range of /i/-commencing prefixes, the child overgeneralizes a NC9 prefix or the pre-prefix. The child learning Sotho, Tswana, or Swati confronts prefixes commencing with different consonants, a vowel, and a zero morpheme. The child tackles this range of forms in a different manner, by using a filler syllable, variably identified as a partial prefix, a shadow prefix, or a placeholder morpheme.

As shown in Table 6.10 the vowel-commencing Zulu prefixes cleave along a high-front and high-back vowel axis, maximizing phonetic oppositions. Although

TABLE 6.10
Acquisition Strategies

NC	ZULU			Tswana and Sotho	
1	*umu*			*mo*	
1a	*u:*			*Ø*	
5	*i:*	Overgeneralization		*le*	Shadow prefixes
7	*isi*	of NC9 /i/		*se*	/a~e~ʌ~ə/
9	*iN*			*N*	

the phonetic values of the vowels in Tswana and Sotho are not that different, the consonant-commencing prefixes make the adult shape of the prefix less accessible to the child and he falls back on placeholder morphemes. In this view, the shadow prefix and overgeneralized prefix reflect alternative morphological strategies of acquisition depending on the morphophonological properties of the system being learned.

Support for this interpretation comes from other similarities between shadow prefixes and overgeneralized prefixes. Neither overgeneralized nor shadow prefixes spread to the "human" classes, NC1 and 1a (/um/ and /u:/) in Zulu, /mo/ and /Ø/ in Sotho). Nor did prefixal /e/ in Tswana overgeneralize to common and rote-learned nouns like *mama* 'mother', *mmu* 'soil' or *metsi* 'water' (Tsonope, 1987). This suggests that semantic or phonological factors play a role in the restriction of the shadow prefix and overgeneralizations to the same range of noun classes in related languages. Furthermore, overgeneralizations and shadow prefixes occur between the no prefix stage and the full adult prefix system. For Tswana, Tsonope (1987) reported frequent occurrence of shadow prefix between 1;11 and 2;6. In Zulu, overgeneralizations are frequent at the same time, with gradual development of accurate forms. Finally, neither shadow vowel nor overgeneralized vowel delay the overall age of acquisition of the prefix, as illustrated in Table 6.6.

Zulu children were using recognizable adult prefixes while Sotho and Tswana children were using shadow prefixes, a type of placeholder morpheme, but their functions were arguably the same. Peters discussed empty morphemes as "filler syllables which seem to be used as placeholders to fill out not yet analyzed parts of a phrase" (1983, p. 72). This learning strategy would plausibly occur when language-specific structure was not perceptible to language learners. The greater perceptual salience of the Zulu system, due to the pre-prefix, is reflected in a learning strategy that results in the pre-prefix being used as a general prefix for /i/-commencing classes.

CONCLUSION

This study has shown that the timetable and strategies of acquisition of the noun class systems in closely related Bantu languages are similar, despite differences in perceptual salience and input frequencies. Similarities are attributed to noun classes being characteristic features of these languages and to prosodic effects (the trochaic foot structure of Bantu stems and, in Zulu, elision rules preserving CV structure) that bring the morphological system to the child's attention.

Differences were found in the detail of the acquisition strategy. It was proposed that overgeneralization and placeholder were alternative strategies determined by the morphophonological properties of the noun class system in surface input. Comparatively, Zulu prefixes are longer, hightoned, vowel-commencing, maximally contrastive phonetically ([i] versus [u]), and are used consistently in input, properties that were argued to make Zulu morphology more transparent to the language-learning child than the Sotho and Tswana prefixes that are monosyllabic and lowtoned, commence with a range of consonants, and are optional in input. The Sotho languages present a less perceptually salient noun class system to the language learner, a factor that influences the way in which prefixes are learned.

Bantu languages provide a particularly clear example of noun classification that minimally interacts with other systems like case and number (in the early stages at least) and allows the researcher a felicitous linguistic framework in which to investigate questions about the determinants of acquisition of morphological systems. This study identifies a constellation of morphophonological features that differentiate morphological systems in a range of Bantu languages. Patterns of acquisition in the different languages show how the similarities and differences influence the language acquisition task.

Results of this study indicate that morphophonological properties of surface input are the principle determinants of variation in patterns of acquisition across these languages. In this respect, these findings support a number of other studies such as Karmiloff-Smith (1979), Slobin (1966) and Smocyznska (1985), where phonological or phonetic factors influence perception or acquisition.

The study also raises the issue of differences in input consistency between Zulu and the Sotho language prefixes, where the noun class prefix may be omitted when there are agreement markers in the utterance. The data available provide little insight into the possible influence this factor might have on the learnability of the system. As suggested by Tsonope (1987), one reason why Sotho children use placeholder prefixes may be simply that they have less input information than Zulu children do about prefixes. More research on contextualized adult-child interaction is necessary in these languages in order to investigate the relevance of this factor.

Crosslinguistic studies of related linguistic systems contribute to the question of what is general and what is language-specific in the language acquisition process. This study provides information from Bantu languages on the kinds of variation within general development that can be expected in the study of morphological systems, and in particular, gender systems.

ACKNOWLEDGMENTS

This chapter was presented as a paper at the Sixth International Congress for the Study of Child Language, Trieste, Italy, July 18–24, 1993. Thanks go to Dan Slobin and Ann Peters for suggestions on the paper and to Lynne Murphy for comments on the proofreading of the text. I would also like to thank two anonymous readers of an earlier draft of the paper for their comments. Responsibility for the contents of the final product rests with me.

REFERENCES

Berman, R. (1986). A crosslinguistic perspective: Morphology and syntax. In P. Fletcher & M. Garman (Eds.), *Language acquisition* (2nd ed., pp. 429–447). Cambridge, England: Cambridge University Press.

Brown, R. (1973). *A first language.* Harmondsworth, England: Penguin.

Connelly, M. (1984). *Basotho children's acquisition of noun morphology.* Unpublished doctoral dissertation, University of Essex, England..

Corbett, G. (1991). *Gender.* Cambridge, England: Cambridge University Press.

Demuth, K. (1988). Noun classes and agreement in Sesotho acquisition. In M. Barlow & C. A. Ferguson (Eds.), *Agreement in natural languages: Approaches, theories and descriptions* (pp. 305–321). Stanford: Center for the Study of Language and Information..

Demuth, K. (1992). The Acquisition of Sesotho. In D. I. Slobin (Ed.), *The crosslinguistic study of language acquisition* (Vol. 3, pp. 557–638). Hillsdale, NJ: Lawrence Erlbaum Associates.

Denny, J. P., & Creider, C. (1986). The semantics of noun classes in Proto-Bantu. In C. Craig (Ed.), *Noun classes and categorization: typological studies in language* (Vol. 7, pp. 217–239). Amsterdam: John Benjamins.

Doke, C. M. (1954). *Textbook of Zulu grammar* (6th ed.). Cape Town, South Africa: Maskew, Miller, Longman.

Herbert, R. K. (1978). Morphological reanalysis in the Bantu nasal class. *African Studies, 37,* 125–37.

Herbert, R. K. (1991). Patterns in language change, acquisition and dissolution: Noun prefixes and concords in Bantu. *Anthropological Linguistics, 33,* 103–134.

Karmiloff-Smith, A. (1979). *A functional approach to child language: A study of determiners and reference.* Cambridge, England: Cambridge University Press.

Kunene, E. C. L. (1979). *The acquisition of Siswati as a first language: A morphological study with special reference to noun prefixes, noun classes and some agreement markers.* Unpublished doctoral dissertation, University of California at Los Angeles.

Limber, J. (1973). The genesis of complex sentences. In T. E. Moore (Ed.), *Cognitive development and the acquisition of language* (pp. 169–185). New York: Academic Press.

Peters, A. (1983). *The units of language acquisition* (Cambridge Series of Monographs and Texts in Applied Psycholinguistics, S. Rosenberg, Ed.). New York: Cambridge University Press.

Peters, A. (in press). Language typology, prosody, and the acquisition of grammatical morphemes. In D. I. Slobin (Ed.), *The crosslinguistic study of language acquisition, Vol. 4.* Hillsdale, NJ: Lawrence Erlbaum Associates.

Slobin, D. I. (1966). The acquisition of Russian as a native language. In F. Smith & G. A. Miller (Eds.), *The genesis of language: A psycholinguistic approach* (pp. 129–148). Cambridge, MA: MIT Press.

Smoczynska, M. (1985). The acquisition of Polish. In D. I. Slobin (Ed.), *The crosslinguistic study of language acquisition, Volume 1: The data* (pp. 595–686). Hillsdale, NJ: Lawrence Erlbaum Associates.

Suzman, S. M. (1980). Acquisition of the noun class system in Zulu. *Papers and Reports on Child Language Development, 19,* 45–52.

Suzman, S. M. (1991). *Language acquisition in Zulu.* Unpublished doctoral dissertation, University of the Witwatersrand, Johannesburg, South Africa.

Tsonope, J. (1987). *The acquisition of Setswana noun class and agreement morphology, with special reference to demonstratives and possessives.* Unpublished doctoral dissertation, State University of New York, Buffalo.

Welmers, W. E. (1973). *African language structures.* Berkeley: University of California Press.

Ziervogel, D. (Ed.). (1967). *Handbook of the speech sounds and sound changes of the Bantu languages of South Africa.* (Unisa Handbook Series No. 3E). University of South Africa, Pretoria.

7

"Guillaume I Va Pas Gagner, C'est d'Abord Maman" Genesis of the First-Person Pronoun

Mireille Brigaudiot
Aliyah Morgenstern
Catherine Nicolas
Université Paris III—Sorbonne Nouvelle

Since the turn of the 20th century, we have known that between the ages of 2 and 3 children use several linguistic forms to refer to themselves as the subject of the utterances they produce. In French and in English, the two languages we have studied for this work, the following forms have been analyzed by various authors:

1. Preverbal vowels. For example, Bloch's (1924) daughter said [ə] before nouns but also before verbs. This phenomenon has been described more recently by Bloom (1970), who gave two possible explanations for the occurrence of [ə] in her subject Eric's data at 1;7, in expressions such as "[ə] sit" and "[ə] home." According to Bloom, "One possible source for /ə/ may have been the pronoun 'I', this interpretation of /ə/ in constructions with verbs became more tenable at Eric III [1;10], when the form was often 'I' in context before verbs only. A second possible source may have been the prenoun article 'a' or 'the' " (p. 106).

2. First name or nickname. For example, at 1;8 Bain's (1936) daughter Sheila used her name to refer to herself, as in "Seebee eat."

3. Pronouns *me* and *my*, in French *moi*. Grégoire (1937) described his son Charles at 1;9 as saying /mapapet/ ('me not potty', meaning "I don't want to go on the potty").

4. *You,* in French *tu:*. When Cooley's (1908) daughter said "you want cake" at 2;2, she was the one who wanted a piece of cake.

5. *I,* in French *je*. At 1;11, Bain's daughter said "I help Mama."

6. Null form. Another phenomenon to which some of these authors have referred is the absence of any form before verbs when *I* is mandatory in adult English and *je* in adult French. For example, at 2;1 Bloch's daughter said /papome/ ('hat put', meaning "I want to put on the hat").

These examples show that acquisition of the pronoun *I* is in progress when children are around the age of 2. But how can the use of these several competing forms by young speakers be explained? Are there stages that prepare for the use of *I*? What are the problems we are presented with when we study the acquisition of this tiny, slippery pronoun? Several authors go beyond the simple record of these various forms and attempt to explain the genesis of the first person pronoun by referring to problems that for us correspond to three different points of view.

A Psychological Problem: Self-Awareness

Since the middle of the 19th century, psychologists have insisted on the relation between first person pronouns (*me*, *I*) and an important stage in the psychological development of self-awareness. They claim that children become aware of themselves only when they acquire "self-pronouns" (Lobish, 1851). Whether they use those pronouns is directly related to the "feeling of personality" (Wallon, 1934). "Before the appearance of *je*. . .children . . . have not understood that the representation they have of themselves is different from the one others have of them" (translated from Piaget, 1926, cited in Pichon, 1936, p. 95). Even if this feeling of self is sometimes acknowledged to be already present in the child before these productions, they correspond to psychological processes that can be considered "a fact of introspective awareness generated by a realization of differential awareness" (translated from Pichon, 1936, p. 95). This explanation of the absence of a form in terms of a psychological "lack" has been severely criticized.

A Linguistic Problem

According to Pavlovitch (1920), observers of child language often confuse the notion of person and the acquisition of pronominal forms. Indeed, self-awareness cannot be said to be less intense when children use their first names instead of the pronoun *je*. The appearance of first-person pronouns does not necessarily correspond to the first setting up of self-awareness (Stern & Stern, 1907) and the distinction between the self and the other, but is rather related to difficulty in using the linguistic system (Jespersen, 1922; Sabeau-Jouannet, 1975).

However, a number of works show that the reference of each word-for-self used by the child is not the same. *Baby* and first name refer to the physical self, to the image, the shadow, whereas the pronoun *I* refers to the social self in interaction with the others (Nelson, 1989). In her analysis of Emily's monologues, Nelson presented the "different temporal contents" of self-reference. From 1;8 to 1;11, *Emmy* is the term the little girl used most often to mark an "objective self." After 1;11, she preferred the pronoun *I* to mark her "subjective self" when the system of temporal reference also emerged. Two systems, self-reference and temporal reference, therefore develop over the same period.

According to Budwig (1985, 1989, 1990), who took both linguistic forms and discursive functions into account in her analysis, children code internal states with *I* and agentivity with *my*. *Agentivity* is treated as a prototype and corresponds to responsible actions with "intent to bring about a change." *Internal states* correspond to assertive utterances, as when Jeff said "I wear it" after he had negotiated with the researcher and been allowed to wear the microphone. When they want to mark their status as experiencer, children prefer the form *I*.

Besides the question of locutory intention expressed by the children, we must also deal with the question of the referent. Indeed, because pronouns do not have a stable and objective referent (Benveniste, 1066; Jakobson, 1963), children encounter great difficulties with these forms, leading to the famous "pronominal reversal." The problem is to find out whether, when they say *you* instead of *I*, children consider pronouns to refer to specific persons, therefore making them equivalent to proper names (Clark, 1978) or to roles in discourse (Charney, 1980; Chiat, 1982, 1986; Oshima-Takane, 1992). In order to analyze this problem, we must consider the conditions under which acquisition takes place.

An Interaction Problem

It is important to understand the consequences of the linguistic "input." There is a tight connection between the errors children make and certain uses of pronouns and proper names in the language addressed to them (Preyer, 1887). Some authors have even shown that French mothers use a variety of terms instead of *tu* ('you') when they speak to their children, including *il /elle*, *on*, *nous*, *moi*, and *je*. This motherese might paradoxically both help and hamper the children in their acquisition process (Rabain-Jamin, 1984; Rabain-Jamin & Sabeau-Jouannet, 1989; Sabeau-Jouannet, 1975).

In contrast to previous work, instead of wondering why children *do not say I*, we asked ourselves: What *do* children mean when they use the various forms we have mentioned? Our task is to seek coherence in children's speech in their ways of expressing self with their own markers.

DATA, METHOD, AND RESULTS

We studied three corpora of dialogues between adults and children in their natural environments. One of the children, Peter, is an English speaker; the data, collected by Bloom and her team (Bloom & Lahey, 1978), is part of the CHILDES database (MacWhinney, 1991). The two other children, Guillaume and Juliette, are French speakers; the data was collected by Brigaudiot and Nicolas (1990).

We have systematically listed and analyzed their words-for-self, beginning with the first production of each child's name in subject position. The three children were 1;8. We ended when they all stopped using their names in subject position, at which time the children were 2;10. We paraphrased each utterance in which the children expressed self, according to the linguistic and extralinguistic context. As an example, (1) shows how we interpreted Peter's utterance in its context:

TABLE 7.1
Use of Self-Reference by Peter, Guillaume, and Juliette: Categories of Uses and Linguistic Forms

	From 1;8	
	Will/Project	Turn-Taking/Opposition
		<u>Peter</u>
English	Ø I, [a], [ə] (+ want, get, do)	me, my, I
	Ø	<u>Juliette, Guillaume</u>
French	[a], (+ *veux*)	*moi*

	From 2;3	
	Will/Project/Affect Comments Narratives	Turn-Taking Opposition Comparison
	I	<u>me</u>
English	ø	my, I
	ø	<u>Guillaume, moi,</u> Juliette
French	*tu*, [ə], *je*	*moi aussi, c'est moi*

	From 2;10	
	First Person in Time-Mode-Aspact	
English	I	
French	*je*, Ø (+ *veux*), *moi je*	

Note. The underlined forms are the most frequent.

(1) Peter (2;0) is looking at Lois and Pat, who are going to put the toys away and leave.

Lois: We're gonna put our toys away and go home.
Peter: Peter go home
Mother: I think the toys are gonna go home.

We know the child was sorry each time the team left and took the toys away. We therefore assign the meaning 'I want to go home too' to "Peter go home," implying "not only the toys and not only you go home."

Such paraphrases have enabled us to categorize uses that we are now going to list as they appear diachronically. We thus successively analyze the categories of use and the forms within each period (See Table 7.1).

Beginning at Age 1;8

Categories. Two categories can be distinguished. We have named them *Will/Project*, and *Turn-taking/Opposition* (Brigaudiot, Morgenstern & Nicolas, 1994). The Will/Project category includes all utterances in which the children say *I want to* or *I am going to*, with the meaning 'I am able to do it like a grownup,' 'I succeed,' as shown in example (2), from Juliette:

(2) *aller là-dessous*   'go there-under'
(said just before crawling under the bed to get a toy)

In the Turn-taking/Opposition category, children emphasize their actions versus others' actions. The words-for-self are first used in utterances meaning "my turn," or "not you, me," as shown in example (3):

(3) The Brigaudiot family is going on a trip.
Mother: *Je vais faire ta valise.* 'I'm gonna make (pack) your suitcase'
Guillaume: *Guillaume*   (meaning '*I* and not you am going to pack my suitcase')

Forms. Various forms correspond to the two categories of uses. In the Will/Project category, the most frequent form used in both languages is the null form. It seems that the verb is sufficient to express actions (*do*), desires (*get*), and volition (*want*). We find the first-person pronoun *I* only in Peter's data. This might be explained by the fact that the data was transcribed orthographically, which could lead to overinterpretation. According to Chiat (1986), various phonemes produced by children before verbs can be interpreted as either *I* or as *you*. However, the transcription problem might not be the only explanation for the occurrence of *I* at such an early age in Peter's data. Indeed, according to Bloom, Lightbown, & Hood (1975), Peter is considered as a *pronominal style* child, who uses a preponderance of proforms such as *I* and *my* as agents, in contrast to *nominal style* children, who predominantly use names.

In order to express Turn-taking and Opposition, the three children mainly use their proper names. We also find *me*, *my*, and *moi*, in the data, but Peter uses *I* here, too. This use, which we only find in the English data, might be due to syntactic differences between the two languages. In the situation where several protagonists are present and one of the speakers would like to stress the fact that he wants to be the agent, an English speaker would say *I'm gonna do it* (stress on *I*), wheras a French speaker would say *c'est moi qui vais le faire* (use of *moi* in a set expression).

From Age 2;3

Categories. Within the framework of self-designation, the children said more and used a greater number of forms. The Will/Project category kept its subjective nature. The children expressed their feelings, emotions, and desires (see example 4), but also made comments and evaluations (example 5), and narrated their past actions (6):

(4) Juliette: *t'as soif* 'you have thirst' (meaning "I'm thirsty")

(5) Peter: I just fixing this guitar (when asked what he is doing)

(6) Guillaume: *fait des bêtises aujourd'hui* 'did naughty things today' (talking about his day at school)

The Turn-taking/Opposition category at this time also included comparisons between self and others, as shown in an exchange between Juliette and her mother, who was describing a picture of an animal in a book (7).

(7) Mother: *il donne la patte*   'he gives the (his) paw'
     Juliette: *moi aussi, donne la patte*   'me too, give the paw'

Forms. In the Will/Project category, *I* became the privileged marker in English, and *je* appeared in French, as did *tu* (*you* meaning *I*). In addition, the null form remained quite frequent. In the Turn-taking/Opposition category, there was an important use of *me* in English, and the proper name was dropped from subject position. The French children still frequently used their names, along with *moi*.

The chief feature of this period in the genesis of the first-person pronoun is the large number of the forms used: five for Peter, six for Guillaume, and eight for Juliette.

At Age 2;10

At this age the two categories merge into one, as the children express a subjective *I* inside their relation to the other. Their utterances now involve Time, Mode and Aspect. Examples are:

(8) Adult: *T'es un petit*   'You're a little boy'
     Guillaume: *non, je suis grand*!   'no, I am big!'

(9) Peter: I am Peter, I'm not Patsy   (said as he is checking out everybody's name)

(10)   Juliette: *regarde, je siffle comme les enfants*
                       'look, I (can) whistle like the children'
                       (said to her mother when they are talking about their status
                       and their abilities)

Some forms disappeared from the children's language, such as *tu* and first name in French, *me* and *my* in English. Other grammatical markers at this point replaced the various words-for-self the children used before. For example, whereas Peter had previously said *my do*, he now says the adultlike *I'm doing*, with *I* to designate himself and the complete *-ing* form.

ANALYSIS

Our analysis of the three children's data has enabled us to distinguish two categories, with forms that evolve when the children are between the ages of 1;8 and 2;10, in agreement with Budwig (1989). Our two categories of use cover the contrasted use of *I* versus *my* by the three youngest children in her study (1;8 to 2;6). Indeed, the Will-Project/Affect/Comment-Evaluation/Narrative category corresponds to internal states found in assertions. The Turn-taking/Opposition/Comparison category corresponds to *high agentivity* as defined by Budwig (1993), involving two or more participants, highly kinetic verbs, telic situation, purposeful action, and affirmation. Our results are consistent with the semantic meaning she attributed to the two types of form: experiencer and agent.

We now consider all the data in order to hypothesize how these two categories help us understand the genesis of the first-person pronoun. We went back to the children's first words, which we found to be the basis of all further development, as we now proceed to demonstrate.

For a long time, children's language is deictic. Children do not need to mark the person of the verb, because they are learning to speak about what *they* want in the present situation. Guillaume says *ouvrir* and Peter says *open* when they mean 'I want to open'. They already have the ability to verbalize their desires and their will before the age we have chosen as the starting point for our study. For example, Guillaume says *humhum* at 1;2 when asking his mother to open a box. In addition, we think that the ability to verbalize agentivity is precocious. Very young children are particularly likely to put agentivity into words in routine games that involve opposition to another. The importance of these contexts is well known, especially the give-and-take games described by Bruner (1975), in which the marking of the agent is particularly clear.

The children also have the means to deal with their competition with adults. When Guillaume says *raconter* 'tell', his mother starts to read a story. Guillaume then has to protest *non Guillaume* for her to understand that *he* wants to read.

This locutory force is fundamental to the genesis of words-for-self. We have

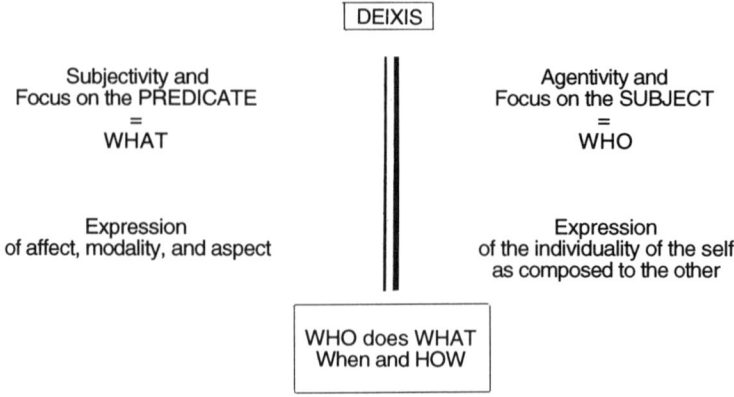

FIG. 7.1. Two sources of the first person pronoun.

taken up phenomena that testify to this importance in two other languages. In Spanish, Emilio, studied by Vila and his team in Barcelona (Vila, Gonzalez, & Zanon, 1987), overuses first-person markers. He says *me lo como yo* 'me, I eat it'. In French Sign Language, Laurene, studied by Morgenstern (1994), over-marks the self-pointing gesture, where an adult only needs to use the verb, because the speaker is implicitly the subject of the sentence; instead of signing *drink*, she signs *me drink*.

Fig. 7.1 summarizes our view of the process of acquiring self-designation. During the period in which the children's language is entirely deictic, there are two main sources of the first-person pronoun in their speech. The children either express affect, modality, aspect, and, in this case, their person-marked utterances mainly focus on the predicate (*what*). The children stress what they have achieved, what they feel, and what they want. Their utterances are, of course, entirely subjective, and the enunciator is fully responsible for them; the predicate is therefore constructed through the speaker's subjectivity. The children may also focus on the subject of the utterance (*who*), that is, on who is doing the action, expressing the individuality of the self as opposed to the other.

By hypothesizing two sources of the genesis of the first person, we do not consider the various forms produced by the children to be overextensions of *I* (Rispoli, 1994). In our analysis, *I* and *me* are two different words in Peter's language. For example, when he says "me found it, I find it," we interpret it to mean '*I* found it, not you *and* I was able to find it even if I am just a little boy'.

At the end of this process, the children will then say *who* does *what* (when and how) in and outside of deictic contexts, as shown in (11) and (12):

(11)   Juliette: *tout à l'heure j'ai baillé parce que j'étais sommeil*
'awhile ago, I yawned because I was tired'

(12)   Guillaume: *quand je suis trois ans, je peux souffler les bougies*
'when I am 3 (years), I can blow out the candles'

We here agree with Nelson's (1989) results: the stabilization of *I* is contemporary with that of temporal markers such as *tout à l'heure* 'a while ago', *quand je suis trois ans* 'when I am 3 years old'. When we evoke what is not present, we are able to talk about what we do and feel without having to position ourselves in opposition to another. That is when we use a fully fledged *I*. In a situation where the other is present, the ability to say *je* 'I' on its own on the one hand, and *moi* 'me' in order to oppose oneself to others on the other hand, enables the children to say *moi je* (stressed 'I'). They are then verbalizing what we call *intersubjectivity*.

All these hypotheses are of a psycholinguistic nature, because we have tried to find regular uses over a long period in two languages. Among the processes involved in the acquisition of self-reference, we also take into account how children deal with the language they hear. For example, Guillaume and Juliette only use *tu* 'you' instead of *je* 'I' in expressions they have heard adults say to express prohibitions, achievements, or internal states. Juliette says *t'as mal* 'it hurts you' when something hurts *her,* and Guillaume says *t'allumes* 'you put the light on' when *he* has finally succeeded in putting the light on. Our study would, therefore, be more complete if it included a precise analysis of the mothers' speech. This would enable us to discover whether preverbal vowels first appear in repetitions just like *tu* 'you'. For example, in Juliette's case at 1;9:

(13)   Mother: *Oh! tu as fait un trou! Tu as abimé le livre!*
                   'Oh! you've made a hole! You wrecked the book!'
       Juliette: [ame]
       Mother: *Oui, abîmé.*
                   'Yes, wrecked'
       Juliette: [olabim]
                   'oh wreck it'
       Mother: *Oui, t'as abîmé!*
                   'Yes, you've wrecked it!'
       Juliette: [əbim alatabim]
                   'wreck you wreck'

CONCLUSION

The fact that children do not use *I* to mark the first person in subject position from the earliest stages of language acquisition was interpreted, in the beginning of the century, as a lack of self-awareness. However, whether the children say *veux ça* 'want that' or *je veux ça* 'I want that', adults know they are unambiguously expressing their own desires. In addition, children also use their names, and *me* and *my* (*moi* in French). In this case, they are claiming responsibility for the ongoing action in a turn-taking process. We have therefore proposed two categories of use beginning at the age of 1;8, with the characteristics Will/Project in one and Turn-taking/Opposition in the other. When children begin to talk about their feelings or past events, they take possession of the forms they have heard in those contexts (*I, you*). Finally, when they are able to position themselves in relation to the other *and* to verbally express their subjectivity (*I'm hungry, I fell, I don't want to stay here*), they have the means to verbalize their own feelings within the intersubjectivity of discourse (e.g., when told *I love meatballs; let's have some for lunch*, they can answer *But I don't like them*).

This genesis of words-for-self is formally easier to trace in French than in English, in which the forms *I* and *I* (stressed) are hard to differentiate, even though they refer to two different values. This may be the reason why English-speaking children use the forms *me* and *my* (a phonic and syntactic combination of *me* and *I*) in subject position. It would therefore be interesting to take stress into account in further analyses of the development of the first person pronoun.

When we study the process of acquiring self-reference, it is, of course, important to distinguish phenomena of a psycholinguistic nature from those that are strictly linguistic and linked to the formal acquisition of the mother tongue. A study of various languages, especially non Indo-European languages, would confirm that there are two problems: the formal linguistic phenomena should take on different forms, whereas the psycholinguistic hypothesis would be validated.

ACKNOWLEDGMENT

We would like to thank Professor Laurent Danon-Boileau, Director of the Groupe Langage Acquisition Lecture Apprentissages, Université Paris III, for his continuous and constructive participation in this research.

REFERENCES

Bain, R. (1936). The self-and-other words of a child. *The American Journal of Sociology, 41,* 765–775.

Benveniste, E. (1966). De la subjectivité dans le langage [On subjectivity in language]. In *Problèmes de linguistique générale* (Vol. 1, pp. 258–266). Paris: Gallimard.

Bloch, O. (1924). La phrase dans le langage de l'enfant [The sentence in the language of the child]. *Journal de Psychologie Normale et Pathologique, 21,* 18–24.

Bloom, L. (1970). *Language development: Form and function in emerging grammars.* Cambridge, MA: MIT. Press.

Bloom, L., & Lahey, M. (1978). *Language development and language disorders.* New York: Wiley.

Bloom, L., Lightbown, P., & Hood, L. (1975). Structure and variation in child language. *Monographs of the Society for Research of Child Development, 40* (2, Serial No. 160).

Brigaudiot, M., & Nicolas, C. (1990). *Acquisition du langage: Les premiers mots* [Acquisition of language: The first words]. Unpublished doctoral dissertation. Université de Paris VII.

Brigaudiot, M., Morgenstern, A., & Nicolas, C. (1994). "Me found it, I find it." A la recherche de 'je' entre deux et trois ans [On the investigation of 'I' between two and three years]. *Faits de langue—La personne. 3,* 123–130.

Bruner, J. (1975). The ontogenesis of speech acts. *Journal of Child Language, 2,* 1–19.

Budwig, N. (1985). I, me, my and 'name': children's early systematizations of forms, meanings and functions in talk about self. *Papers and Reports on Child Language Development, 24,* 30–37.

Budwig, N. (1989). The linguistic marking of agentivity and control in child language. *Journal of Child Language, 16,* 263–284.

Budwig, N. (1990). Do young children linguistically encode the notion of agent? *Papers and Reports on Child Language Development, 29,* 133–147.

Budwig, N. (1993, July). *The notion of reorganization and the construction of grammar.* Paper presented at the Sixth International Congress for the Study of Child Language, Trieste.

Charney, R. (1980). Speech roles and the development of personal pronouns. *Journal of Child Language, 7,* 509–528.

Chiat, S. (1982). If I were you and you were me: The analysis of pronouns in a pronoun-reversing child. *Journal of Child Language, 9,* 509–528.

Chiat, S. (1986). Personal pronouns. In P. Fletcher & M. Garman (Eds.), *Language acquisition* (2nd ed., pp. 339–355). Cambridge, England: Cambridge University Press.

Clark, E. (1978). From gesture to word: On the natural history of deixis in language acquisition. In J. Bruner & A. Garton (Eds.), *Human growth and development* (pp. 85–120). Wolfson College Lectures, 1976. Oxford: Oxford University Press.

Cooley, C. (1908). A study of the early use of self-words by a child. *Psychological Review, 15,* 339–357.

Grégoire, A. (1937). *L'apprentissage du langage* [Language learning]. Liège: Bibliothèque de la Faculté des Lettres.

Jakobson, R. (1963). *Essais de linguistique générale* [Essays in general linguistics]. Paris: Le Seuil.

Jespersen, O. (1922). Language: Its nature, development and origin. London: Allen & Unwin.

Lobisch, G. E. (1851). *Entwicklungsgeschichte der Seele des Kindes* [The developmental history of the child's soul]. Vienna: Die Seele des Kindes.

MacWhinney, B. (1991). *The CHILDES Project. Tools for analyzing talk.* Hillsdale, NJ: Lawrence Erlbaum Associates.

Morgenstern, A. (1994). *Selfsigns and selfwords.* Paper presented at the First Lisbon Meeting on Child Language with Special Reference to Romance Languages. Faculdade de Letras, Universidade de Lisboa, Lisbon, Portugal.

Nelson, K. (1989). Monologue as the linguistic construction of self in time. In K. Nelson (Ed), *Narratives from the crib* (pp. 284–308). Cambridge, MA: Harvard University Press.

Oshima-Takane, Y. (1992). Analysis of pronominal errors: A case study. *Journal of Child Language, 19,* 111–131.

Pavlovitch, M. (1920). *Le langage enfantin (acquisition du serbe et du français par un enfant serbe)* [Child language (Acquisition of Serbian and French by a Serbian child)]. Paris: Champion.

Piaget, J. (1926). *La représentation du monde chez l'enfant* [The child's conception of the world]. Paris: Felix Alcan.

Pichon, E. (1936). *Le développement psychique de l'enfant et de l'adolescent* [The psychic development of the child and the adolescent]. Paris: Masson & Cies.

Preyer, W. (1887). *L'âme de l'enfant* [The soul of the child]. Paris: Felix Alcan.

Rabain-Jamin, J. (1984). De quelques formes paradoxales de l'échange mère-nourrisson [On some paradoxial forms in mother-infant interaction]. *Neuropsychiatrie de l'Enfant et de l'Adolescent, 32,* 545–551.

Rabain-Jamin, J., & Sabeau-Jouannet, E. (1989). Playing with pronouns in French maternal speech to prelingual infants. *Journal of Child Language, 16,* 217–238.

Rispoli, M. (1994). Pronoun case overextensions and paradigm building. *Journal of Child Language, 21,* 157–172.

Sabeau-Jouannet, E. (1975). Les premières acquisitions syntaxiques chez des enfants français unilingues [The first syntactic acquisitions of unilingual French children]. *La linguistique, 2,* 105–122.

Stern, C., & Stern, W. (1907). *Die Kindersprache: Eine psychologische und sprachtheoristiche Untersuchung* [Child language: A psychological and language theoretical investigation]. Leipzig: Barth.

Vila, I., Gonzalez A. M., & Zanon, J. (1987). *Emergence and use of the Castellian pronominal system in early language*. Unpublished manuscript, University of Barcelona, Department of Evolutive Psychology and Education.

Wallon, H. (1934). *Les origines du caractère chez l'enfant* [The origins of character in the child]. Paris: Boivin.

8 Complex Sentence Acquisition in Italian: A Case Study

Donella Antelmi
University of Venice

Between the ages of 2 and 3, children begin to use multiclausal sentences in which the syntactic-semantic relation between the clauses is expressed by an explicit complementizer. This phase, which is marked by developmental steps, immediately follows the so-called *successive sentence stage* (Cipriani, Chilosi, Bottari, & Pfanner, 1993). *Successive sentences* are sentences that are syntactically unrelated, but semantically (or pragmatically) connected, as shown in (1):

(1) *casca. poi male*
'falls. after pain' (from Cipriani et al., 1993)

This strategy shows that the inability to connect clauses by syntactic means cannot be attributed, from a given age onwards, to the child's cognitive or logical limitations. Instead, it could depend on some grammatical constraints, which, therefore, have to be explained.

The problem is to identify the lexical and syntactic mechanisms that must be acquired by the child in order to attain the target ability to produce complex sentences. This is the question I address in this chapter. I consider spontaneous linguistic data from a child at the crucial age where the production of complex sentences begins.

This case study is presented in the Government and Binding (GB) framework (Chomsky, 1981, 1986). An aspect of this theory relevant to the topic of the present study is that it distinguishes between *lexical categories* (LC) and *functional categories* (FC). The former are Noun, Verb, Adverb, and Adjective, the latter Inflection (INFL), Determiner (DET), and Complementizers (COMP). A developmental delay in the acquisition of conjunctive elements may thus be due to their different categorial status.

A second relevant aspect of GB Theory is its parametric approach. In the Principles and Parameters framework it is assumed that, while some grammatical principles are given by biological endowment (i.e., are *universal*), a number of options are parameterized and need to be specified in the course of language acquisition. Given that parameters relate primarily to the nonsubstantive elements of the lexicon—that is, to the functional categories—one should expect to find differences between child and adult grammar, or crosslinguistic variation, precisely in these categories.

Developmental data support a position recently argued within this theory, according to which child grammars initially lack functional categories (Meisel & Müller, 1992; Platzack, 1992; Radford, 1988, 1990, 1992). Radford (1990), for example, claimed that such categories emerge later than lexical/referential ones, because they are (in a sense, similar to physiological growth) subject to maturation. A contrasting theoretical position defends the idea that functional categories are initially present, but parameters are set to wrong values (i.e., to values deviating from adult grammar) (Hyams, 1986, 1992).

The Italian acquisition data discussed here confirm the first hypothesis, namely, that functional categories are initially missing—in particular, that COMP is missing. However, the developmental pattern in the acquisition of complex sentences shows that there is a gradualness that cannot be explained by referring to maturation alone. In a strictly maturational view, the acquisition of a category should imply the simultaneous acquisition of all its grammatical functions. Maturation is therefore coupled with some kind of *bootstrapping*: certain linguistic abilities grow over time and influence the child's ability to pay attention to specific input data. New data will trigger other constructions (and so on).

The analysis of data shows that the first elements used to introduce embedded sentences are wh-elements (Italian *chi* 'who', *che cosa* 'what') already used by the child in main questions, with complementizers (Italian *che, se, di*) acquired only later. This process can be accounted for by considering the various features that characterize the COMP node, along the lines proposed by Penner and Müller (1992).

This chapter is organized as follows. In the next section I present the subject and method of the study. I then briefly describe the grammar of the functional category COMP in adult Italian. In the fourth section I present developmental data. The last two sections are devoted, respectively, to the discussion of the Maturational Hypothesis with respect to the acquisition of COMP and a description of a model of language acquisition.

SUBJECT AND METHOD

The subject of the study was a first-born child, Camilla, whose language development I have reported elsewhere (Antelmi, 1992, forthcoming). I collected the corpus of Camilla's spontaneous speech by both daily annotations and by recording at regular intervals. Camilla's corpus is available on CHILDES (MacWhinney, 1991).

From the whole corpus, which consists of 4,224 utterances covering the age range of 1;5–3;4, I have extracted all the sentences containing a wh-element as well as complex sentences. The amount of data extracted following these requirements is 351 utterances. By complex sentences I mean every sentence formed by a main and an embedded clause, be it a complement (i.e., selected by the main verb), or an adjunct (i.e., a relative or adverbial clause). Indirect questions and subject and object clauses are in the former set; temporal, causal, final, and hypothetical clauses are in the latter group. In this study I have not considered connected clauses that extend across utterance boundaries. Sentences that involve CP projection (focalized, comparatives, cleft, and pseudo-cleft sentences) have not been considered either (with or without explicit connectives or complementizers).

The interpretation of meaning relations between clauses was not always without problems. This issue has to do with the fact that several of the semantic relations between clauses were themselves ambiguous. For example, some adverbial temporal clauses were ambiguous with a relative interpretation. For the purpose of this study, however, the issue of the distinction between adjuncts was only partially relevant. For this reason such distinctions were left out.

COMP IN ADULT ITALIAN

Before analyzing Camilla's developing grammatical system, I briefly summarize the relevant facts in the corresponding adult grammar. The functional category of complementizers is COMP. Its projection, CP, dominates the Inflection Projection, IP. The grammar of COMP, in adult Italian, concerns elements basically generated in the head C, as well as elements moved from another head or projection. The head C may contain the complementizers *che* 'that' and *se* 'if' basically generated, or raised verbal heads (in main and embedded questions), as shown in (2):

(2) (a) *speravo* [$_{CP}$ [$_C$ *che* [$_{IP}$ *Gianni arrivasse presto*]]]
          'hoped that G arrived soon'
          = I hoped G would arrive soon

     (b) [$_{cp}$ *che libro* [$_c$ *hai*] [$_{IP}$ *e letto* ?]]
          'which book have read?'
          = which book have you read?

     (c) *mi domando* [$_{CP}$ *quale libro* [$_C$ *hai*] [$_{IP}$ *e letto*]]
          'myself wonder which book have read'
          = I wonder which book you have read

The SpecCP position is the landing site of wh-movement, which is involved in main as well as embedded questions. In these sentences the wh-phrase must be adjacent to the verb, which, therefore, is raised from I to C. This adjacency requirement is expressed by the WH-Criterion (Rizzi, 1991), as follows:

(3) The WH-Criterion:
    (a)   A WH Operator must be in a Spec-head configuration with $X^{\circ}{}_{+WH}$.
    (b)   An $X^{\circ}{}_{+WH}$ must be in a Spec-head configuration with a Wh Operator.

The WH-Criterion is a well-formedness requirement; it allows the formal licensing of a feature $[+Q]$ (question) in COMP, and it explains why, in Italian as well as in other languages, lexical material cannot appear between the wh-element and the verb, as the ungrammatical examples in (4) show:

(4)   (a)   *quale libro Maria ha letto?
              'which book Mary has read?'
    (b)   *mi domando quale libro Maria ha letto[1]
              'I wonder which book Mary has read'

As far as questions are concerned, children must be aware that the WH-Criterion must be satisfied, given that the Criterion is thought to be a principle of Universal Grammar. However, if we adopt a maturational point of view, we can hypothesize that the realization of such a principle may undergo maturation, or may be parametrized, for example, with regard to the projection in which the Criterion itself has to be satisfied.

Concerning relative clauses, the traditional view is that the dependent clause modifies a head noun, the antecedent, which is base generated externally to the CP. The SpecCP of the relative clause contains a wh-operator, which inherits the semantic features of the antecedent, as in (5a), or a null operator, from which the complementizer *che* inherits features as well (5b) (Chomsky, 1980; Cinque, 1981):

(5)   (a)   la casa $_j$ [$_{CP}$ nella quale $_j$ [abitavo . . . t $_j$]]]
              'the house in which lived'
              = the house where I lived
    (b)   la casa $_j$ [$_{CP}$ 0 $_j$ [$_C$ che $_j$ [$_{IP}$ avevi comprato t $_j$]]]
              'the house that had bought'
              = the house you bought

According to this analysis, the grammar of relative clauses is characterized by movement of a wh-constituent. In contrast, this movement does not hold in

---

[1]For the possibility of sentences like "Mi domando quale libro Maria abbia letto," that is, with an embedded subjunctive; see Rizzi (1991).

pseudorelative constructions of this kind (Burzio, 1986; Cinque, 1992; Guasti, 1988):

(6)   *ho visto Gianni che ballava*
      'have seen Gianni who danced'
      = I saw John dancing

Pseudorelatives are then like small clauses, because a predication relation holds between a NP-subject and a CP-predicate, without wh-movement. Other sentential adjuncts (modal, temporal, etc.), in order to be properly interpreted, must be connected to the matrix verb with some instance of coindexation at the clause level (mediated by C-projection). We can refer to all these instances of coindexation as a feature [+REF] in COMP (Penner, 1992; Penner & Müller, 1992). Argument clauses (to which I will refer as *subject, object,* and *question* dependent clauses), being selected by the matrix verb, do not need any kind of coindexation (i.e., the corresponding feature is [−REF] in COMP).

Summing up, the presence of COMP in child grammar is revealed by complementizers, wh-movement, and (verbal) head movement. In order to properly connect clauses, two requirements must be satisfied. The [Q] feature must be formally licensed (i.e., the WH-Criterion must be satisfied in COMP), and one of the two clausal licensing requirements must be encountered: the coindexation with an antecedent at clause level (for adjuncts), or the saturation of selectional requirements of the matrix verb (for arguments).

DEVELOPMENTAL DATA

A Prefunctional Phrase?

Many facts suggest that at an early stage COMP is missing in child grammar. This claim is also supported by studies of languages other than Italian, in particular V2 languages, where the presence of COMP is overtly manifested by verb movement in the second position of the sentence, and its absence by the fact that the verb remains in VP (Clahsen, 1990; Clahsen & Penke, 1992; Meisel & Müller, 1992). (On the other hand, many scholars reject the equation "missing data = missing categories," so the claim that COMP is present in child grammar is equally supported, at least on theoretical grounds, even if empirical evidence is dubious; see Hyams, 1992; Verrips & Weissenborn, 1992; Weissenborn, 1990.)

Camilla's early productions show that COMP is initially missing in her grammar. Heads base generated in C° (that is, the complementizers *che* and *se*) are absent until 2;1; at this age *che* ('that') appears in her grammar, but its categorial status is again unclear, as I show in the next section.

As regards head movement to C—that is verb movement in questions— Camilla's data neither confirm nor disprove that movement has taken place.

However, Shaeffer (1993) showed that Italian children do not raise the verb to C. In a comprehension task administered to preschool children, the answers violated the WH-Criterion. Sentences submitted were of the type:

(7)   *che ragazze stanno suonando?*
       'what girls are playing?'

Children (erroneously) identified *che* 'what' as the object of the verb, answering, for example, "the piano." In this case the wh-element was interpreted as the operator that binds the object position instead of the determiner of the NP subject (i.e., [DP *che ragazze*] 'what girls'). According to this interpretation, the NP subject is between the wh-operator and the verb, resulting in a violation of the WH-Criterion and showing that the verb does not move outside IP.

In contrast, preposed wh-elements are frequent from an early stage, given that questions are acquired precociously. However, alongside sentences like that in (8), for some time there are no sentences where the wh-element refers to the object, as in (9):

(8)   *itto la bua?*
       'seen the hurt?'
       = have you seen my injury?

(9)   *che cosa $_j$ faie e $_j$?*
       'what do?'
       = what are you doing?

Not only did Camilla not produce sentences like (9) before 1;11, but, until that age, she never understood questions of this type and, when asked them, did not answer. Again, this observation matches an analogous developmental pattern in other languages (Radford, 1988, 1990).

The explanation I suggest for this asymmetry is that, in early questions, the wh-element is not moved to SpecCP, but is generated in SpecIP (or SpecVP). If this is the case, the wh-phrase has been misanalyzed as a N-phrase. The analysis of her early productions leads me to conclude that until Camilla was able to ask questions about the object of a sentence (i.e., until 1;11), CP was not present, and wh-elements were not recognized as operators.

This explanation raises a problem for the WH-Criterion, which is, presumably, a principle of Universal Grammar. Nothing, however, prevents us from hypothesizing a parametric choice as to where such a criterion must be met. Therefore, I propose:

(10)   The WH-Criterion is met in the root.

Given that it is independently admitted that children can optionally instantiate the root as CP (Rizzi, 1992),[2] the possibility of the WH-Criterion being satisfied in IP follows.

Other Developmental Data

In this section I present developmental data from Camilla's spontaneous speech related to the grammar of main and embedded questions, pseudorelatives, relatives, and other dependent clauses. The first embedded sentences she produced were infinitives after modals (*voglio* 'want') or motion verbs (*andare* 'to go'). These dependent clauses are (sometimes) introduced, in adult Italian, by prepositions. In child grammar, however, the prepositions are initially omitted:

(11)   2;0   *andiamo vedere treno*
            = *andiamo A vedere IL treno*
            'go-1st.pl. see train'
            = let's go to see the train

This is not a surprising fact, given that prepositions are omitted in other contexts, too. Until 2;0, Camilla's only complex utterances were of the type exemplified earlier, with matrix control verbs like *volere* and *andare*. It is worth noticing that these sentences have been analyzed as not really biphrasal, given that they can undergo the *restructuring* process (which allows the object clitic to move in front of the main verb) (Rizzi, 1982). Crosslinguistic data confirm that this kind of verbal predicate always precedes explicit biphrasal sentences (Clark, 1985; Radford, 1990).

Embedded infinitives were preceded by prepositions, as in the target language, when Camilla was 2;0:

(12)   (a)   2;0   (*papa e andato fuori*) *a lavorare!*
                    '(daddy has gone outside. .) to work'
        (b)   2;1   *vieni a giocare*
                    'come to play'
                    = come and play
        (c)   2;2   *stai a vedere*
                    'stay to see'
                    = look at

Indirect questions are a second type of embedded clause. In adult Italian these are argument clauses introduced by a complementizer (*se* 'if' in yes/no ques-

---

[2]Recent research has shown that children may admit a projection lower than CP as root (Rizzi, 1992). The same studies, however, show that questions 'activate' the whole CP projection. These findings do not challenge my proposals, given that the children's ages do not correspond; I refer to an earlier stage.

tions) or by a wh-element. Early embedded questions appear in Camilla's grammar at 1;11, but they are exclusively fronted by a wh-element. Interestingly enough, indirect questions (13b) emerge when, in a direct question, the wh-element would refer to the object (13a), that is, when there is an overt wh-movement:

(13) (a) 1;11 *che $_j$ fai e $_j$? lavori?*
                 'what do? work?'
                 = what are you doing? are you working?
      (b) 1;11 *guarda chi $_j$ c'e e $_j$*
                 'look who there is'
                 = look who is there

However, only subject and direct object wh-elements can be fronted in the embedded clause; that is, pied-piping is avoided (e.g., *hai sentito a chi ho telefonato?* 'have you heard to whom I phoned?'). Another observation is related to the main verb: embedded questions depend on perception verbs (e.g., *visto, guarda*), but never on a predicate with the illocutionary force of a question, or on a verb of doubt (e.g., *ask, wonder*).

Interrogative pronouns and adverbs are the lexical elements that introduce the embedded sentence. The order of emergence of these elements in Camilla's grammar is provided in Table 8.1, showing that elements that do not appear in

TABLE 8.1
Sequence of Emergence of Camilla's Wh-Phrases in Questions and Other Sentences

Age	Main Clause Questions	Embedded Questions	Others
1;6 - 1;9	*chi*		
1;7 - 1;10	*dove*		
1;11	*che*	*chi*	
	perché		
2;0	*quanti*	*che*	*che* (pseudorelative)
			perché (causal)
2;1	*come*	*cosa*	*che* (relative)
	cosa		
2;2	*quale*		*ché* (final)
2;3			*quando*
			dove
			che (object)
			come
2;5		*come*	*se* (hypothetical)
2;10	*che cosa*	*se*	
		perché	

main questions cannot be used to introduce an embedded question. In the third column other types of argument and nonargument clause are reported (e.g., pseudorelative, causal, final, object, hypothetical). The table makes it clear that each element begins to be used in one context, gradually becoming available for the other contexts.

Adverbial dependent clauses appeared after 2;0. These were introduced by connectives with a causal value, as shown in examples (14 a) and (b). Other dependent clauses are final, after *perché, (affin) ché, che, a* plus infinitive (examples 15 a and b). *Quando* introduces temporal clauses (examples 16 a and b):

(14) (a) 2;0 *prendo ciuccio, perche e sporco*
            'take pacifier, because is dirty'
            = I take the pacifier, because it's dirty

      (b) 2;2 *sto tagliando, perche sono rotti*
            'am cutting, because are broken'
            = I'm cutting, because they are broken

(15) (a) 2;2 *sono stata a Azelio a fare male a giardino*
            'am been to Azelio to do bad to garden'
            = have been to Azelio, to hurt the garden

      (b) 2;3 *te vai fori, che vengo io*
            'you go outside, that come I'
            = you go outside, I'm coming

(16) (a) 2;3 *quando sono malata sto poco bene*
            'when am ill, am little well'
            = when I'm ill, I'm not very well

      (b) 2;3 *quando vado in piscina, mi metto questo*
            'when go to swimming pool, (on) me put this'
            = when I go to the swimming pool, I put this on

These embedded sentences are introduced by elements which, in adult Italian, have adverbial status and are not true complementizers. It must be stressed, however, that in this developmental phase main verbs that subcategorize argument clauses (subject, object) are also missing.

Other languages show the same developmental pattern (see Lieko, 1992, for Finnish and Radford, 1990, for English, among others). For German, Meisel and Müller (1992) reported that complex sentences are formed using adverbs and prepositions with semantic functions and formal properties analogous to complementizers, but that the latter are not represented in child grammar at this stage. Guilfoyle and Noonan (1988) and Radford (1988, 1990), on the basis of similar observations, also concluded that COMP is lacking in early grammar.

Subcategorized finite clauses introduced by *che* appear after 2;3. Main predicates are perception verbs and modals. Initially, omissions are frequent:

(17)   OBJECTIVE   [+finite]CHE realized:
    (a)   2;3   *piange, hai visto che piange?*
                      'cries, have seen that cries?'
                      = she's crying, did you see she's crying?
    (b)   2;3   *visto che sono bruciati i piedi di Pinocchio?*
                      'see that are burns the feet of Pinocchio?'
                      = did you notice P's feet are burnt?
    (c)   2;8   *facciamo finta che era una gomma*
                      'make pretence that was a (chewing) gum'
                      = let's pretend-that-it was a piece of chewing gum
    (d)   2;8   *ho detto che non si puo*
                      'have said that not one can'
                      = I said you-impers. couldn't
[+finite] CHE omitted:
    (e)   2;8   *hai visto—mi sono tuffata*
                      'have seen—myself am dived?'
                      = did you see I dived?
    (f)   2;7   *lo sai—la mamma mi rompe tutti i giochi?*
                      'it-obj. know—the mommy to-me breaks all the toys'
                      = do you know mommy is always breaking my toys
    (g)   2;8   *spero—non cada!*
                      'hope—not fall'
                      = I hope [it] doesn't fall down

Finally, argument clauses appeared after *verba dicendi*, with a subcategorized complementizer, only at 2;6. Examples in (18) show that Camilla avoided indirect speech until 2;6 and beyond. Examples of reported speech are given in (19). Camilla began to produce subject clauses at about this stage, as shown in (20):

(18)   (a)   2;6   *dice: no no pigiare questo*
                  'says: no no press this'
                  = she says: (no) don't press this
    (b)   2;6   *dice Paperone: no lo toccare*
                  'says Donald Duck not it touch'
                  = Donald Duck says: don't touch it
    (c)   2;6   *io ho detto: dammi bacino*
                  'I have said: give me little kiss'
                  = I said: give me a little kiss
    (d)   2;6   *questo qua e rosso, io dico*
                  'this here is red, it say I'
                  = this one's red, I say so

(19)   (a)   2;8   *ho parlato con Livia, e li diciamo di venire qua*
                  = *per dirle, le ho detto*
                  'have spoken with Livia, and to-her say of come here'
                  = I spoke to Livia and told her to come here

    (b)   2;9   *dice a Sorellina di andare sull'elefante*
                     'says to little sister of go on the elephant'
                     = she tells her little sister to ride on the elephant

    (c)   2;1   *digli di stare stretti stretti di qui*
                     'tell him of be near near of here'
                     = tell him to more close up

(20) (a)   2;6   *vero che son piccole, queste, guarda*
                     'true that are small, these, look'
                     = they really are small, these, look

    (b)   2;10 *ma da qui e vero che non si apre?*
                     'but by here is true that not itself opens'
                     = but can't you really open it here?

The developmental pattern outlined in this section supports the conclusion that, in Italian as in other languages, complementizers emerge later than other embedding connectives. This fact is due to their being functional elements, as pointed out by Radford (1988, 1990).

A MATURATIONAL ACCOUNT

As stated in the last section, the developmental data presented here offer evidence that contravenes the presence of COMP in early grammar. Complementizers are often omitted until a given age, but wh-movement—apart from a very early stage in which it seems to be precluded—is used from very early on. On the other hand, not all the syntactic contexts in which wh-movement is required are simultaneously realized, showing that some constraints in child grammar do not depend on the presence or absence of the functional category COMP, but are related to some more subtle feature.

Following Penner and Müller (1992), I have argued that COMP must satisfy the licensing requirement of two features, namely, a *question* feature, $[+/-Q]$, and a *referential* feature, $[+/-REF]$. The former is the interrogative feature in C, which must be instantiated via Spec-Head feature sharing in COMP, as stated by the WH-Criterion in (3). The latter is a feature that covers all instances of coindexation between clauses; it must be instantiated as an index whose value is assigned by a matrix element or is obtained from the discourse.

According to Penner and Müller, embedded clauses can be defined as clusters of $[+/-Q, +/-REF]$, as follows: (a) Complement clauses (e.g. embedded questions, reported speech, object clauses) must instantiate both Q and REF features. (b) Adjunct clauses (e.g., relatives, adverbials) must instantiate only the REF feature. Penner and Müller accounted for the lack of complement clauses in child language by arguing that in early grammar sentential complements are not in their canonical position (X'), but in adjunct position (XP). For this reason, given that Q occurs only in X' configurations, it fails to be properly assigned, yielding the asymmetry observed in the production of embedded clauses: adjuncts produced versus complements missing.

With respect to Italian data, this proposal must be slightly modified. According to Penner and Müller, in the first phase (i.e., when Q cannot be assigned) interrogative complements should be absent, but this is not the case in Camilla's corpus. From the earlier examples, it seems that [Q] is properly assigned before 2;6 (i.e., before the second phase age). Moreover, if children are able to utter sentences where only REF must be assigned, we should find conditionals (where Q is not required); on the contrary, these complements only appear a few months later. Given these inconsistencies, one cannot explain why there is a development in the production of embedded clauses like the one I briefly described in the last paragraph.

Before attempting to adapt Penner and Müller's proposal to explain idiosyncratic Italian data, I would like to summarize the development of Camilla's production of the required Q and REF features, shown in Table 8.2. This developmental pattern indicates that: (a) The Q feature can be assigned in a projection other than CP (e.g., IP or VP), when CP is not yet activated in child grammar; and, (a) the REF feature is assigned according to a decreasing degree of referentiality. Points (a) and (b) may reflect some constraints that undergo maturation. Point (a) does not need further comment. As regards (b), we can observe that children begin with a maximum degree of coreferentiality, given by the trans-

TABLE 8.2
The Development of Camilla's Production of [Q] and [REF]

Age			Features
before	1;11	main clause question without WH-movement: *chi è* ?	+[Q] assigned in IP/VP
	1;11	main clause question with WH-movement *che fai* ?	+[Q} assigned in CP
	2;0 - 2;2	sentential adjuncts pseudorelatives relatives	+[REF] must be instantiated as co-indexation
after	2;3	*hai visto che piange* ?	+[Q], +[REF]
after	2;6	interrogative complement after complementizer, reported speech, conditionals	+[Q], -[REF] - [Q], -[REF] - [REF]

ference of referential features by wh-movement (1;11). Afterwards, REF assignment is obtained by coindexation at the clause level, through wh-elements (2;0–2;2). Finally, argument clauses selected by the matrix verb do not need coindexation (2;6).

From this analysis some problems emerge. First, why is pied-piping avoided in both matrix and embedded interrogatives? Nothing from earlier the discussion seems to prevent such a construction, which is, however, unattested (see Guasti & Shlonsky, in press; Labelle, 1990).[3] My opinion is that pied-piping involves phonological and grammatical difficulties that do not depend on the constraints singled out in this chapter and that require more detailed treatment elsewhere. Therefore, I will leave this question unanswered.

A second problem is related to the possibility, in child grammar, of producing interrogative clauses at a time when other argument clauses are not attested. Here it should be noted that matrix verbs of these constructions do not have the illocutionary force of "question." Early embedded Italian questions are not selected by verbs of "doubt" or "question." They depend, instead, on perception verbs, that is, verbs that generally select pseudorelatives, such as:

(21)   Pseudorelative:
        hai visto Luisa $_j$ che e $_j$ balla?
        'have seen Luisa that dances?'
        = did you see Luisa dancing?
        Embedded question:
        hai visto che $_j$ ho fatto e$_j$
        'have seen what have done'
        = did you see what I've done?

These observations lead to the following considerations:

1. Early dependent interrogative clauses are, actually, free relative clauses originated by the wh-movement of the head (along the lines discussed for headed relatives by Guasti & Shlonsky, in press).

2. Consequently coindexation of matrix and embedded clauses is performed via wh-operator,[4] which acts as a "bridge" for transferring semantic and/or

---

[3]According to Guasti and Shlonsky (in press), pied-piping in relatives is avoided because relatives are formed by wh-movement of the head antecedent from the base position. This strategy is not allowed when the indirect object must be relativized, so pied-piping is not admitted in relatives. Labelle (1990) argued against wh-movement in child relatives, thus excluding pied-piped relatives, which are, in fact, not attested in child language.

[4]Guasti and Shlonsky (in press) argue against this option, which they call linking operators. Their opinion is sustained by the absence of pied-piping in relatives, which is the only structure in which it is evident that the head of the relative is base-generated in the matrix sentences, and which is coindexed with the embedded position by means of the linking operator in SpecCP. I think that the absence of pied-piped relatives is due to other reasons, and that linking elements are not available unless they are provided with referential features. (Wh-elements have such features.)

quantificational features from the matrix to the embedded clause. A maturational constraint should account for these observational patterns, that is:

(22)   Until a certain age (after 2;6) linking between clauses is allowed only by means of elements with referential or quantificational features (e.g. wh-elements), while recoverability of referential features by COMP is not available.

The last problem is one of learnability. What triggers the acquisition of complementizer, and, therefore, the possibility of transferring indexes via subcategorization? Camilla's data strongly support the hypothesis that the acquisition of prepositions triggers the acquisition of complementizers or that complementizers are, in the beginning, categorized as prepositions, an idea already advanced for Creoles (Bickerton, 1981, among others). Prepositions and the connective *che* appear at the same time in Camilla's grammar (2;0), but at this stage *che* is used only in pseudorelatives, that is, in dependent clauses connected by a wh-operator. *Che* reaches its full function when constraint (22) is discarded by child's grammar, for maturational reasons.

A MODEL OF LANGUAGE ACQUISITION

Figure 8.1 represents a possible model of language acquisition that takes both maturational factors and lexical factors (bootstrapping) into account. My view is that maturation makes functional projection available and/or allows constraints to be discarded in child grammar. These facts, however, cannot guarantee that the grammar will be restructured accordingly. As we have seen, neither does the acquisition of COMP suffice so that complex sentences are immediately and correctly produced, nor is the abandonment of constraint (22) a sufficient reason to produce complement clauses, if some lexical element (i.e., *che*) is not already in use.

In my view, then, lexical acquisition and maturation both act as "triggers" for restructuring child grammar towards the target. This sort of "double track" may also explain children's different acquisition times of the same phenomenon. Whereas maturational processes are more or less contemporary in all children, lexical acquisition can take varying amounts of time to occur, yielding well known individual differences.

Setting of parameters occurs when functional categories are active in child grammar. According to this model it may be that functional categories are acquired and parameters are fixed, but due to insufficient vocabulary, specific grammatical phenomena emerge later (e.g., complex sentences after the acquisition of COMP)—or, on the contrary, that the necessary elements are acquired, but parameters are unsettled or constraints are active, so that Functional Elements are miscategorized as lexical (e.g., *che* in the period between 1;11 and 2;3 in this study).

.

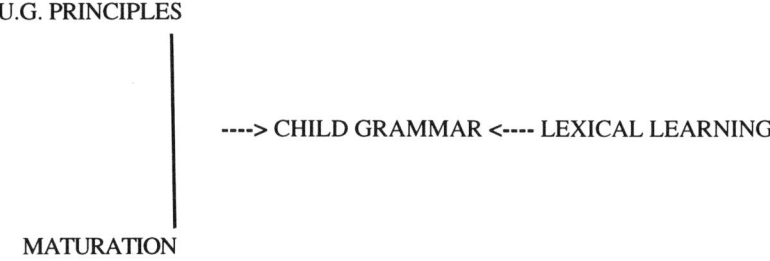

FIG. 8.1. A Model of Language Acquisition.

CONCLUSIONS

Italian learners show two developmental stages in the acquisition of complex sentences. In the first stage only nonargument clauses are produced; a few months later the second stage begins, during which subcategorized clauses are correctly uttered. This delay can be attributed to the fact that the functional category COMP must licence two features in it: Q and REF. Feature licensing is subject to a maturational constraint that, in the first stage, does not allow assignment of [−REF]; that is, the clauses connected must be in some sense coreferential.

The claim that COMP is not completely operative at the beginning is supported by the fact that at a very early stage, COMP seems to be completely missing. I interpret these results as evidence that functional categories may undergo maturation, as claimed in the recent literature on language development.

Notwithstanding this, the maturational hypothesis fails to explain the differences between children in the time of acquisition of several phenomena. For this reason a model of language acquisition must embody a lexical-learning module, which "anchors" language development to real-time learning, thus explaining individual differences.

REFERENCES

Antelmi, D. (1992). *L'Ipotesi maturazionale nell'acquisizione del linguaggio. Indagine longitudinale su una bambina* italiana [The maturational hypothesis of language acquisition. Longitudinal investigation of an Italian infant]. Unpublished doctoral dissertation, Universita di Padova, Italy.

Antelmi, D. (forthcoming). *La prima grammatica dell'italiano. Indagine longitudinale sull'acquisizione della morfosintassi italiana* [The first grammar of Italian. Longitudinal investigation of the acquisition of Italian morphosyntax]. Bologna: Il Mulino.

Bickerton, D. (1981). *Roots of language.* Ann Arbor, MI: Karoma.

Bloom, L., Lahey, M., Hood, L., Lifter, K., & Fiess, K. (1980). Complex sentences: Acquisition of syntactic connectives and the semantic relations they encode. *Journal of Child Language, 7,* 235–261.

Burzio, L. (1986). *Italian syntax: A government-binding approach.* Dordrecht: Reidel.

Chomsky, N. (1980). On binding. *Linguistic Inquiry, 11,* 1–46.

Chomsky, N. (1981). *Lectures on government and binding.* Dordrecht: Foris.

Chomsky, N. (1986). *Knowledge of language: Its nature, origin, and use.* New York: Praeger.

Cinque, G. (1981). On the theory of relative clauses and markedness. *The Linguistic Review, 1,* 243–294.

Cinque, G. (1992). *The pseudo-relative and acc-ing constructions after verbs of perception* (Working Papers in Linguistics). Venice: University of Venice.

Cipriani, P., Chilosi, A. M., Bottari, P., & Pfanner, L., (1993). *L'acquisizione della morfosintassi in italiano: fasi e processi* [The acquisition of morphosyntax in Italian: Stages and processes]. Padova: Unipress.

Clahsen, H. (1990). Constraints on parameter setting. *Language Acquisition, 1,* 361–391.

Clahsen, H., & Penke, M. (1992). The acquisition of agreement morphology and its syntactic consequences: New evidence on German child language from the Simone corpus. In J. Meisel (Ed.), *The acquisition of verb placement* (pp. 181-224). Dordrecht: Kluwer.

Clark, E. (1985). The acquisition of Romance. In D. Slobin (Ed.), *The crosslinguistic study of language acquisition, Vol. I: The data* (pp. 687–782). Hillsdale, NJ: Lawrence Erlbaum Associates.

Guasti, M. T. (1988). La pseudorelative et les phenomenes d'accord [The pseudorelative and the phenomena of agreement]. *Rivista di Grammatica Generativa, 13,* 35–57.

Guasti, M. T. (1993).Verbs syntax in Italian child grammar: Finite and nonfinite verbs. *Language Acquisition, 3,* 1–40.

Guasti, M. T., & Shlonsky, U. (in press). The acquisition of French relative clauses reconsidered. *Language Acquisition.*

Guilfoyle, E., & Noonan, M. (1988, October). *Functional categories and language acquisition.* Paper presented at the Boston University Conference on Language Development, Boston, MA.

Hyams, N. (1986). *Language acquisition and the theory of parameters.* Dordrecht: Reidel.

Hyams, N. (1992). The genesis of clausal structure. In J. Meisel (Ed.), *The acquisition of verb placement* (pp. 371–400). Dordrecht: Kluwer.

Labelle, M. (1990). Predication, wh-movement, and the development of relative clauses. *Language Acquisition, 1,* 95–119.

Lieko, A. (1992). *The development of complex sentences. A case study of Finnish.* Helsinki: Suomalaisen Kirjallisuuden Seura.

MacWhinney, B. (1991). *The CHILDES Project: Tools for analyzing talk.* Hillsdale, NJ: Lawrence Erlbaum Associates.

Meisel, J., & Müller, N. (1992). Finiteness and verb placement in early child grammars: Evidence from simultaneous acquisition of French and German in bilinguals. In J. Meisel (Ed.), *The acquisition of verb placement* (pp. 109–138). Dordrecht: Kluwer.

Penner, Z. (1992). The ban on parameter resetting, default mechanisms and the acquisition of V2 in Bernese Swiss German. In J. Meisel (Ed.), *The acquisition of verb placement* (pp. 245–282). Dordrecht: Kluwer.

Penner, Z., & Müller, N. (1992). On the early stages in the acquisition of finite subordinate clauses. *Geneva Generative Papers, 1–2,* 163–181.

Platzack, C. (1992). Functional categories and early Swedish. In J. Meisel (Ed.), *The acquisition of verb placement* (pp. 63–82). Dordrecht: Kluwer.

Radford, A. (1988). Small children's small clauses. *Transactions of the Philological Society, 86,* 1–43.

Radford, A. (1990). *Syntactic theory and the acquisition of English syntax: the nature of early child grammars of English.* Oxford, England: Basil Blackwell.

Radford, A. (1992). The acquisition of the morphosyntax of finite verbs in English. In J. Meisel (Ed.), *The acquisition of verb placement* (pp. 23–62). Dordrecht: Kluwer.

Rizzi, L. (1982). *Issues in Italian syntax*. Dordrecht: Foris.

Rizzi, L. (1991). Residual verb second and the WH-Criterion (Technical Reports in Formal and Computational Linguistics, 2). Geneva, Switzerland: University of Geneva.

Rizzi, L. (1992). Early null subjects and root null subjects. *Genève Generative Papers, 0* (1–2), 102–114.

Shaeffer, J. (1993). Non-inverted main Wh-questions in Italian and English child language. Unpublished master's thesis, University of California, Los Angeles.

Verrips, M., & Weissenborn, J. (1992). Verb placement in early German and French: The independence of finiteness and agreement. In J. Meisel (Ed.), *The acquisition of verb placement* (pp. 283–332). Dordrecht: Kluwer.

Weissenborn, J. (1990). Functional categories and verb movement in early German: the acquisition of German syntax reconsidered. In M. Rothweiler (Ed.), Spracherwerb und Grammatik. Linguistische Untersuchungen zum Erwerb von Syntax und Morphologie [Language development and grammar. Linguistic investigations of the development of syntax and morphology]. *Linguistische Berichte, Sonderheft 3*, 189–224.

9

Similarities Between SLI and L2 Children: Evidence From the Acquisition of Swedish Word Order

Gisela Håkansson
Ulrika Nettelbladt
Lund University

This chapter combines two hitherto separate research areas, namely, research on children with specific language impairment (SLI) and research on second language (L2) acquisition. Direct comparisons are made between children with specific language impairments and children learning a second languge who are approximately the same age. The data has been collected and analyzed within the same research project. Such direct comparisons have, to our knowledge, not yet been pursued, not even in an international perspective.

Swedish Word Order

The present research focuses on the development of Swedish word order rules, specifically the position of the subject in relation to the verb. Swedish, as well as the other Scandinavian languages and also German and Dutch, belongs to the so-called *V2 languages*. In V2 languages the finite verb always occurs in second position in a main clause; that is, only one constituent may precede the finite verb (XVX). This implies that subject-verb inversion is obligatory whenever a constituent other than the subject occurs in the first position. Examples (1) and (2), from a recording of Niklas (2;6), illustrate this rule:

(1) han står där   [Subj-Verb-Adv]
    'he stands there'
(2) nu står motorcykla   [Adv-Verb-Subj]
    'now stands motorbike'

In a sociolinguistic study of spoken Swedish, an analysis of word order revealed 1515 different word order patterns in a corpus of 6808 sentences (Jörgensen, 1976). About 60% of the main clauses had a subject in first position, whereas 40% had an adverbial, object or verb in the first position. As mentioned earlier, a nonsubject in initial position requires subject-verb inversion. This means that the uninverted pattern (SV) is used in 60% of the main clauses and the inverted pattern (VS) in 40%. This ratio seems to be quite consistent, both in adult-adult conversations, across different regional, social and stylistic varieties of the language (Jörgensen, 1976), and in adult-child interaction (Håkansson, 1988).

Acquisition of V2

What seems to be characteristic of early Swedish is that normally developing children have considerable variation in the order of sentence elements. All logically possible combinations in clauses with three elements have been documented, along with orders that do not appear in adult Swedish. Thus not only SVX and XVS have been found, but also VSX, SXV, VXS and XSV. There is, however, a strong preference for SVX and XVS in declaratives (see examples (1) and (2), and Håkansson, 1988; Henningson & Håkansson, 1989; Lange, 1975, 1976; Lange & Larsson, 1973, 1977; Platzack, 1990).

The variable pattern found in early speech of Swedish L1 children stands in striking contrast to the word order used in L2 Swedish. A number of studies of adult L2 learners of Swedish have shown that the verb-second rule is one of the longest lasting problems for L2 learners (e.g. Bolander 1987, 1988; Hyltenstam 1977, 1978). What seems especially difficult for the L2 learners is to dissolve the subject-before-verb pattern and use inverted word order, that is, place the verb before the subject. The first occurrences of subject-verb inversion in learner language is normally found in questions. This has been explained by the fact that subject-verb inversion has a clear function in question formation, because this is a means to differentiate between questions and statements (Håkansson, 1992). In declaratives, subject-verb inversion is a purely grammatical phenomenon, and many studies have shown that L2 learners tend to keep a rigid subject-verb order in declaratives when a nonsubject is in initial position. In other words, L2 learners favor SVX and XSV patterns. Interestingly, this preference for a canonical subject-verb order has also been found in L2 acquisition of other V2 languages, such as German (Clahsen, Meisel & Pienemann, 1983) and Danish (Holmen, 1993). Because most L2 learners in these studies have a first language with SVO word order, the preference for a canonical SVO order has been explained as cases of negative transfer from the first language.

Studies of Swedish Children With Specific Language Impairment

There is empirical evidence that Swedish children with specific language impairment also exhibit problems in the area of word order. In a pilot study analyzing grammatical errors made by five SLI children within the preschool age range, Hansson and Nettelbladt (1990) found that noninverted word order after a non-subject was one of the most common errors both intra- and interindividually. Other common word order errors were omission of obligatory sentence elements and use of extrasentential negation. Nettelbladt, Sahlén, Ors, and Johannesson, (1989) examined 10 SLI children of varying ages in a cross-sectional study. This study was done within an interdisciplinary research framework, focusing on not just linguistic aspects, but on psychological and medical aspects as well. Problems related to word order were found in 8 of the 10 children; the remaining 2 children were at a presyntactic stage of development. The word order problems consisted of a rigid subject-verb pattern, problems with negation, and omission of obligatory sentence elements. Finally, Sahlén and Nettelbladt (1992, 1993) studied 10 SLI children from preschool age onwards. Systematic errors of word order of the same kind as described in the earlier studies were made by all children at ages 4 and 5. Five of the children still made word order errors at 8 years of age. It is thus evidenced from the aforementioned studies, which include different groups of children, that mastery of subject-verb word order is a long-lasting problem area for Swedish SLI children.

Combining SLI and L2 Perspectives

In reviewing earlier research on Swedish L2 learners and Swedish SLI children, we have found interesting parallels (Nettelbladt & Håkansson, 1991; Håkansson & Nettelbladt, 1993). Problems in the acquisition of word order are typical of both groups, whereas such problems do not seem to exist for monolingual, normally developing Swedish children. As was mentioned earlier, the present research makes direct comparisons of the acquisition of word order by SLI and L2 children. With this in mind, it is surprising that such direct comparisons have not been made in earlier research, at least to our knowledge. Moreover, in the standard definitions of SLI exclusive criteria are used (Fey & Leonard, 1983; Stark & Tallal, 1981; Watkins, 1994). Of particular interest for the present study is that children who are not monolingual speakers are usually excluded from SLI research according to such criteria and tend to be viewed as confounding the data. Because of this, there is very limited knowledge of the relationship between SLI and L2.

Previous Research on Specific Language Impairment

Research on specific language impairment has been particularly prolific during the last two decades and has been conducted from several different perspectives. Most studies have been based within a clinical tradition, in particular within the disciplines of speech-language pathology, developmental and cognitive psychology, and special education (Watkins, 1994). Some researchers have mainly been concerned with the search for the underlying nature of specific language impairment in terms of neuropsychological or cognitive factors (Aram, Morris & Hall, 1993; Bishop, 1992; Johnston, 1994; Tallal, 1975). In recent years, linguists have become increasingly interested in the case of specific language impairment, and they have approached data from SLI children using different theoretical models of language and of language acquisition, for example Clahsen (1989), Gopnik and Crago (1991), Håkansson and Nettelbladt (1993), Leonard (1989), Leonard, Bortolini, Caselli, McGregor, and Sabbadini (1992), and Loeb and Leonard (1988).

Most published studies on specific language impairment refer to English-speaking children. Recently, however, SLI data are accumulating from other languages as well, in particular German (Clahsen, 1989; Kaltenbacher & Lindner, 1991; Lindner & Johnston, 1992), but also Italian and Hebrew (Dromi, Leonard, & Shteiman, 1993; Leonard et al., 1992). A more recent trend in SLI research is crosslinguistic comparisons (Leonard, 1992), which appear to be a very promising research direction because differences and similarities among SLI children are directly and systematically explored within different languages.

Delay or Deviance?

One of the most important research questions in specific language impairment research is to determine to what extent SLI children differ from children with normal language development. Thus, comparisons with normally developing children have been the rule. Comparisons are usually made with younger children matched to the SLI children in terms of language age in MLU (in words). Matching is often also made to normally developing children of the same chronological age. The matching procedures allow the researcher to determine types of delay or deviance of various language components in the SLI children as compared to the normal children.

The notions of delay versus deviance have been discussed in the SLI literature for several years, and the results of various studies are conflicting. Some studies favor a delay position, for example research on the acquisition of the lexicon (e.g., Schwartz & Leonard, 1985) and on pragmatic aspects (e.g., Skarakis & Greenfield, 1982) but also on grammatical aspects of development (Leonard, 1972). More inclined toward a deviance position is research on phonology, where persistence of abnormal phonological processes has been noted (e.g., Ingram, 1976) and in syntax, where deviant syntactic structures were noted in German SLI children (Grimm & Weinert, 1990).

As Curtiss, Katz, and Tallal (1992) recently pointed out, there is a tendency for studies claiming a delay position to base their arguments on data focusing on one single aspect of language. Advocates of a deviance position, on the other hand, usually include data from different aspects of development and show an asynchronous development between these.

In later years, the notions of delay versus deviance have been subjected to critical reevaluations, and a number of problems have been identified. In reviewing research on language development in adverse conditions, Bishop and Mogford (1993) state: "Language is not a unitary skill, but rather a collection of component abilitites that can be delayed or disordered in many different ways" (p. 28). Furthermore, there is a large range of individual variation in normal language acquisition that has to be accounted for. It is thus problematic to define what would or would not be found in normal development, because it is likely to be a matter of degree.

Within L2 acquisition variability is a key concept. It is a rule rather than an exception that learner language exhibits a great deal of variation, both within the same individual and across individuals. The variation has been dealt with, for example, in terms of cognitive style (Rubin, 1975), age (Long, 1993), social factors (Gardner & Lambert, 1972; Giles & Johnson, 1987), linguistic context (Hyltenstam, 1977, 1978) and amount of instruction (Pienemann, 1984, 1989).

AIM AND HYPOTHESES

The aim of the present study is to compare Swedish SLI children with children acquiring Swedish as a second language. To that end we have chosen to use a syntactic phenomenon typical of the interlanguage of L2 learners as a yardstick, namely, the position of the subject in relation to the verb. The comparisons are not primarily made with normally developing L1 children. Data from such children are used as reference. Furthermore, our frame of reference is not the superimposed norm of the language, but rather actual structures used by real speakers in communication of daily life (Linell, 1982). Five hypotheses were set up to be tested by our empirical findings:

1. The order of development is the same for L1 and L2 children but is different for SLI children, because of the impaired language faculty in the latter group.

2. The order of development is the same for L1 and SLI children but is different for L2 children. The two former groups are L1 acquirers, whereas the latter group already has a first language and is acquiring Swedish as an L2.

3. The order of development is the same for L2 and SLI children but is different for L1 children. The L1 children are neither impaired in their language faculty nor do they have another language, which can interfere with their development of Swedish.

4. The order of development is the same for all groups of children. The assumption behind this claim is that language development tends to proceed from the unmarked to the marked. Also, it can be assumed that the biologically based language acquisition device works in the same way in all groups of children, irrespective of learning conditions.

5. The order of development is different for all three groups of children. The underlying assumption is that the different language learning conditions for the groups involved are crucial.

METHOD

Subjects and Data Collection

A total of 15 children—5 children with specific language impairment (SLI children), 5 normally developing children acquiring Swedish as their first language (L1 children) and 5 children acquiring Swedish as their second language (L2 children)—participated in the study. All children were followed longitudinally at regular intervals.

The SLI children were selected by speech-language pathologists in southern Sweden according to criteria for SLI (Fey & Leonard, 1983; Stark & Tallal, 1981; Watkins, 1994). They all exhibited both grammatical and phonological impairment of at least a 1-year delay. The children had not been exposed to any long-term language therapy. The language comprehension of all the children was tested with the Reynell Test (Reynell, 1985) or with the Swedish Test of Language Comprehension (Hellquist, 1982). Their productive language was tested with the Lund Test of Phonology and Grammar (Holmberg & Stenkvist, 1978). All of the SLI children were developing normally, except for language. The SLI children were recorded either in their homes or in the language clinic, with which they were well acquainted. They either talked to one of their parents or to their own clinician.

The L1 children were selected from monolingual Swedish families and were judged by their parents, their preschool teachers, and the researchers to have normal language development as well as normal cognitive and motor development, and to be healthy in all other respects. The recordings began when the children had started to combine two to three words in a single utterance. The children were recorded at monthly intervals for about one year, talking to one of their parents or one of the researchers (who, in the latter case, the child knew beforehand).

The L2 children were selected from families that had arrived recently in Sweden. McLaughlin's (1987) definition of L2 acquisition was used; that is, children over 3 years of age when first exposed to the target language are defined as second language learners of that language. The L2 children in the present study were well over that limit. They were assessed to be developing normally in all respects, including their first language competence (as judged by their parents and/or an interpreter). The recordings of the L2 children started as soon as they began to make themselves understood in Swedish and continued until they moved from the refugee camp to different parts of Sweden. They were recorded in a free play situation in the preschool unit talking to one of the researchers.

TABLE 9.1
Age and MLU Range for the SL1, L2, and L1 Children

Name	Age Range	MLU Range	Sex
		SL1 Children	
Annika	4;11 - 6;11	2.24 - 3.07	Girl
Elvis	5;3 - 7;0	3.00 - 2.31	Boy
Frans	5;3 - 7;0	2.29 - 3.29	Boy
Beda	5;7 - 8;4	2.70 - 3.22	Girl
Alfons	5;11 - 8;3	2.64 - 3.71	Boy
		L2 Children	
Helena	4;0 - 4;3	3.17 - 2.83	Girl
Ali	4;6 - 5;2	3.53 - 3.09	Boy
Cynthia	4;7 - 4;10	3.82 - 4.18	Girl
Leila	5;1 - 5;3	3.17 - 3.52	Girl
Hannibal	5;5 - 6;0	2.42 - 3.43	Boy
		L1 Children	
Karin	2;0 - 3;1	2.18 - 3.38	Girl
Martin	2;2 - 3;1	1.26 - 2.83	Boy
Joakim	2;3 - 3;4	1.53 - 2.90	Boy
Niklas	2;4 - 3;1	1.40 - 2.76	Boy
Erik	2;5 - 3;0	1.84 - 2.05	Boy

Table 9.1 displays the code name, age, MLU and gender of each child in the three groups (SLI, L2 and L1).

Data and Transcription

The data consist of audio- and videotaped conversations from the 15 children. We tried to keep the conversational context as constant as possible. All children talked to an adult: either a parent, clinician, or researcher. The topics of conversation differed to some extent as a function of the child's age. The recordings were thus either play-oriented, with the youngest children, or focused on pictorial material, as with the older children. From each dialogue a sequence of approximately 20 minutes of continuous conversation was selected and transcribed. In order to facilitate quantification, the data were transcribed according to the conventions of the SALT program (Systematic Analysis of Language Transcripts, Miller & Chapman, 1986).

The transcriptions were done by the second author, or by two research assistants and then checked by the first or the second author. Consensus in cases of disagreement was arrived at through discussion.

Analysis

All utterances containing a subject and a verb were extracted and used for the syntactic analysis. Two different types of analysis were undertaken: an error analysis and a performance analysis. In the error analysis, V3 patterns; that is, the nontarget XSV (*Här den ska sova*, "Here it will sleep") were calculated as percentage of the total number of clauses containing a subject and a verb, for all groups of children. In the performance analysis the proportion of subject-verb versus verb-subject was measured. In this analysis, grammatical as well as ungrammatical clauses were counted.

RESULTS

The presentation of results is organized as follows. In the first section the results of the analysis of V3, or XSV, patterns are presented. In the second section the analysis of the proportion subject-verb versus verb-subject is presented. In order to get a direct mode of comparison, the section is subdivided into three sections. First, MLU matches are made between the first recordings of the five SLI children and recordings from the L1 children of the corresponding level of MLU. Second, age matches are made between the first recordings of the five SLI children and the first recordings of the L2 children of approximately the same age. In the third section, the developmental paths of the SV/VS ratio are presented. Individual patterns are also discussed.

XSV(V3) Patterns

Compiling the data on V3 patterns demonstrates that such patterns do occur in all three groups of children, but to a very different extent. In the L1 children the V3 patterns occur to a very limited extent (only nine examples across five L1 children). One of the L1 children, Karin, has no V3 examples at all. This is in glaring contrast to the SLI and the L2 children, who have a much greater number of such patterns (57 and 82 occurrences, respectively). Exceptions are the SLI children Beda and Elvis, and the L2 children Cynthia and Helena, who have relatively few occurrences of V3 sentences. As is shown in Table 9.3, however, all of them have a high proportion of the subject-verb pattern, thus indicating a

TABLE 9.2
Number of Occurrences of V3 Patterns for Each Child

L1	V3	SLI	V3	L2	V3
Erik	2	Annika	25	Ali	30
Joakim	3	Alfons	16	Cynthia	8
Karin	-	Beda	8	Hannibal	16
Martin	1	Elvis	1	Helena	6
Niklas	3	Frans	4	Leila	22
Total	9		54		82

preference for a rigid word order without topicalization. By choosing a strategy of avoiding topicalization, they use a rigid word order without making errors. Table 9.2 shows the compilations of V3 patterns from the three recordings of each child.

Examples (3)-(5) illustrate the V3 patterns in the children's production:

(3) där man äta mat med armarna   (Martin, L1 child, 2;11)
     'there one eat food with the arms'

(4) sen jag fick en kompis där   (Alfons, SLI child, 5;11)
     'then I got a friend there'

(5) nu dom har byttat   (Leila, L2 child, 5;0)
     'now they have changed'

Proportion of Subject–Verb
Versus Verb–Subject Patterns

In order to make direct comparisons between the different groups of learners, the first recordings from the SLI children are first matched to recordings from the L1 children in terms of MLU. As can be seen in Table 9.3, there is a clear difference between the SLI children on the one hand and the L1 children on the other. The former have a great preponderance of subject–verb word order, whereas the latter use proportions of SV/VS similar to the ratio of older children and adults (approximately 60%). Although there is some variation among individuals, a robust difference is found when looking at the group means, namely, 91% subject–verb for the SLI children and 64% for the L1 children.

Second, the first recording of each SLI child is compared to the first recording of the L2 children. All of the children are approximately within the same age range except for Helena, who is younger (age 4;0) than the youngest SLI child,

TABLE 9.3
Subject-Verb Versus Verb-Subject Ratio as Percentages. Comparison Between
SLI Children and L1 Children Matched for MLU

Name	MLU	SV/VS	%SV
		SLI	
Frans	2.29	36/5	88
Annika	2.24	23/1	96
Beda	2.70	16/1	94
Elvis	3.00	48/10	83
Alfons	2.64	26/2	93
Mean			91
		L1	
Joakim	2.28	17/15	53
Erik	2.22	29/19	74
Niklas	2.76	14/8	64
Martin	2.83	46/18	72
Karin	2.93	12/9	57
Mean			64

TABLE 9.4
Subject-Verb Ratio in the First Recordings of the SLI and L2 Children

Name	Age	SV/VS	%SV
		SLI	
Annika	4;11	23/1	96
Frans	5;3	36/5	88
Elvis	5;3	48/10	83
Beda	5;7	16/1	94
Alfons	5;11	26/2	93
Mean			91
		L1	
Helena	4;0	29/1	96
Cynthia	4;6	22/1	96
Ali	4;6	114/4	97
Leila	5;0	91/7	93
Hannibal	5;5	74/5	94
Mean			95

Annika (age 4;11), and Alfons, who is older (age 5;11) than the oldest L2 child, Hannibal (age 5;5). The results are displayed in Table 9.4.

Interestingly, the pattern is dramatically different from the pattern displayed in Table 9.3. Both the SLI and the L2 children exhibit a strong preference for subject–verb word order, as is clearly shown by their group means, and they do not show the pattern of word order variation which is typical for adult Swedish and also for the younger L1 children.

In an earlier study Hansson and Nettelbladt (1994) have shown that normally developing Swedish children in the age range of 4;5–6;7 have a mean proportion of subject-verb pattern of 57.7%, one that is very close to the adult proportion of 60%.

Developmental Profiles

Figures 9.1–9.3 illustrate the development of word order patterns used by SLI, L2, and L1 children. As has been discussed earlier, there is a clear difference between the L1 children at one extreme, and the SLI children and the L2 children at the other. Both the SLI and the L2 children start with almost 100% subject–verb order, indicating a strong preference for a rigid pattern. The L1 children, on the contrary, start with relatively low proportions of subject–verb patterns. This pattern of word order variability is stable through the three recordings.

A few individual differences can be seen. One of the SLI children, Alfons, and one of the L2 children, Hannibal, undergo a development in syntactic patterns and use more variation in the later recordings than in the first recording. They seem to have acquired a targetlike variation in word order in their later record-ings. The other SLI children and L2 children use the stable SV pattern through all the recordings. This implies that, although they might have an error-free syntax

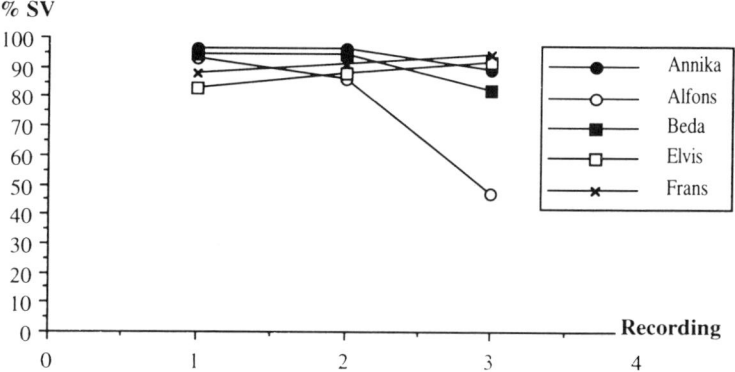

FIG. 9.1. Proportion of clauses with subject–verb word order from three recordings in the speech of the SLI children—Annika, Alfons, Beda, Elvis, and Frans.

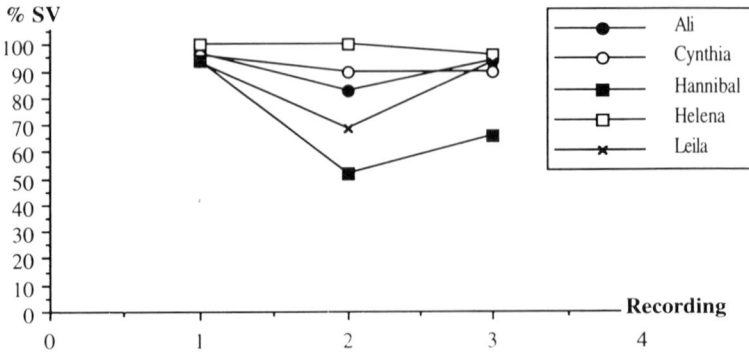

FIG. 9.2. Proportion of clauses with subject–verb word order from three recordings in the speech of the L2 children—Ali, Cynthia, Hannibal, Helena, and Leila.

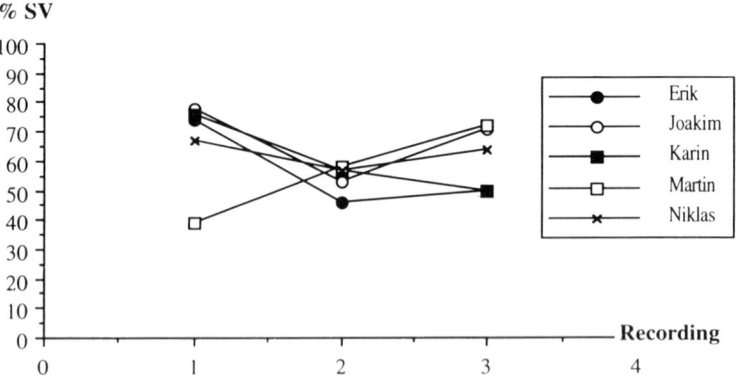

FIG. 9.3. Proportion of clauses with subject–verb word order from three recordings in the speech of the L1 children—Erik, Joakim, Karin, Martin, and Niklas.

with almost no V3 sentences (as for example Frans and Elvis), they do not use the potential for variation that is characteristic of Swedish word order.

DISCUSSION

The results of the analysis of subject–verb order in the different groups of children support our hypothesis 3; that is, L2 and SLI children are similar and that they differ from L1 children. In terms of an innate language acquisition faculty (Lenneberg, 1967), this might suggest that the faculty is not working in an optimal way in L2 and SLI conditions. Both SLI and L2 children acquire the Swedish word order pattern in a stepwise and effortful way, by making use of a canonical subject–verb strategy. Normally developing L1 children, on the other hand, show a surprisingly rapid acquisition of the specific features of Swedish word order.

To conclude, the present results show that the combination of two separate research areas, specific language impairment and second language research, has proven to be fruitful in more than one way. First, the difference between L1 and L2 acquisition is by no means as clear-cut as has been claimed earlier (e.g., Clahsen & Muysken, 1986, 1989), if we include SLI as cases of L1 acquisition. Our results on the development of Swedish word order show that, contrary to expectations, Swedish monolingual SLI children resemble L2 learners of Swedish more than they resemble young monolingual L1 learners (or L1 learners of the same age).

Second, in order to reach a full understanding of the nature of specific language impairment, it is not sufficient only to look at monolingual conditions of language acquisition. In fact, looking at other complicated or adverse conditions can shed new light on the language impairment problem. This has recently been discussed by Bishop and Mogford (1993), who scrutinized a number of exceptional conditions: for example, extreme deprivation, twinship, hearing children with deaf parents, visual impairment, recurrent otitis media, Down Syndrome, autism, and focal brain damage. In examining the possible influence of these conditions on language development, the authors showed that, although normal language development is compatible with many of the conditions reviewed, a transient delay is often found. However, children with specific language impairment still puzzle us because, in the absence of adverse and different conditions, they still show a persisting language impairment.

Third, this research also gives a new perspective on the question of transfer and markedness in L2 acquisition. Hitherto, it has been assumed that the preference for subject–verb word order in adult L2 Swedish is due to transfer from an L1. Because most L2 learners of Swedish have an L1 with subject–verb word order, this assumption has been hard to refute. With the present data of SLI children preferring subject–verb patterns, however, we might instead speculate on the role of markedness in language acquisition. Because SLI children do not have any L1 to be transferred into their Swedish, the transfer hypothesis does not fit their case. It is plausible that markedness conditions play a more important role in language acquisition than has been assumed to date.

Fourth and finally, our results indicate that the Swedish children with specific language impairment are not only delayed, but also deviant in terms of their development of subject–verb word order. The present research has shown that, by taking a syntactic phenomenon typical of L2 acquisition as our point of departure, it is possible to discern signs of deviance in SLI children (Hansson & Nettelbladt, 1995). This is not possible if we only look for phenomena typical of early L1 acquisition. Thus, our results are important in the continuing discussion of language delay versus language deviance in SLI children.

The results of the present study show the importance of interdisciplinary research. It is our firm belief that a deeper knowledge of the language learning process in general cannot be gained without direct and systematic comparisons across different groups of language learners under a variety of conditions.

ACKNOWLEDGMENTS

The authors wish to thank Kristina Hansson for her assistence in data collection and transcription. This research has been supported by grants 86—105 and 90—211 from the Bank of Sweden Tercentenary Foundation awarded to Ulrika Nettelbladt and Gisela Håkansson, and a grant from the Medical Faculty, Lund University to Ulrika Nettelbladt. Our special thanks go to the children and their parents for participating in the time-consuming recordings, and to the speech-language clinicians for helping us to select children for the study and participating in the recordings.

REFERENCES

Aram, D., Morris, R., & Hall, N. (1993). Clinical and research congruence in identifying children with specific language impairment. *Journal of Speech & Hearing Research, 36,* 580–591.

Bishop, D. (1992). The underlying nature of specific language impairment. *Journal of Child Psychology and Psychiatry and Allied Disciplines, 33,* 3–66.

Bishop, D., & Mogford, K. (Eds.). (1993). *Language development in exceptional circumstances.* Hove, England: Lawrence Erlbaum Associates.

Bolander, M. (1987). *"Man kan studera inte så mycket." Om placering av negation och adverb i vuxna invandrares svenska* [On the placement of negation and adverbs in adult immigrant Swedish] (SUM Report No. 5). University of Stockholm.

Bolander, M. (1988). Is there any order? On word order in Swedish learner language. *Journal of Multilingual and Multicultural Development, 9,* 97–113.

Clahsen, H. (1989). The grammatical characterization of developmental dysphasia. *Linguistics, 27,* 897–920.

Clahsen, H., Meisel, J., & Pienemann, M. (1983). *Deutsch as Zweitsprache. Der Spracherwerb ausländer Arbeiter* [German as a second language. The language development of foreign workers]. Tubingen, Germany: Gunter Narr.

Clahsen, H., & Muysken, P. (1986). The availability of universal grammar to adult and child learners—A study of the acquisition of German word order. *Second Language Research, 2,* 93–119.

Clahsen, H., & Muysken, P. (1989). The UG Paradox in L2 acquisition. *Second Language Research, 5,* 1–29.

Curtiss, S., Katz, W., & Tallal, P. (1992). Delay versus deviance in the language acquisition of language-impaired children. *Journal of Speech & Hearing Research, 35,* 373–383.

Dromi, E., Leonard, L., & Shteiman, M. (1993). The grammatical morphology of Hebrew-speaking children with specific language impairment: Some competing hypotheses. *Journal of Speech and Hearing Research, 36,* 760–771.

Fey, M., & Leonard, L. (1983). Pragmatic skills of children with specific language impairment. In T. Gallagher & C. Prutting (Eds.), *Pragmatic assessment and intervention issues in language* (pp. 65–82). San Diego: College-Hill Press.

Gardner, R., & Lambert, W. (1972). *Attitudes and motivation in second-language learning.* Rowley, MA: Newbury House.

Giles, H., & Johnson, P. (1987). Ethnolinguistic identity theory: A social psychological approach to language maintenance. *International Journal of the Sociology of Language, 68,* 69–100.

Gopnik, M., & Crago, M. (1991). Familial aggregation of a developmental language disorder. *Cognition, 39,* 1–50.

Grimm, H., & Weinert, S. (1990). Is the syntax development of dysphasic children deviant and why? New findings to a new question. *Journal of Speech and Hearing Research, 33,* 220–228.

Håkansson, G. (1988). "Hungry I am—Breakfast I want." On the acquisition of inverted word order in Swedish. *Working Papers, 33* (pp.123–130). Lund, Sweden: University of Lund, Department of Linguistics.

Håkansson, G. (1992). Variation och rigiditet i ordföljdsmönster [Variation and rigidity in word order patterns]. In M. Axelsson & Å. Viberg (Eds.), *Förhandlingarna från symposiet Nordens språk som andraspråk* [The first symposium on research in Scandinavian languages as second languages] (pp. 314–324). University of Stockholm, Department of Linguistics.

Håkansson, G., & Nettelbladt, U. (1993). Developmental sequences in L1 (normal and impaired) and L2 acquisition of Swedish syntax. *International Journal of Applied Linguistics, 3,* 131–157.

Hansson, K., & Nettelbladt, U. (1990). The verbal interaction of language impaired preschool children. *Clinical Linguistics and Phonetics, 4,* 39–48.

Hansson, K., & Nettelbladt, U. (1994). Grammatical profiles of Swedish language-normal and SLI-children *(Working Papers in Logopedics & Phoniatrics, 9,* pp. 7–38). Lund, Sweden: University of Lund.

Hansson, K., & Nettelbladt, U. (1995). Grammatical characteristics of Swedish children with SLI. *Journal of Speech and Hearing Research, 38,* 589–598.

Hellquist, B. (1982). *SIT—Språkligt impressivt test för barn [Language Comprehension Test for children].* Malmö, Sweden: Tryckeriteknik.

Henningsson, L., & Håkansson, G. (1989). Etablering av subjektspositionen. [Establishing subject position]. In R. Söderbergh (Ed.), *Proceedings from the Second Scandinavian Child Language Symposium* (pp. 67–74). Lund, Sweden: University of Lund, Lund Child Language Research Institute.

Holmberg, E., & Stenkvist, H. (1976). *Lundamaterialet. Kartläggning och bedömning av barns språkliga förmåga* [The Lund test of phonology and grammar. Description and assessment of children's linguistic abilities]. Malmö, Sweden: Utbildningsproduktion AB.

Holmen, A. (1993). Syntactic development in Danish L2. In K. Hyltenstam & Å. Viberg (Eds), *Progression and regression in language* (pp. 267–288). Cambridge, England: Cambridge University Press.

Hyltenstam, K. (1977). Implicational patterns in interlanguage syntax variation. *Language Learning, 27,* 383–411.

Hyltenstam, K. (1978). *Variation in interlanguage syntax* (Working Papers, 18). Lund, Sweden: University of Lund, Department of Linguistics.

Ingram, D. (1976). *Phonological disability in children.* New York: Elsevier.

Johnston, J. (1994). Cognitive abilities of children with language impairment. In R. Watkins & M. Rice (Eds.), *Specific language impairments in children* (pp. 107-121). Baltimore: Paul H. Brookes.

Jörgensen, N. (1976). Meningsbyggnaden i talad svenska. [Sentence structure in spoken Swedish]. Student literature, Doctoral dissertation, Lund, Sweden.

Kaltenbacher, E., & Lindner, K. (1991). Some aspects of delayed and deviant development in German children with specific language-impairment. In P. Mjaavatn, B. Hagvedt, & J. Feilberg (Eds.),

Proceedings of the Conference on Child Language Disorders (pp. 216–231). Trondheim, Norway: Norwegian Center for Child Research

Lange, S. (1975). *En preliminär grammatisk analys av språket hos Freja från 20 till 41 månaders ålder. Del 2. Freja 6–10. Ålder 22–24 månader* [A preliminary grammatical analysis of Freja's speech from 20 to 41 months of age. Part 2. Freja 6–10. Age 22–24 months] (Report No. 8). University of Stockholm, Institutionen för Nordiska Språk.

Lange, S. (1976). *En preliminär grammatisk analys av språket hos Freja från 20 till 41 månaders ålder. Del 3. Freja 11–15. Ålder 25–27 månader* [A preliminary grammatical analysis of Freja's speech from 20 to 41 months of age. Part 3. Freja 11–15. Age 25–27 months] (Report No. 10). University of Stockholm, Institutionen för Nordiska Språk.

Lange, S., & Larsson, K. (1973). *Syntactical development of a Swedish girl, Embla, between 20 and 42 months of age. Part 1. Age 20–25 mo.* (Report No. 1). University of Stockholm, Institutionen för Nordiska Språk.

Lange, S., & Larsson, K. (1977). *Studier i det tidiga barnspråkets grammatik* [Studies in early child language grammar] (Report No. 11). University of Stockholm, Institutionen för Nordiska Språk.

Lenneberg, E. (1967). *Biological foundations of language.* New York: Wiley.

Leonard, L. (1972). What is deviant language? *Journal of Speech & Hearing Research, 15,* 427–446.

Leonard, L. (1989). Language learnability and specific language impairment in children. *Applied Psycholinguistics,10,* 179–202.

Leonard, L. (1992). The use of morphology by children with specific language impairment: Evidence from three languages. In R. Chapman (Ed.), *Processes in language acquisition and disorders* (pp. 186–201). Chicago: Mosby Yearbook.

Leonard, L., Bortolini, U., Caselli, C., McGregor, C., & Sabbadini, L. (1992). Morphological deficits in children with specific language impairment: The status of features in the underlying grammar. *Language Acquisition, 2,* 151–179.

Lindner, K., & Johnston, J. (1992). Grammatical morphology in language-impaired children acquiring English or German as their first language: A functional perspective. *Applied Psycholinguistics, 13,* 115–129.

Linell, P. (1982). *The written bias in linguistics* (Studies in Communication, 2). Linköping, Sweden: University of Linköping.

Loeb, D. F., & Leonard, L. (1988). Specific language impairment and parameter theory. *Clinicial Linguistics and Phonetics, 2,* 317–327.

Long, M. (1993). Second language acquisition as a function of age: Research findings and methological issues. In K. Hyltenstam & Å. Viberg (Eds). *Progression and regression in language* (pp. 196–221). Cambridge, England: Cambridge University Press.

McLaughlin, B. (1987). *Theories of second language learning.* London: Edward Arnold.

Miller, J., & Chapman, R. (1986). *SALT: A computer program for the systematic analysis of language transcripts.* Madison: University of Wisconsin, Waisman Center, Language Analysis Laboratory.

Nettelbladt, U., & Håkansson, G. (1991). Towards an integrated view of language acquisition. Can clinical work with language disordered children profit from heories of first and second language acquisition? *Scandinavian Journal of Logopedics & Phoniatrics, 16,* 29–35.

Nettelbladt, U., Sahlén, B., Ors, M., & Johannesson, P. (1989). A multidisciplinary assessment of children with severe language disorder. *Clinical Linguistics & Phonetics, 3,* 313–346.

Pienemann, M. (1984). Psychological constraints on the teachability of languages. *Studies in Second Language Acquisition, 6,* 186–214.

Pienemann, M. (1989). Is language teachable? Psycholinguistic experiments and hypotheses. *Applied Linguistics, 10,* 52–79.

Platzack, C. (1990). A grammar without functional categories: A syntactic study of early Swedish child language. *Nordic Journal of Linguistics, 13,* 107–126.

Reynell, J. (1985). *The Reynell developmental language scales—revised.* Windsor, England: NFER-Nelson Publishing Co.

Rubin, J. (1975). What the 'good language learner' can teach us. *TESOL Quarterly, 9,* 41–51.

Sahlén, B., & Nettelbladt, U. (1993). On language production in severe developmental language disorders and the concept of linguistic levels. A longitudinal study of ten children with severe developmental language disorders. *Scandinavian Journal of Logopedics & Phoniatrics, 18,* 15–28.

Schwartz, R., & Leonard, L. (1985). Lexical imitation and acquisition in language-impaired children. *Journal of Speech & Hearing Research, 50,* 141–149.

Skarakis, E., & Greenfield, P. (1982). The role of new and old information in the verbal expression of language-disordered children. *Journal of Speech & Hearing Research, 25,* 462–467.

Stark, R., & Tallal, P. (1981). Selection of children with specific language deficits. *Journal of Speech and Hearing Disorders, 46,* 114–122.

Tallal, P. (1976). Rapid auditory processing in normal and disordered language development. *Journal of Speech & Hearing Research, 19,* 561–571.

Watkins, R. (1994). Specific language impairments in children. An introduction. In R. Watkins & M. Rice. (Eds.), *Specific language impairments in children* (pp. 1–15). Baltimore: Paul H. Brookes.

APPENDIX

Individual proportions of subject-verb word order in each of three recordings of each child in the three groups of SLI, L2, and L1 children. The numbers are given as a percentage of the total number of clauses containing a subject and a verb.

SLI Children

Annika	96-96-89
Alfons	93-86-47
Beda	94-94-82
Elvis	83-88-92
Frans	88-91-94

L2 Children

Ali	97-83-94
Cynthia	96-90-90
Hannibal	94-52-66
Helena	100-100-96
Leila	93-69-93

L1 Children

Erik	74-46-50
Joakim	78-53-71
Karin	76-57-50
Martin	39-58-72
Niklas	67-57-64

10 The Acquisition of Object Shift in Swedish Child Language

Gunlög Josefsson
Lund University, Sweden

Object shift is a syntactic operation that raises a weak object pronoun to a position to the left of a negation or a sentential adverbial. This position is not available for NP objects and strong pronouns:

(1) (a) *Mamman tvättade inte barnen*
'mother-the washed not children-the'
(b) *Mamman tvättade dem/*barnen inte*
'mother-the washed them/*children-the not'

In this chapter I present a pilot investigation of the acquisition of object shift by Swedish children. The result is, in short, that object shift is acquired rather late in the language acquisition process. Even if isolated examples of this construction are found early, it seems to be the case that even older children (4 to 5 years of age) who are fluent speakers have a tendency to avoid the construction. The explanation I propose is that weak object pronouns in the target grammar are classified as heads (Josefsson, 1992, 1993a, 1993b, 1994), but that children tend to classify them as full phrases—NPs—on a par with proper nouns and names.

The organization of this chapter is as follows. The first section describes how and when object shift applies in adult Swedish. In the next section, the investigation of the acquisition of object shift is presented. This is followed by a discussion, and then a summary. The Appendix contains the elicitation test.

OBJECT SHIFT IN SWEDISH

In this section I briefly discuss the phenomenon of object shift in adult Swedish. Object shift has been described previously by Holmberg (1986, 1991), Vikner

(1990), and Josefsson (1992, 1993a, 1993b, 1994), among others. The reader is referred to these works for a deeper discussion of the phenomenon.

Object shift is the raising of a weak object pronoun to a position to the left of a negation or a sentence adverbial. An example of this was given in (1). Weak pronouns do not differ morphophonemically from strong pronouns. However, as Holmberg (1991) has shown, a weak pronoun displays all three criteria of Kayne's (1975) test on clitichood; it cannot be stressed, conjoined or modified:

(2)   *Mamman tvättade *DEM[1]/*dem och oss/*dem båda inte*
      'mother-the washed *THEM/*them and us/*them both not'

Object shift applies only in simple main clauses. It is thus ruled out in subordinate clauses (3), in auxiliary constructions (4) and (5), in PP complements (6), and in verb particle constructions (7). Common to all these constructions is that the verb remains in its base generated position in V. It thus seems as though the raising of the object pronoun is dependent on the raising of the verb.[2]

(3)   (a)   *Jag vet att Anna den inte ser*
            'I know that Anna it not sees'
      (b)   *Jag vet att Anna inte ser den*

(4)   (a)   *Anna har den inte sett*
            'Anna has it not seen'
      (b)   *Anna har inte sett den*

(5)   (a)   *Anna lovade att dem inte tvätta*
            'Anna promised to them not wash'
      (b)   *Anna lovade att inte tvätta dem*

(6)   (a)   *Anna talar mej inte med*
            'Anna speaks me not with'
      (b)   *Anna talar inte med mig*

(7)   (a)   *Anna gav den inte bort*
            'Anna gave it not away'
      (b)   *Anna gav inte bort den*

This chapter deals with object shift in Swedish. It should, however, be mentioned that there are some differences between the Scandinavian languages with

---

[1]Throughout the chapter I use majuscules when referring to strong pronouns (in isolation) and minuscules when referring to weak pronouns.

[2]As opposed to Mainland Scandinavian, the verb raises to Infl in Icelandic also in subordinate clauses. As we would expect, object shift applies also in subordinate clauses in Icelandic, yielding sentences like (i):

(i)   Að Frída sá hann ekki
      'that F saw him not'

respect to the properties of object shift. In Icelandic full NPs may also shift (provided they are definite) and in Danish the verb particle does not block object shift. (Note, however, that the order between the verb and the verb particle is reversed in Danish, compared to Swedish.)

It is sometimes said that object shift is an obligatory operation. It is, however, not immediately evident that this is the case. All we can say is that strong pronouns are banned in the object shift position (to the left of the negation or the sentence adverbial), and that all stressed, conjoined, or modified pronouns must remain to the right of the verb. An unstressed object pronoun may also remain to the right of a negation or a sentence adverbial. Even though it is a bit circular, in this chapter I use the term *weak object pronoun* only for pronouns that undergo object shift.[3] It is necessary, however, to stress that a factor having to do with focus also seems to be involved. In an object-shifted construction the object never contains any new or focused information. An interesting attempt to explain object shift in terms of informational structure is made by Diesing and Jelinek (1993), who compared object shift in the Scandinavian languages to a similar construction in Egyptian Arabic and suggested that only presupposed objects, not asserted objects, undergo object shift (see also Josefsson, 1993b, 1994).

There have been different proposals regarding the structural description of object shift. The crucial point seems to be how to analyze weak pronouns in X' terms, that is, whether the pronoun is a head or a phrase. As will become evident, this question is important for my description of the acquisition of object shift in Swedish child language. Holmberg (1991) described weak pronouns as belonging to an N* category. The Scandinavian pronouns of the N* type have some properties in common with clitic heads of the Romance type (they cannot be stressed, modified or conjoined), but as far as movement is concerned, they move as full phrases. Object shift is thus considered a VP adjunction of an N* category above the sentence adverbial, according to Holmberg's description. Vikner (1990) also described object shift as a VP adjunction. A different analysis is given in Josefsson (1992, 1993a, 1993b 1994), where object shift is described as cliticization or incorporation of a head to a functional projection situated above

---

[3]Note, however, that there are certain "true" clitic pronouns that may remain to the right of the sentence adverbial:

  (i) *Jag såg inte'na*
      'I saw not-her (CL)'

'na is not a reduced form of the personal pronoun *henne*, but is a remainder of the no longer used object pronoun *hana*. The pronoun *'na* may undergo object shift too:

  (ii) *Jag såg'na'nte*
       'I saw her-CL not-CL'

I will not discuss this kind of clitic pronominal this chapter.

the VP.[4] This analysis is supported by the fact that a weak object pronoun under some circumstances may raise to a position between the finite verb (in the second position in the clause) and a nonsentence-initial subject.[5] The most general and simple account of the two possible positions for an object shifted pronoun seems to be to assume that object shift is a head-to-head movement of a head to a functional head, either to Infl or to C. See Josefsson (1992, 1993a, 1993b, 1994) for further discussion.

THE ACQUISITION OF OBJECT SHIFT
BY SWEDISH CHILDREN

In order to determine when and how object shift is acquired by Swedish children, I have used two methods. First, I have examined two corpora to find out how many instances of object shift were found. Second, I have used the method of elicited imitation (see Slobin & Welsh, 1973) to explore when the children acquire this construction. In the following subsections I present the result of these

---

[4]The background assumption is that the clause has three domains, the CP, the IP and the VP:

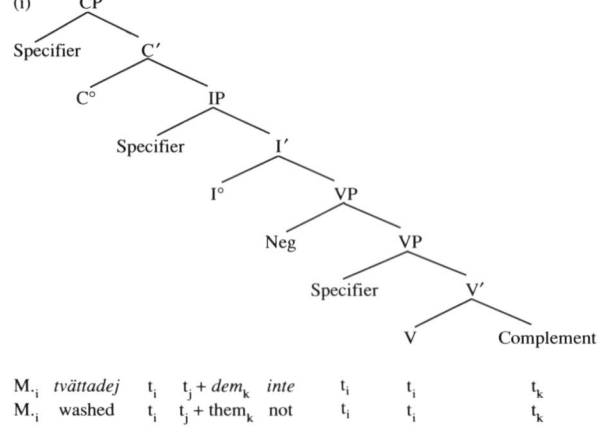

The verb is generated as the head of the VP, and raises to Infl to check its tense features, and further to C to check the finiteness features (which accounts for the verb second phenomenon in main clauses). According to the proposed analysis, a weak object pronoun (*dem* in this tree) is analyzed as the head of the complement NP, which raises to Infl and cliticizes to this (empty) head.

[5]An example of a weak object pronoun between the finite verb and a nonsentence initial subject is given in (i):

(i) *Därför ger mig Tutanchamons förbannelse inte någon ro*
    'therefore gives me T's curse not any peace'

investigations. As is shown, the object shift construction is rather rare in the investigated corpora, and the conclusions are therefore mainly based on the results of the elicited imitation investigation.

The Corpus Investigation

The first part of the investigation is an examination of two corpora collected by Söderbergh (1973) and Schlyter (1993). Söderberg's corpus contains 40 recordings of five Swedish children from the age of 1;8 to 3;6. I have used the recordings of four of the children in my study: Freja and Embla in total, the recordings of Tor up to sample 36, and the recordings of Ask up to 19,[6] finding only five instances of object shift :

(8) (a) *hon når det inte—fast jag har den där*   (Freja 35:59, 3;4)
          'she reaches it not—though I have it there'
     (b) *ta den inte*   (Ask 7:141, 2;2)
          'take it not'
     (c) *ta dom inte, bara DEN också*   (Ask 9:72, 2;4)
          'take them not, only IT too'
     (d) *ej VILL det in/ Jag VILL det/ /n/ jag vill inte. läsa den där mamma*
          (Ask 12:21–24, 2;5)
          'not WANT it not/ I WANT it /n/ I want not. read that mommy'
     (e) *vi vågar honom /int/*   (Embla 39:85, 3;5)
          'we dare him not'

The part of Schlyter's corpus I have examined contains recordings of three bilingual children, two of whom had Swedish as their stronger language. The children were recorded from the age of 1;10 to 4;2. In neither of these recordings have I found any example of object shift.

The Elicited Imitation Investigation

The natural conclusion to draw from the scarcity of examples of object shift in the corpora is that object shift is not very common in spontaneous child language up to about 4 years of age, at least. In order to get more information about when children acquire this construction I have also made a pilot investigation using the method of elicited imitation (see Slobin & Welsh, 1973). The investigation proceeded as follows: 15 children from age 2;5 to 7;5 were asked to repeat a fairy tale sentence by sentence (see Appendix). Eight of the 30 sentences contained an object-shift construction. At the time of the investigation the children all attended preschool or school. All the children have at least one Swedish-speaking parent.

---

[6]Not all recordings are available in transcriptions. The following notation is used in this section— recording sample number:utterance number,years; months.

TABLE 10.1
Elicited Imitation--Results

Number of example Sentences containing the object shift construction[a]

	Age	1	2	3	4	5	6	7	8	#OK
Pia	2;5	NegPn	NegPn	NegPn	PnNeg	WrPn	(OK?)_	OK	-	1
David	3;0	NegPnNeg	OK*	OK*						0
Fanny[b]	3;3	OK	NegPnNeg	OK	OK*		OK	PnNeg	OK	5
Johan[b]	3;6	OK*		-	OK*	OK	OK	OK*		2
Robert[c]	4;1	Unan	Unan	OK	?NegNeg	OK*	OK	OK	OK*	3
Sam	4;3	OK	OK	OK	OK	OK	PnNeg	OK	OK	7
Axel	4;5	WrPn	WrPn	OK*	OK	-	-	-	OK*	1
Josef	4;6	OK*	-	OK	PnNeg	OK	PnNeg	-	OK	3
Lisa	4;10	OK	-	NegPnNeg	OK	OK	OK	-	OK	5
Filip	4;11	OK	OK	OK*	-	OK*	PnNeg	(OK?)	OK	4
Julia[d]	4;11	PnNeg	PnNeg	NegPn	NegPn	NegPn	PnNeg	PnNegAl	PnNeg	0
Anna	5;2	OK	-	OK	OK	OK	PnNeg	OK	OK	6
Linda	5;4	OK	PnNeg	OK	OK	OK	PnNeg	(NegAl?)	OK	5
Rosa	5;	OK	OK	OK	OK	OK	OK	OK	OK	8
Erika	7;4	OK	OK	OK	OK	OK	OK	OK	OK	8

[a]The eight sentences are in the Appendix. OK = correct repetition; OK* = correct rep. after having heard the pattern sentence more than once; NegPn = Inversion (see Acquisition of Object Shift section); PnNeg = Deletion of the pronoun; Unan = Unanalyzable structure; WrPn = wrong object pronoun repeated; PnNeg = deletion of the negation (see section 2); Al = addition of the adverbial *aldrig* (never).
[b]Finnish as first language.
[c]Adopted at 0;9.
[d]English as first language.

(I have made a remark on those cases where a second language may have influenced the result.) Results of the elicitation are shown in Table 10.1.

It is not immediately obvious how to interpret the results. First of all, the fact that a child is able to repeat a sentence containing an object-shift construction does not prove that the child has acquired the construction in question. As with all experiments of this type, it could be the case that the child is simply good at repeating word by word. This might, for example, be the case with Johan (3;6). Johan had trouble in understanding what the task was, and in continuing the repetition. Like some of the other children, Johan was "caught by the story," and frequently started commenting on the sentences instead of repeating them. It was therefore necessary to repeat the sentences several times before Johan would imitate them. (When this was done the result is marked with an * in the table.) Second, several children did not produce an object shift construction in the beginning of the recording, but succeeded at the end. This could either be due to the fact that they had "learned" the construction quickly, that they had a vague and unstructured idea about the construction, or that they got used to "the game" of imitating.

Bearing all these caveats in mind, I shall point out the most interesting results from the investigation. First, the youngest child does not seem to have the construction at all. The example in 7 is marked OK, but it is the only example with the adverb *aldrig* 'never'. *Aldrig* is semantically a time adverb, but in adult Swedish it is always used as a sentential adverb. If the child uses the semantic criterion she will probably analyze *aldrig* as a time adverb, placing it in the canonical time adverbial position to the right of the object. Only the two oldest children repeated all the object shift examples correctly at once. It is clear from the outcome of the investigation, I think, that even fairly old children have trouble with this construction, and therefore tend to avoid using it.

In trying to avoid the object-shift construction, the children used different strategies. The table shows six different "strategies of avoidance":

1. Inversion. One example of this is from Pia (2;5)

(9) Adult: *Ser du mej inte?*
     'see you me not'
  Pia: *ser du inte mej?*

Here Pia inverts the order between the negation and the pronoun. By doing so she has "restored" the canonical order between a sentence adverbial and an object; see the example in (1a). This is a strategy also used by other children.

2. Deletion of the pronoun. This strategy also creates a canonical construction, where the object is deleted. One example (Anna 5;2) of the use of this strategy is shown in (10):

(10) Adult: *Jag vågar det inte*
      'I dare it not'

> Anna: *jag vågar inte*
> Adult: *Jag vågar det inte*
> Anna: *jag vågar inte*

As this example shows, Anna insisted on deleting the object pronoun even after repetition of the model sentence.

3. Deletion of the negation. This strategy occurs only once. The result is a correct and canonical sentence, but it of course deviates semantically from the model sentence:

(11) Adult: *Jag ser dej inte*
            'I see you not'
      Josef: *jag ser dej* (4;3)

4. Negation + pronoun + negation. This strategy is exemplified by the following sentence by Fanny (3;3):

(12) Adult: *Hör du mej inte?*
            'hear you me not'
      Fanny: *hör du inte mej in . . . te*

The child apparently gets into a conflict whether to repeat the sentence word by word or to repeat the meaning. Another interpretation is that the child has a vague idea what it is all about. The repeated sentence does not conform to the target grammar.

5. Wrong object pronoun. Two children produce what looks like an object-shift construction but use the wrong object pronoun. One example, the interpretation of which is unclear, is given below:

(13) Adult: *Jag pussar dej inte. Kan du säga det? Jag pussar dej inte*
            'I kiss you not. Can you say that? I kiss you not'
      Pia: *(?jag) pussar mej inte* (2;5)
            '(I?) kiss me not'

6. Unanalyzable sentences. Some children produce what seems to be a mish-mash. This is apparently what happens to Robert (4;2), who quickly and without problem repeats the initial sentences (without any object shift constructions), but apparently gets confused when an object-shift construction turns up:

(14) Adult: *Dom såg henne inte*
            'they saw her not'
      Robert: *då såg dom honn . . . då såg hon inte honom henne*
            'then saw they [honn] . . . then saw she not him her'

Apart from the youngest child (discussed earlier), there is only one child who fails in all her attempts to repeat the object shift constructions, namely Julia (4;11). This girl has an English-speaking father and a Swedish-speaking mother. She speaks Swedish well, however, and has attended a Swedish preschool for several years. The strategies she uses are inversion (three times) and deletion of the object pronoun (five times). Even more interesting is that Julia, at a second try on the first object-shift example, uses the English object pronoun *her*:

(15)   Adult: *Dom stora såg henne inte*
                      'The bigs saw her not'
          Julia: *dom stora såg inte*
          Adult: *Dom stora såg henne inte*
          Julia: *dom stora såg her inte*

She may be translating in a word-by-word fashion, hence the English pronoun.

DISCUSSION

Object shift is apparently a construction mastered rather late in the language development. Children around 2;6–3;0 do not seem to have the construction at all. At later stages the construction can be elicited to a varying degree. Only at the age of 5 to 7 years does the construction seem to be completely mastered. Why is this so?

As mentioned earlier, I analyze object shift as involving a head-to-head movement of the weak pronoun to Infl° (or a functional projection contained in Infl, using a split IP analysis). Object shift is, as also mentioned earlier, allowed only in simple main clauses. In other constructions, object pronouns have the same distribution as ordinary NPs. This means that a child has rather poor evidence of the possibility of classifying weak object pronouns as heads. Weak and strong pronouns are morphophonemically indistinct, so the child has no support for the weak-strong distinction by morphology either. My suggestion is, therefore, that children by a rule of default classify all object pronouns as XPs. In light of this description, the aforementioned strategies 1–3 could well be explained; according to the child's grammar the object pronouns are phrases. The sentences the child is asked to repeat, however, contain a pronoun in a position disallowed for full phrases. The child solves the dilemma by restoring a pattern where the pronoun is placed in the same position as a corresponding NP.

If this analysis is correct, we also might expect to find the same pattern for weak subject pronouns.[7] Josefsson (1992, 1993a, 1993b, 1994) proposed that

---

[7]The term *weak subject pronoun* refers to unstressed subject pronouns.

weak subject pronouns should be classified as heads as well. The line of reasoning is, in short, as follows.

Sentence adverbials have two canonical positions in Swedish (apart from topicalization), namely VP adjunction or IP adjunction (Holmberg, 1991; Platzack, 1986):

(16) (a) [[$_C$·*Har* [$_{IP}$*Lisa* [$_{VP}$*inte* [$_{VP}$*tvättat kläderna än?*
'has Lisa not washed clothes-the yet?'

(b) [[$_C$·*Har* [$_{IP}$*inte* [$_{IP}$*Lisa* [$_{VP}$*tvättat kläderna än?*

A sentence adverbial is not allowed between a weak subject pronoun and the verb,[8] indicating that the weak pronoun is incorporated in C (or cliticized). It thus seems as though weak subject pronouns and weak object pronouns have the same classification from a categorical point of view. If the analysis of weak object pronoun is correct (weak object pronouns are classified as full phrases in child language) we would suspect that children tend to treat weak subject pronouns equally as full phrases. This prediction seems to be borne out in some parts of the material. When considering the topicalized sentences of Freja in Söderbergh's corpus, we find a great number of what must be analyzed as weak subject pronouns preceded by a sentence adverbial (the negation *inte*).

(17) (a) *nu TAR inte han den*   (Freja 2;10)
'now TAKES not he it'
(b) *HÄR kan inte dom SOVA där*   (Freja 3;2)
'here can not they SLEEP there'

This pattern seems, however, to be specific to Freja; the other children in the investigation display a seemingly adult pattern at once. One might speculate why Freja treats subject pronouns as full phrases to a much higher degree than the other children in the investigation. It is, however, expected that children learn that weak subject pronouns are heads earlier than they acquire the classification of weak object pronouns, because constructions with a weak subject pronoun and a sentence adverbial or negation is much more common, occurring both in root and nonroot clauses.

---

[8]An example of a sentence adverbial intervening between the finite verb in C and a weak subject pronoun is shown in (i). A sentence adverbial intervening between the finite verb and a strong subject pronoun or an NP subject is grammatical, as shown in (ii):

(i)   **Därför tvättade inte hon sig*
'therefore washed not she REFL'
(ii) *Därför tvättade inte HON/flickan sig*
'therefore washed not SHE/girl-the REFL'

The question whether the acquisition of object shift covaries with anything else is not easy to answer at this stage. One thing that might be of importance is the fact that object shift is dependent on a certain kind of intonation. The object pronoun is unstressed, but the verb or the negation must be stressed. One observation was that children who were able to imitate the special intonation pattern of an object shift construction also were able to imitate the word order. However, very little is known at the moment about the relation between intonation pattern and syntactic structures, and even less is known about the role of intonation in acquiring syntax. Nevertheless, I think the understanding of what object shift is and how it is acquired would profit from such an investigation.

SUMMARY

In this chapter I have presented a pilot study of the acquisition of the object shift construction in Swedish. A study of two child language corpora shows that little evidence of this construction is found in spontaneous child language. An elicitation test on 15 children from the age of 2;5 to 7;4 confirms the picture that children have a tendency to avoid this construction. I have illustrated six different strategies used by children to avoid the construction. Only the two oldest children in the study repeated all eight object-shift constructions in the elicitation test correctly. The result of the test reveals no clear progression in the acquisition of the construction in question, but the fact that all children except the two oldest ones failed to various degrees to repeat the pattern sentences indicates that the object-shift construction is acquired rather late in language development.

My suggestion to explain the late acquisition of object shift involves an analysis where object shift is described in terms of head-to-head movement of the object pronoun to a functional projection to the left of the negation or sentence adverbial. Because object shift is allowed only in simple main clauses, a child has very little evidence that object pronouns could be heads. I therefore suggest that children tend to classify weak object pronouns as full phrases, that is, on a par with NPs, following a default rule. When asked to repeat a sentence where an object pronoun is placed in a position where NPs are disallowed, the child responds by giving a canonical sentence with the object pronoun in an NP position.

Children who mastered the intonation pattern correlating with the object shift construction had less trouble repeating the object-shift construction. I have therefore suggested that the acquisition of the object-shift construction involves the acquisition of intonation pattern as well. Because little is known about the interaction between the acquisition of intonation patterns and syntax, I will have to leave this as an issue for future research.

ACKNOWLEDGMENTS

I wish to thank those who commented on this work at the time it was presented at the Sixth International Congress for the Study of Child Language. Thanks also to Christer Platzack and Lynn Santelmann for extensive comments on earlier versions of this chapter. I am also in great debt to Suzanne Schlyter and Ragnhild Söderbergh for letting me use their child language corpora.

REFERENCES

Diesing, M., & Jelinek, E. (1993). The syntax and semantics of object shift. *Working Papers in Scandinavian Syntax, 51,* 1–54. Lund, Sweden: University of Lund, Department of Scandinavian Languages.

Holmberg, A. (1986). *Word order and syntactic features in the Scandinavian languages and English.* Unpublished doctoral dissertation, University of Stockholm.

Holmberg, A. (1991). The distribution of Scandinavian weak pronouns. In H. van Riemsdijk & L. Rizzi (Eds.), *Clitics and their hosts* (ESF-Eurotyp Working Papers, Vol. 1, pp. 155–174). Tilburg, The Netherlands: University of Tilburg, Grammatical Models Section.

Josefsson, G. (1992). Object shift and weak pronominals in Swedish. *Working Papers in Scandinavian Syntax, 49,* 59–94. Lund, Sweden: University of Lund, Department of Scandinavian Languages.

Josefsson, G. (1993a). Object shift and weak pronouns in Swedish. In L. Hellan (Ed.), *Clitics in Germanic and Slavic* (ESF-Eurotyp Working Papers, Vol. 4, pp. 51–82). Tilburg, The Netherlands: University of Tilburg, Grammatical Models Section.

Josefsson, G. (1993b). Scandinavian pronouns and object shift. *Working Papers in Scandinavian Syntax, 52,* 1–28. Lund, Sweden: University of Lund, Dept. of Scandinavian Languages, University of Lund, Sweden.

Josefsson, G. (1994). Scandinavian pronouns and object shift. In H. van Riemsdijk & L. Hellan (Eds.), *Clitics: Their origin, status, and position* (ESF-Eurotyp Working Papers, Vol. 6, pp. 91–120). Tilburg, The Netherlands: University of Tilburg, Grammatical Models Section.

Kayne, R. (1975). *French syntax.* Cambridge, MA: MIT Press.

Platzack, C. (1986). The position of the finite verb in Swedish. In H. Haider & M. Prinzhorn (Eds.), *Verb second phenomena in Germanic languages* (pp. 27–47). Dordrecht: Foris.

Schlyter, S. (1993). [The Swedish-French bilingual child language corpus]. Unpublished raw data. Department of Romance Studies, University of Lund, Sweden.

Slobin, D. I., & Welsh, C. (1973). Elicited imitation as a research tool in developmental psycholinguistics. In C. A. Ferguson & D. I. Slobin (Eds.), *Studies of child language development* (pp. 485–497). New York: Holt, Rinehart & Winston.

Söderbergh, R. (1973). [Project Child Language Syntax]. Unpublished raw data University of Stockholm.

Vikner, S. (1990). *Verb movement and the licensing of NP positions.* Unpublished doctoral dissertation, University of Geneva.

APPENDIX

The Elicitation Test

Det var en gång en prinsessa.
it was one time a princess
Hon var söt.
she was pretty
Men hon var ensam.
but she was lonely
De stora hade bråttom.
the big had busy
("the grown-ups were busy")

1. De såg henne inte.
they saw her not
Då hörde hon ett ljud.
then heard she a sound
-Kvack, kvack.
quack quack
-Kvack, kvack.
quack quack

2. -Hör du mig inte?
hear you me not
-Jag är en groda.
I am a frog

3. -Ser du mej inte?
see you me not
-Lilla söta flicka, vem är du?
little sweet girl, who are you
-Jag är prinsessan.
I am princess-the

4. -Men jag ser dej inte. Var är du?
but I see you not . where are you
-Jag är här.
I am here
-Pussa mig!
kiss me

5. -Jag pussar dig inte!
I kiss you not
-Du är ju en groda!
you are a frog
-Nej jag är en förtrollad prins!
No I am an enchanted prince

6. -Jag vågar det inte.
I dare it not
-Jag leker gärna med grodor.
I play happily with frogs

7. -Men jag pussar dem aldrig.
but I kiss them never
-Snälla!
please
-OK, sa prinsessan.
OK, said princess-the
Och vips blev grodan en prins!
and oups became frog-the a prince
Sen levde de lyckliga.
then lived they happy
Prinsessan leker gärna med en groda
princess-the plays happily with a frog
om hon hittar en.
if she finds one

8. Men hon pussar den inte.
but she kisses it not
Det räcker med en prins!
it suffices with one prince

11 Children's Comprehension of Swedish Nominal Compounds

Ingmarie Mellenius
Lund University, Sweden

This chapter examines children's ability to detect the formal structure of a set of words, that is, *morphology*. Traditionally, the analysis of word structure is divided into the two areas of inflection and derivation, the latter being the part of morphology that is concerned with the creation of "new words." In the following, I report on an experiment that was designed to capture children's notions of the rules that are involved in the formal interpretation of novel compounds in Swedish.

In the study described here, a picture-identification experiment was administered to 60 children, aged between 2;0 and 5;4. On hearing a novel compound, the task of the children was to point to the one picture out of four that best represented the word that they just had heard. From the results, it seems clear that children learn to master the rules for compound interpretation, which implies that the last part is the head of the construction, with the first part functioning as a modifier, around 3 years of age. The results are compared to those of Clark, Gelman, and Lane (1985), concerning English-speaking children, and to those of Berman and Clark (1989), concerning Hebrew-speaking children.

Another significant result of the present study is that detecting the head noun is easier for the children when the compound contains a modifying noun appearing in a special shape, here called *liaison form*. Several Swedish nouns have to appear in this form (which is different from what the noun looks like when it is an independent word) when they are in modifying position.

The first section, on the attention that children's word formation has received, and the second section, on compounding in Swedish, set the scene for the present experiment, which is described in the third section along with its results. The final section contains a discussion of the implications of the results obtained, together with some concluding remarks.

WORD FORMATION IN
LANGUAGE ACQUISITION THEORY

Whereas children's first words and early vocabulary growth, as well as the first signs of syntax and early syntactic development, are of paramount importance to child language research and receive due attention as important disciplines in their own right, morphology does not have the same independent status. For instance, there is not one word on word formation in a standard work like *Language Acquisition* (de Villiers & de Villiers, 1978).

From before 2 years of age children can, at least occasionally, form new words such as, *kepsmössa* 'cap-cap'[1] (1;9) (said of a cap with a visor; does not exist in Swedish), *konstboll* 'art-ball' (1;10). Novel compounds like these show that the children have taken units they already have in their respective mental lexica and put them to use in a new setting, where they are combined with other morphemes to form a word that the child could not ever have heard before. This feat, however, has attracted comparatively little attention. There are several possible reasons for this neglect:

1. The lack of interest in the development of word formation rules may be due to a general unconcern for morphology. In this area, linguistics suffers from its bias towards English as the main language of investigation. English is not a morphologically complex language, so there are few opportunities to marvel at English-speaking children's sensitivity and skill in detecting morphemes and discovering morphological relationships.

2. The view of many linguists has been that words are basic irregularities (Bloomfield, 1933) or idiosyncracies (Di Sciullo & Williams, 1987), and hence not of interest to linguistic theory.

3. The creative aspect of language use is typically illustrated by the fact that we can produce or understand sentences we have never said or heard before; the fact that it is just as possible for us to produce or understand *words* we have never said or heard before is seldom noticed.

4. The uncertain status of morphology is a stumbling block. In scientific contexts, the human language capacity is mostly seen as consisting of two major parts: lexicon and grammar. The problem of where to place morphology within this dichotomy is a subject that has been much debated over the years, primarily within the Chomskyan tradition (see, e.g., Anderson, 1982), but the question is still open.[2]

---

[1]All through this chapter, verbatim translations from Swedish are written within single quotation marks, and the equivalent words or expressions in English are within double quotation marks, for example, *sovsäck* 'sleep sack' "sleeping bag."

[2]It is worth noticing, however, that the latest bids from the Chomskyans have been to place morphology firmly within the domain of syntax (Baker, 1988; Lieber, 1992).

The first work I know of that treats children's word formation at length is a book by the Russian literary critic Kornei Chukovsky (1882–1969), a leading figure in the field of Russian children's literature. His pioneering work *From Two to Five* was published in 21 editions between 1925 and 1970.[3] This book is full of examples of innovative language use by children:

> When Serjozja was two and a half years old, he saw for the first time a bonfire out of doors. The sparks were jumping from the fire, and he clapped his hands and shouted: Look at the fire and the fire-kids! The fire and the fire-kids! (In Russian, young animals are called the name of the animal plus the ending -jónok, plur. -játa.) (Tjukovskij, 1975, p. 30, translated by I. M.)

Chukovsky's (1963) goal is

> to show that in the process of assimilating his native spoken language the child, from the early age of two, introduces a critical evaluation, analysis, and control. It seems to me that, beginning with the age of two, every child becomes for a short period of time a linguistic genius. Later, beginning with the age of five to six, this talent begins to fade. There is no trace left in the eight-year-old of this creativity with words, since the need for it has passed; by this age the child already has fully mastered the basic principles of his native language. If his former talent for word invention and construction had not abandoned him, he would, even by the age of ten, eclipse any of us with his suppleness and brilliance of speech. Not in vain did Leo Tolstoy, addressing himself to adults, write: " . . . [the child] realizes the laws of word formation better than you because no one so often thinks up new words as children." (pp. 7–8).

In a sense, children's novel words can shed some light on the eternal question of what comes first, the chicken or the egg—in this case, the concept or the word. When a child has coined a new word, this is surely evidence that there was, inside the child's mind, a notion of something, a "concept" in the widest sense, that could be singled out and given a name. This concept existed before the actual word that later was created to convey it. The concept, however, is not a "pre-linguistic" one; it is an idea that is formed by the help of meanings that are already coded lexically. Thus the new words that a child construes are actually evidence of the level of lexical refinement the child has reached, as well as proofs of an awareness of word-formation rules.

Whenever there is an occasion where a concept needs a linguistic realization, the child finds herself at the intersection between concepts, lexicon, and syntax. We can imagine that, first of all, the lexicon is checked for an appropriate term. If none is found, the child turns to her rule inventory, in order to make up a new expression that could fit the concept she has in mind. The situation can be

---

[3]The Swedish translation (Tjukovskij, 1975), based on the 19th edition, is much less abbreviated than the English one (Chukovsky, 1963).

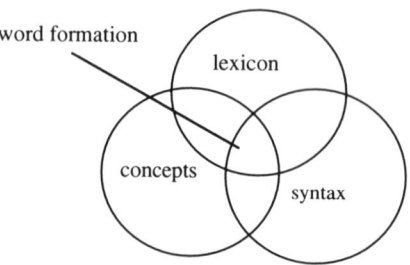

FIG. 11.1. Borromeic knot representing the way the lexicon, semantic concepts, and syntactic
rules interact in word formation.

illustrated by the help of the borromeic knot diagram in Fig. 11.1. The reasons
why the child in this situation would ever choose to create a new word (and to
what extent she does so) rather than forming a syntactic expression is a matter for
future research. Here, I only hint at a few possible explanations:

1. The compound is shorter than a group of words with comparable meaning
(e.g., *tungkoppa* 'tongue vesicle' for "chickenpox vesicle on the tongue" (4;10).

2. It might be that the word is sensed to be a more stable construction (which
it is, in the sense that it can receive its own lexical entry).

3. In forming a compound, the child does not have to be as explicit about the
exact relation between the head and the modifier as in a corresponding phrasal
construction. A phrase could, for instance, require the child to find the one
correct preposition for the context; this might be something that is sensed as
being so difficult that the child tries to avoid it.

4. The formation of a new word might give the child a sense of achievement.
Maybe the word gives its creator a concession on the concept, as it were.

To summarize, it would seem that the development of word formation in
children deserves closer scrutiny. Through an examination of a child's novel
words, we could gain insights into how the child conceptualizes, and organizes
semantically, as well as how the rules for formally expressing the conceived
concepts emerges.

A DESCRIPTION OF COMPOUNDING IN SWEDISH

In Swedish, as in other North Germanic languages, compounding is an old and
well-established word-formation process. This means that the language contains
a large number of lexicalized compounds. However, compounding is above all a
very practicable and powerful process for creating new words: Around one fourth
of the words in newspaper text are compounds, out of which one tenth can be
considered lexicalized.[4]

---

[4]Reevaluated estimates based on Blåberg (1988).

At first glance, compounding in Swedish seems to have few formal or semantic restrictions: There are examples of compounds containing words from almost all word classes, as well as phrases of different types. (Descriptions of word formation in Swedish can be found in Teleman, 1970, or Thorell, 1981.)[5] A closer scrutiny, however, reveals that there are restrictions: A comparison of the different Germanic languages with respect to possible or preferred compounds should reveal interesting patterns. By definition, a compound has to contain at least two morphemes (the upper limit is set by intelligibility) that also may appear as independent words.[6] Traditionally, compounds are divided into two main groups: *exocentric* compounds,[7] which is the least common type and which are not going to be discussed here further, and *endocentric* ones, in which one of the lexical morphemes of the compound is commonly called the *head*; that is, the word as a whole denotes an instance of the head morpheme. In Swedish, as in the other Germanic languages, it is the last lexical morpheme that functions as the head of the construction. The function of the preceding morpheme or morphemes is to modify the meaning of the head somehow. This also means that in the case of nominal compounds, an indefinite article before the word must agree in gender and number with the head, and not with any previous morpheme.

A list of the productive two-part compounds is provided here. The extent to which the compounds are productive varies, however; the order in which they appear here resembles their decreasing order of productivity, with N–N compounds first as the most productive, and V–V and NUM–V at the end as the least productive.

N–N:
barn#barn	'child child'	"grandchild"
last#bil	'load car'	"lorry"
åker#bär	'field berry'	"arctic raspberry"

A–N:
röd#beta	'red beet'	"beetroot"
bar#mark	'bare ground'	"no snow on the ground"
låg#stadiet	'low level'	"the junior level of compulsory school"

P–N:
med#känsla	'with feeling'	"compassion"
över#fall	'overfall'	"assault"
in#land	'in land'	"interior"

V–N:
sug#rör	'suck pipe'	"straw"
res#väska	'travel bag'	"suitcase"
sov#säck	'sleep sack'	"sleeping bag"

[5]These texts do not contain any attempt at a full description of the constraints on compounding in Swedish that do exist, nor does any other literature that I know of.

[6]Note, however, that modifying morphemes often appear in a shape which they cannot have as independent words; see following discussion.

[7]Within this group, only the so-called coordinate compounds are formed according to a process that is still productive.

ADV–N:
ute#grill	'outdoor grill'	
hit#vägen	'here way'	"the way here"
fjärr#värme	'far heat'	"district heating"

NUM–N:
fem#krona	'five crown'	"five-crown coin"
tio#tiden	'ten time'	"around ten o'clock"
mång#miljonär	'many millionaire'	"multimillionaire"

N–A:
hälso#farlig	'health dangerous'	"injurious to the health"
morgon#pigg	'morning alert'	"lively in the morning"
grod#lik	'froglike'	

A–A:
ljus#grön	'light green'	
tvär#brant	'abrupt steep'	"precipitous"
söt#sliskig	'sweet sickly'	"sickly sweet"

V–A:
härsk#lysten	'rule desirous'	"domineering"
tänk#värd	'think worthy'	"worth considering"
skjut#glad	'shoot happy'	"trigger happy"

N–V:
allergi#sanera	'allergy renovate'	
hals#hugga	'throat chop'	"decapitate"
värde#sätta	'value put'	"appreciate"

A–V:
vit#lacka	'white lacquer'	"lacquer white"
ny#inreda	'new decorate'	"decorate anew"
dubbel#arbeta	'double work'	

P–V:
genom#stråla	'through beam'	"beam through"
på#fylla	'on fill'	"refill"
under#blåsa	'under blow'	"heighten"

V–V:
kryp#köra	'creep drive'	"drive very slowly"
tork#tumla	'dry tumble'	"tumble dry"
bränn#märka	'burn mark'	"brand"

NUM–V:
noll#taxera	'zero assess'	"be a tax dodger"
fyr#dubbla	'four double'	"multiply by four"
tu#dela	'two split'	"divide into two"

A compound is pronounced with a particular stress pattern, called *compound stress*, which is an instance of the Swedish *grave accent*, or *accent 2*. This is an intonation contour that contains two stressed syllables: The first where the stress was originally placed in the first root morpheme of the compound when this is pronounced as an isolated word, and the second at the place of the stress of the last root morpheme of the compound, when it is pronounced in isolation. Consequently, in more complex compounds, there can be several unstressed syllables in the middle of the word (e.g., *'utrikeshandelsmi'nister* 'minister for foreign trade', which has five syllables between the two that are the most prominent). This also reveals that an important function of the compound stress pattern is to keep the word together intonationally: The relative pitch of the middle part of a long compound word tells us that we have not reached the end of the word yet. Also, the compound stress pattern always indicates where there is a compound, so that we do not confound them with instances of the same morphemes occurring in a phrase, as is illustrated in Fig. 11.2. In Fig. 11.2(a), the words *lång klänning* 'long dress' are pronounced. The intonation curve shows the two peaks in the contour which demonstrate that *klänning* has grave accent. In Fig. 11.2(b), the word *klänning* and the adjective *lång* have been combined into the compound *långklänning* 'long dress' "evening gown." The grave accent of *klänning* has disappeared; instead, the compound has its own grave accent, whose twin peaks appear distinctly in the figure.

Apart from the intonation contour, there is another feature that sometimes reveals the compound nature of juxtaposed words, namely a special "liaison form" of a modifying noun. Sometimes a final vowel is deleted (*pojke* 'boy', but *pojkcykel* 'boy's bike'; *ficka* 'pocket', but *fickpengar* 'pocket money'), and sometimes a final vowel is substituted (*vara* 'merchandise', but *varuhus* 'merchandise house' "department store"; *hälsa* 'health', but *hälsokost* 'health food'). Historically, the liaison forms are either the stem, or an old genitive—a fact that explains why the property of having this liaison form is a feature of our native Swedish words, and therefore is a property of many of the more frequent words in the language (and also a property of many of the words that are acquired early). There are also cases where an -s is inserted (*nöje* 'pleasure', but *nöjesresa* 'pleasure-trip'). The -s ending can appear on both native and Latinate words, and it is common to add an -s to a compound that functions as modifier: *rödvin* 'red wine', but *rödvinsflaska* 'red wine bottle'. Potentially, this -s could occasionally serve to disambiguate compounds with three parts: the -s should appear between the modifying compound and the head noun, not within a compound that functions as head of the construction (*trätakplatta* 'wood ceiling tile' "ceiling tile made of wood," but *trätaksplatta* "tile for wooden ceilings").

Although the reasons for the alternations between different liaison forms of a modifying noun are partly morphological (e.g., depending on reasons like the presence of derivational affixes) and partly phonological (e.g., depending on reasons like the length and the sound pattern of the modifying element), there are no comprehensive rules for their application.[8]

---

[8]Holmberg (1992) has suggested that, from the point of view of synchronic description, the shape of the modifying noun depends on its being either a root or case marked.

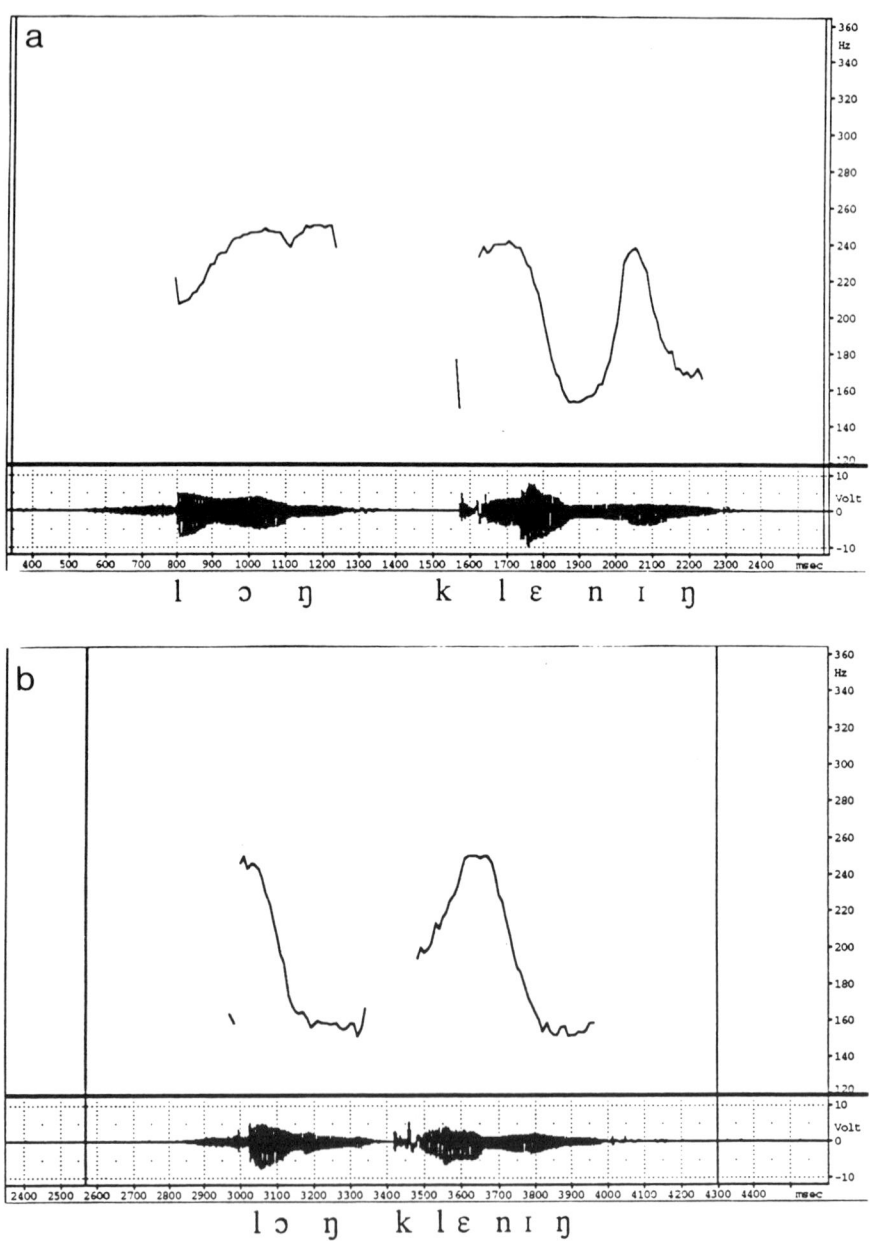

FIG. 11.2. Intonation display (a) for the words *lång klänning,* (b) for the word *långklänning.*

In the present experiment, I have examined children's use of noun-noun compounds. Although there are many kinds of compounds in Swedish, the compounds that consist of two nouns are by far the most common type, and they constitute about two thirds of the compounds in newspaper text, according to Blåberg (1988). At the same time, compounds with a nominal head are the least lexicalized.[9]

THE COMPREHENSION EXPERIMENT

In the first section, a couple of examples of children's earliest compound word formations were given. Although children may produce novel words around the age of 2, data collected from my own children show that it is not until one year later that children abound with testimonies of this ability. At what age could we say, then, that children acquire compounding rules? How large is the correspondence between production and comprehension? In the case of adults, it is usually assumed that it is one and the same ability which, on the one hand, has an overt use in production and, on the other hand, in comprehension. Even though comprehension and production are distinct processes, the assumption is that we should imagine the underlying language ability to be one and the same.

In the case of children, however, this model is probably too coarse, and should be replaced by a model that sets out to show the acquisition of consecutive facets, or aspects, of a particular language phenomenon. The language ability of the child develops gradually, from no knowledge at all to adultlike mastery, so that at a given point in time, the child may have only a partial and unstable knowledge of a certain linguistic construction. Depending on the method of investigation, such a child may be judged by the researcher as having or not having command of the construction in question. The experiment on comprehension of nominal compounds that is described here does not reveal anything about when the children learn about what the semantic relations within a compound may be, nor does it reveal when these children start using the rule for forming compound nouns themselves in a productive manner.

The question that the experiment described here set out to answer was at what age children acquire an adultlike interpretation of the formal structure of compounds: Correct interpretation implies that the child has learned the formal correspondence whereby the second noun is the head of the construction, while the first noun serves as a modifier of the head. Novel words were constructed so that, in order to understand them, children cannot simply rely on what they know about the things being talked about. The lexical properties of the separate nouns give no cues about which relations they should have to each other on this particular occasion; there are no already established roles that the interpretation can have recourse to.

---

[9]Lexicalization of a compound is here, following Bauer (1983), defined as the instances where the relation between the parts of the compound is opaque and fixed.

Method

Materials. For the comprehension experiment, 24 novel noun-noun compounds were constructed on the basis of 48 nouns. Two criteria were used to
select these 48 nouns: The word should be in the lexical repertoire of 2-year-old
children, and it should refer to some concrete object that would be fairly easy to
depict, as well as to recognize in a picture.

Half of the compounds thus created (12 of 24) contained modifying nouns of
the kind that appears in a special liaison form when in modifying position; in the
other half of the words the shape of the modifying noun was unaffected by its
being in a modifying position.

For each of the 24 novel words, four pictures of objects were drawn in black
ink on white cards. The set of four pictures accompanying each word were glued,
in random order, to a large, green cardboard page. The four pictures depicted (a)
the head noun (e.g., for *orm#glas* 'snake glass', it would be the picture of a
glass) (b) the modifier noun (for 'snake glass', it would be a snake), (c) a referent
related to the head noun (for 'glass', we chose the picture of a cup), and (d) a
referent related to the modifier noun (for 'snake', we chose the picture of a fish).
The 24 novel words and the set of four pictures chosen for each one of them are
all given in an appendix.

The motivation behind choosing the four pictures the way we did was to
ensure that correct choices reflect children's mastery of the formal notion of
headedness of a compound. If the target picture were to represent some kind of
combination of the two nouns, and the child, quite correctly, would choose that
one as a possible referent for the novel compound, then all one could be sure of
was that the child understood the semantic content of the separate words. With
this kind of design, however, the child is forced to use his or her linguistic
knowledge concerning the relationship between the two parts of a N-N compound in Swedish in order to arrive at a correct picture choice.

Subjects. The results from 60 children between 2;0 and 5;4 are reported
here; 12 in each of five age groups: group 1 = 2;0–2;7, group 2 = 2;8–3;3,
group 3 = 3;4–3;11, group 4 = 4;0–4;7, and group 5 = 4;8–5;3. Excluded are
children who are growing up bilingual or have a language other than Swedish as
their first language.

Procedure. The experiments took place in a secluded room at a daycare
center, where each child was tested individually. After having shown the child
how to respond in the situation (by pointing), the experimenter went through the
stock of cardboard pages with pictures on them, one by one. For each page, the
child was required to identify, by pointing to the picture representing that word,
the appropriate picture referent for the word that the experimenter pronounced.
The target for each novel word was in each case the picture of the head noun. The

responses of each child were noted by the experimenter, as were hesitations and comments on the pictures, if any.

For the purpose of varying the order of presentation, the materials were divided into three groups, with eight picture sets in each. The three sets of experiment words, with accompanying picture materials, were then given in random order to each child.

Results

Table 11.1 shows the results of the comprehension experiment, both in scores (one point is given for each correct response and no point is given for any kind of incorrect response) and in percentages. Chance level of responding here would give 25% correct answers, because there were four pictures from which to choose. Only one child, a girl in the youngest age group, performed near this level, with 26% correct picture choices. Performance within each age group is more consistent in the older groups; as shown by the standard deviation figures in Table 11.1, the variation within each age group decreases with growing age.

Figure 11.3 gives the scores from Table 11.1 in graphic form. The impression of linear growth given by the graph is confirmed by a one-way analysis of variance, which demonstrated a reliable difference in the number of correct responses across the five age groups, $F(4.55) = 7.56, p < .001$. Planned comparisons show significant differences only between the two youngest age groups ($t = 2.4, p < .05$), but a marginal difference was observed between age groups 2 and 3 ($t = 1.9, p = .06$). From these results I conclude that there is an increase in children's ability to detect the lexical head of the construction in noun–noun compounds during the first half of the period under investigation. It seems that the increase of this ability is the most marked around 3 years of age.

In the section on Swedish compounds, it was hinted that their intonation contour, as well as the fact that some words appear in a particular form when they function as modifying elements, might facilitate the detection, and the analysis,

TABLE 11.1
Correct Picture Choices by Age for Swedish-Speaking Children
(Based on 288 Responses per Group)

Age	2;0 - 2;7	2;8 - 3;3	3;4 - 3;11	4;0 -4;7	4;8 - 5;3
Score	13.4	16.7	19.3	19.6	20.8
Percentage	56%	69%	80%	82%	87%
SD	4.5	3.7	3.0	2.8	1.9

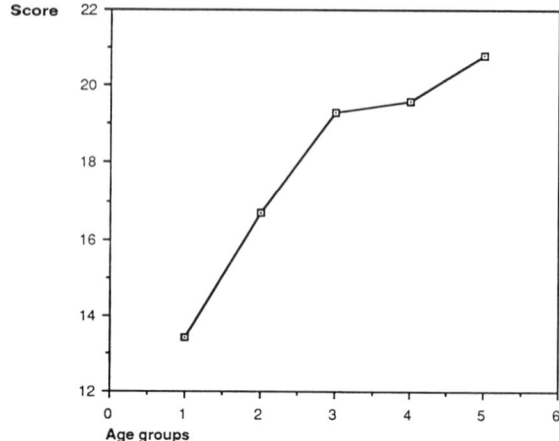

FIG. 11.3. Linear graph representing the scores for age groups 1 (2;0–2;7), 2 (2;8–3;3), 3 (3;4–3;11), 4 (4;0–4;7), and 5 (4;8–5;3).

of compounds. In the case of a possible facilitative effect on the detection of compounds due to the shape of the modifying element, the results of the present experiment support such a hypothesis. The overall correct responses are 9.4 (39%) on the words that contain a modifying noun appearing in liaison form, compared to 8.4 (35%) on the words where the shape of the modifying element is unaffected, $F(1.55) = 5.51, p < .001$. The help that can be gotten from compounds with a liaison form is most probably not limited to these words themselves. By highlighting compound formation, they are likely to help the child in the discovery of compound words and the compounding processes.

Comparison of Swedish, English, and Hebrew

The design of the comprehension experiment above was adapted from a study reported by Clark et al. (1985). The same experimental procedure was later used by Berman and Clark (1989) in a study on the development of compounds in Hebrew-speaking children. As can be seen in Table 11.2, the results obtained by Clark et al. are very similar to those obtained for Swedish: The significant difference in the results for English is the one between the two youngest age groups. Just like the Swedish children, children learning English are helped in their discrimination of compound words from other word combinations by a particular stress contour. The change in the form of some modifying elements, on the other hand, is not to be found in English. The facilitation that the Swedish children get from the compound nouns containing a liaison form does not seem to give Swedish children any overall advantage over the English children in this head noun detection task.

TABLE 11.2
Percentage of Correct Picture Choices by Age
(Based on 120 Responses per Group)

	English-Speaking Children[a]				
Age (mean)	2;4	3;4	4;0	4;10	5;8
Percentage	48%	82%	92%	92%	97%

	Hebrew-Speaking Children[b]				
Age (mean)	2;5	3;5	4;8	5;6	7;0
Percentage	78%	90%	98%	99%	91%

[a]Data from Clark, Gelman, and Lane (1985).
[b]Data from Berman and Clark (1989).

Compounding in Hebrew, on the other hand, is not as common as in the Germanic languages and does not occur until quite late in children's spontaneous speech—around age 4, according to Berman (1987). Another reason why compounding appears late among Hebrew-speaking children, according to Berman and Clark (1989), is that it involves complex morphological alternations in the head noun.

All of the novel compounds made up for the Berman and Clark experiment contained a head noun of the kind that does not require any change in morphological form when in a compound. The modifying part of the compounds was marked with a singular modifier in half of the cases, and with a plural modifier in the other half.[10]

Unlike children learning Swedish or children learning English, the Hebrew-speaking children are not helped in the detection of compound nouns by any particular stress pattern. Nevertheless, identification of the head seems to be easier for children acquiring Hebrew. The explanation for this is that in Hebrew it is the first noun in a N–N compound that is the head, just as the head comes first in all other complex noun phrases in Hebrew. Alongside nominal compounds, where the head comes last in the construction, children learning English or Swedish also come across complex noun phrases where the lexical head of the construction occupies some other position.[11]

---

[10]The plural modifiers were needed to mark these constructions overtly as compounds rather than as sequences of morphologically unmarked nouns (Berman & Clark, 1989).

[11]For example, nouns followed by a prepositional phrase (*katten på taket* 'the cat on the roof').

CONCLUDING REMARKS

What does it mean to say that a child has learned a morphological rule? A critical point in this process must be the discovery of a class of words that could be given the same morphological analysis. In the case of nominal compounding in Swedish, children should hear a sufficient number of those words to be able to discover that the descriptive and grammatical head of such words is the last root morpheme as soon as their language processing capacity is ready for that kind of discovery.

The experiment described in the present chapter was intended to capture when children master the rules concerning the formal interpretation of Swedish endocentric nominal compounds, that is, when they learn that the last lexical morpheme is the head of the construction. It was found that this ability increases with age, and that the most significant increase occurred between the two groups where the mean ages were 2;4 and 3;0, respectively. The interpretation of results from children as young as this presents problems, however. It could be that a fair number of the incorrect answers are due to the fact that children as young as this are inconsistent in their behavior; they point to an erroneous picture because they happen to like it, or for no particular reason at all. The continued increase of correct responses in the older age groups could be a reflection of older children's greater ability to act consistently, rather than to an increased linguistic insight concerning the formal interpretation of compound nouns.

A comparison between children's acquisition of nominal compounds in Swedish, English, and Hebrew indicates that children acquiring Hebrew have the least problem in detecting the lexical head in this kind of construction, although they do not hear nominal compounds as often as children acquiring English or Swedish. This circumstance should imply that English and Swedish children are confused by the existence in their respective languages of phrases with another structure, where the word that functions as the head of the construction occupies a different position from the one that is reserved for the head in compounds. Along with syntactic word-order rules, children acquiring Swedish are also grappling with rules concerning the interior structure of words, which may seem to work in a different way. The question of whether these two kinds of rules operate on different levels, or are parts of one and the same syntactic ability, might be answered by a comparison between the development of word formation rules and the acquisition of hierarchical relationships in other parts of the grammar.

ACKNOWLEDGMENTS

I am grateful to the staff of Kornetten and Stengången daycare centers in Umeå for their cooperation, and to all the children who so willingly judged the words for me. My special thanks go to Tord Söderberg, for drawing the attractive picture material. Thanks are also due to Dawn Behne, for many helpful comments on this chapter, and to Åke Olofsson, for help with the data analysis.

REFERENCES

Anderson, S. R. (1982). Where's morphology? *Linguistic Inquiry, 13,* 571–612.

Baker, M. C. (1988). *Incorporation: A theory of grammatical function changing.* Chicago: The University of Chicago Press.

Bauer, L. (1983). *English word-formation.* Cambridge, England: Cambridge University Press.

Berman, R. A. (1987). A developmental route: Learning about the form and use of complex nominals in Hebrew. *Linguistics, 25,* 1057–1085.

Berman, R. A. & Clark, E. V. (1989). Learning to use compounds for contrast: data from Hebrew. *First Language, 9,* 247–270.

Bloomfield, L. (1933). *Language.* New York: Holt.

Blåberg, O. (1988). *A study of Swedish compounds* (Report 29). Umeå, Sweden: Umeå University, Department of General Linguistics.

Chukovsky, K. (1963). *From two to five.* Berkeley: University of California Press.

Clark, E. V., Gelman, S. A., & Lane, N. M. (1985). Compound nouns and category structure in young children. *Child Development, 56,* 84–94.

de Villiers, J. G., & de Villiers, P. A. (1978). *Language acquisition.* Cambridge, MA: Harvard University Press.

Holmberg, A. (1992). Properties of non-heads in compounds: A case study. *Working Papers in Scandinavian Syntax, 49,* 27–57.

Lieber, R. (1992). *Deconstructing morphology: Word formation in syntactic theory.* Chicago: The University of Chicago Press.

Di Sciullo, M., & Williams, E. (1987). *On the definition of word.* Cambridge, MA: MIT Press.

Teleman, U. (1970). *Om svenska ord* [On Swedish words]. Lund, Sweden: Gleerups.

Thorell, O. (1981). Svensk ordbildningslära [Theory of Swedish word formation]. Stockholm: Esselte Studium AB.

Tjukovskij, K. I. (1975). *Från två till fem år: Om barns språk, dikt och fantasi* [From two to five years: On children's language, poetry and imagination] (2nd ed., S. Skott, Trans.). Stockholm: Gidlund.

APPENDIX

Compounds Used in the Comprehension Experiment

Accompanying Pictures	Target	Rel. to Target	Modifier	Rel. to Modifier
bananpåse 'banana bag'	paper bag	drawer	banana	orange
bulltallrik 'bun plate'	plate	pot	bun	cookie

råttmössa 'rat cap'	cap	hat	rat	lizard
hundtält 'dog tent'	tent	house	dog	turtle
skogskotte 'forest cone'	cone	stone	forest	desert
telefonnyckel 'telephone key'	key	lock	telephone	TV set
handsag 'hand saw'	saw	axe	hand	mitten
babytrumma 'baby drum'	drum	banjo	baby	adult
ängskratta 'meadow rake'	rake	broom	meadow	lake
grodbur 'frog cage'	cage	bowl	frog	snail
ringnäsa 'ring nose'	nose	ear	ring	watch
båtstege 'boat ladder'	ladder	hedge	boat	car
grisstaken 'pig fence'	fence	stool	pig	hen
flicksmörgås 'girl sandwich'	sandwich	blanket	girl	old man
ormglas 'snake glass'	glass	cup	snake	fish
lamppaket 'lamp parcel'	parcel	jar	lamp	candle
tidningsbord 'newspaper table'	table	sofa	newspaper	book
pärlhammare 'bead hammer'	hammer	tongs	beads	buttons
äppelkniv 'apple knife'	knife	fork	apple	cherries
docksko 'doll shoe'	shoe	boot	doll	teddy bear
cykelpensel 'bicycle brush'	brush	pencil	bicycle	chair
månträd 'moon tree'	tree	flower	moon	star
bollkatt 'ball cat'	cat	bird	ball	puck
sängfönster 'bed window'	window	bottle	bed	armchair

12 Parental Scaffolding of Context in Children's Narratives

Carole Peterson
Memorial University of Newfoundland

Allyssa McCabe
University of Massachusetts at Lowell

Personal experience narratives are about events that occurred at some time other than the present, and generally some other place. Instead of talk about the here-and-now, these narratives talk about the there-and-then. According to Brown (1973), this represents a major shift in children's language, and this ability to decontextualize one's language from the physical context within which it is situated is an extremely important skill for children to master (Bruner, 1986; Cazden, 1985; Snow, 1983).

A narrative tells a listener what happened to the speaker. In fact, the definition of a narrative generally includes the notion that it is a verbal recapitulation of the events that occurred within the experience being described (Labov, 1972; Labov & Waletzky, 1967; Peterson & McCabe, 1983; Polanyi, 1982, 1985). But a narrative does more than recapitulate events; it should also tell the listener about the context within which those events took place. Polanyi (1982) has even asserted that in order for a discourse to be a narrative at all, it *must* provide contextualizing orientative information as well as an account of the events that occurred.

Thus, a good narrative should locate itself within a spatial/temporal context; that is, it should tell the listener about the *there* and *then* of the experience. Such contextual embedding is important for at least two reasons: (a) it helps make a narrative comprehensible to a listener (Brewer, 1985; Eisenberg, 1985; Labov, 1972, Labov & Waletzky, 1967; and Polanyi 1982, 1985); and (b) it also seems to be related to literacy acquisition. Information about orienting context is a key component of the "decontextualized language" that seems to be so important to school success (Cazden, 1985; Feagans, 1982; Snow, 1983).

Below are narratives by two children at age 3;7. "R" denotes the researcher, and "C" the child:

Narrative 1

R: Have you ever caught a fish?

C: Yes.

R: Oh, you did?

C: It was a great big one and I, and I lift him off and I lift him up in the boat.

R: And you lift him up in the boat. Uh huh. And?

C: I lift them at the boat.

R: Yeah?

C: And he's a great big one.

R: Uh huh?

C: And he's a yuck one.

R: He's a yuck one?

C: Yes and I sawed him.

R: Uh huh.

C: Purple.

Narrative 2

R: Have you ever gotten stung by a bee?

C: But Mark (her brother) got a big sting when he was just first born.

R: Mark had a big sting when he was first born?

C: Yeah.

R: Well, tell me about it. What happened?

C: I, I was walking with him and, and I just and he falled and he didn't know that he falled right on a bee. And he, and his knee was on a bee and stung, he got stung on a bee.

R: He got stung on a bee?

C: Uh huh. And then I was walking another baby, Randy, and you know what?

R: What?

C: I heard him and me and Randy came running. And you know what?

R: What?

C: Paul, Paul Smith came too.

R: Paul Smith came too.

C: I tried to pick him up but, but he didn't want me to but I had to call my Mommy.

R: You had to call your Mommy, uh huh?

C: My Daddy and everybody who I knowed who was a grown-up. And then everybody who I knowed and who was a grown-up came.

R: They all came, uh-huh.

C: From my house. And I was walking in the park. They came over after Mark and they wanted, they wanted to see what happened to Mark.

R: They wanted to see what happened to Mark? Uh huh?

C: And then I, I told them and I looked down at his knee and there it was, stung.

R: And there it was, stung. Looked at his knee and there it was, stung, uh huh?

C: And I tried to pick him up and he wanted me to pick him up right at that minute.

These two narratives from children of the same age differ on many grounds. The latter is much more informative and provides more detailed information about the events that occurred. More relevant to our present purposes, it also provides extensive orientation to the context of those events: the time of the events (when the narrator's brother was a little baby), their spatial location (the park by her house), who else was there (other children, parents, other grown-ups), and so on. In contrast, the first narrative provides almost no contextual information, although some can be inferred (e.g., the child and others, probably at least some members of his family, were on a body of water somewhere, such as a river, a lake, or the ocean).

There is large individual variation in how much orientation to spatial/temporal context children provide in their narratives (Menig-Peterson & McCabe, 1978; Peterson, 1990; Peterson & McCabe, 1983). Even narratives that are of similar length can differ substantially in terms of how much spatial/temporal information is provided. The question addressed by the present research is *why* this large variation exists among children in their tendencies to include spatial/temporal context in their narratives.

The focus of our search for potential causes for such variation centered on parental discourse. Other research has documented substantial differences between parents in interaction styles when eliciting narratives from their children (Fivush, 1991; Fivush & Fromhoff, 1988; Hudson, 1990; McCabe & Peterson, 1991; Ratner, 1984). In the present study, we investigated how different parental interaction styles related to children's tendencies to include spatial and temporal orientation spontaneously in their stand-alone narratives, that is, when they are providing the entire narrative themselves without being prompted by listeners to provide various specific pieces of information. Such an investigation requires a longitudinal design; our study extended over a period of 18 months.

The theoretical grounding for our study was Vygotskian theory, which suggests a mechanism for how children may learn to incorporate spatial/temporal contextual information into their narratives. A fundamental tenet of Vygotskian theory is that social interactions lay the foundation for an individual's internal processes during development. In a task that is being learned, a skilled person (such as a parent or teacher) provides guidance and feedback to the child while doing the task. Essentially, the adult structures the task for the child and scaffolds his or her performance. At first, adults provide an extensive scaffold, such that they are the ones primarily performing the task, while the child's contributions are quite limited (e.g., appropriately answering yes/no questions). As the child's skill increases, the scaffold is decreased and the child takes over more responsibility for doing the task. Thus, the task is accomplished collaboratively between the adult and child. The scaffold is progressively decreased until eventually the child has internalized its major components and is able to accomplish the task independently.

Researchers have shown that adults progressively change task scaffolds, and this contributes to increasing child skill in a number of skill areas, including memory, problem solving, discourse reference, and communication (e.g., Bruner, 1983; Hickmann, 1985, 1986; McLane, 1987; Paris, Newman, & Jacobs, 1985, Ratner, 1980; Snow & Goldfield, 1983). Vygotskian theory would hypothesize that narrative interactions between adults and children play a key role in the children's acquisition of narrative skills. Parents who frequently engage their children in conversations about past personal experiences show their children that this is a valued activity. Furthermore, the content of what the parents prompt their children to provide in these collaborative narratives point to what sorts of information it is important to include, information such as orientation to spatial/temporal context. Thus, parents who frequently ask questions such as "Where were we?" and "When did that happen?" help their children internalize these cues, and subsequently these should aid the child in providing information about location (*where*) and time (*when*) on their own. Predictions derived from Vygotskian theory are that the style of questioning engaged in by parents when their children are young should be related to children's skill at providing spatial/temporal orientation later, when they are older.

Such a relationship between parental questioning style and child narrative skill was found in a preliminary investigation of two mother–child dyads (Peterson & McCabe, 1992). The present study extends the earlier work by studying 10 parent–child pairs, following them over an 18-month period while the children were approximately 2 to 3 ½ years of age.

We gathered two bodies of data to explore the relationship between parental discourse style and child narrative skill. One set of data was children's narratives collected by a researcher who encouraged narration but who refrained from asking specific questions or scaffolding the children's narratives. Children's spontaneous provision of information about global spatial/temporal context (*where* and *when*) was assessed. These types of context are a universal property of every narrated experience, and needed to be provided by the children. In contrast, a similar assessment of participants (*who*) or objects (*what*–object) could not be done. Often the only participants were the children themselves, who were specified by the researcher when she asked, "Did anything like that ever happen to *you*?" Furthermore, *objects* often did not play a role in various adventures.

The other collected body of data included recordings of parents eliciting narratives from their children. Each parental utterance was classified into one of several categories. Some parental utterances are questions that emphasize context: they prompt the child to fill in the stage scenery of their experience, to locate it in time and space. These questions ask about *when, where, who,* and *what*–objects. Other questions ignore context and instead emphasize action or evaluation. The sorts of utterances made by parents during narrative elicitation were classified into context-eliciting questions versus other sorts of questions or statements.

We predicted that parents who frequently stressed context or stage setting in their narrative elicitations—that is, who frequently asked questions about *when, where, who,* and *what*-object—would have children who were better at providing such context spontaneously to the researcher in their stand-alone narratives. In contrast, parental questions about actions and evaluations (i.e., about everything other than context) would *not* be related to children's provision of orienting information about *when* and *where* the described experiences took place. We also predicted a time-lagged relationship between parent prompts about contextual orientation when children were younger with child skill when they were older.

METHOD

Subjects

Ten families participated; all were middle class, two-parent families with university educations. Each family had a child of approximately 2;2 (range 2;1–2;3) at the beginning of the study. Half of the children were boys and half were girls. Three were singletons at the time of the study, three were the eldest, and four were the second eldest in multiple-child families.

Procedure

To collect the child–researcher narratives, the children were individually visited in their homes at monthly intervals by a researcher for 18 months. In each visit she played with the child for approximately an hour, during which she inserted approximately 15 to 20 prompts for narratives. Some narrative prompts were about events that she knew the children had experienced (such as trips, injuries, or parties) from parent information when she arrived at the house. Other prompts were the product of play interaction. These narrative prompts followed the procedure found to be very successful by Peterson and McCabe (1983): A short prompting narrative is provided by the researcher, followed by "Has anything like that ever happened to you?" For example, "Once I was running in my bare feet and I stepped on a bee and got stung. Have you ever gotten stung by a bee? You have? Tell me about it. What happened?" Once the children began narrating, the researcher maintained the narrative by means of back-channel acknowledgments such as "yeah?" "uh huh," "and?" or repeating what the child had just said. Such responses have been found to be very effective at encouraging a child to continue narrating without simultaneously directing or structuring the narrative that is told.

The second body of data was collected from the parents. At intervals of approximately every other month the researcher gave a tape recorder to parents in each family and asked them to record instances of talk about the past, when they asked their children to tell them about things that had happened to them at some prior time. Because talking about the past is something we all do readily and frequently, no more detailed instructions were necessary.

There was variation in parental compliance, so we divided our 18-month study into three 6-month time intervals and randomly selected for each child two parent tapes for each interval. Thus, a total of six parent-elicitation tapes were analyzed for each child. For two children, only one parent tape was available for two of the intervals, so a total of four tapes was analyzed for each of these children.

Data Analysis

Child Data.   A narrative was defined as an instance of talk about a specific past experience. It consisted of a minimum of two adjacent utterances. This definition of a narrative is similar to that by Peterson (1990) and Umiker-Sebeok (1979). These were not about routine, scriptlike experiences. The average number of narratives produced by each child when talking to the researcher and the average number of utterances per narrative is shown in Table 12.1.

Each of the children's narratives was searched for information on its global spatial/temporal context (*when* and *where*), and scored for such context being present versus absent. Our measures for the children's data are the percentage of their narratives that provide information about temporal context (*when* the events took place) and the percentage that provide information about spatial context (*where* the events occurred). Examples of temporal context include the following: "*Yesterday* I bumped my head"; "*When I was only two* I broke my arm"; "*Last week* my nanny came." Examples of spatial context include: "I was running *outside*"; "I went *to McDonald's*;" "We went for a walk *where the blueberries grow, up a big hill.*" The number of narratives produced by the children differed, and thus frequency counts of how many narratives include orientation to *when* and *where* is not the best measure to use. Instead, we present the percentage of all narratives that provided *when* or *where* information. These percentages were tabulated over three 6-month age intervals.

One of the authors classified the children's narratives in terms of presence or absence of both *when* and *where* information about the described experience.

TABLE 12.1
Number and Length of Narratives (and *SD*s) Elicited by Both Researcher and Parent

Category	Age of Children					
	2;2 - 2;7		2;8 - 3;1		3;2 - 3;7	
Researcher-elicited (unscaffolded)						
# Narratives/child *(SD)*	34.1	(14.24)	51.0	(13.44)	52.3	(8.57)
# Utterances/narrative *(SD)*	4.7	(1.08)	5.3	(0.99)	6.2	(1.05)
Parent-elicited (scaffolded)						
# Narratives/child *(SD)*	14.5	(5.06)	9.8	(7.84)	7.1	(3.63)
# Parent utterances/narrative *(SD)*	16.8	(4.93)	15.8	(11.59)	13.6	(5.82)

Fifteen percent of the narratives were coded by a second rater, and rates of agreement (calculated as number of agreements divided by agreements plus disagreements) were 97% and 95% for *when* and *where* scoring, respectively.

Parent Data.   The transcribed conversations between parents and children were searched for instances of adult questioning about a past specific experience (not habitual behavior). Each such instance that included at least two adjacent utterances was defined as a narrative elicitation. Within these elicitations, each parental utterance was scored.

We particularly focused on *context questions*—questions about *when, where, who,* and *what*–object. These could be phrased as either wh-questions or yes/no questions. Examples of wh-context questions include: "Where did we go yesterday?" and "What did you play with at Nana's house?" Examples of yes/no context questions include: "Was it last summer when that happened?" and "Was grandpa there?" Preliminary analyses indicated that it was necessary to include all types of context questions rather than just *when* and *where* questions in order to have enough data to analyze. Although these various questions differ in terms of the specific sort of context that is being queried, they all share a focus on the contextual background, that is, the stage upon which the events unfolded.

Parents of course ask other sorts of questions too, questions about events and evaluations as well as general prompts. These were classified as *noncontext questions*. These too could be phrased as either wh-questions or yes/no questions. Examples of wh-noncontext questions include: "What happened at Mary's yesterday?" and "What did you do at the Children's Center today?" Examples of yes/no noncontext questions include: "Were you really mad last night?" and "Did you fall down?"

In addition, parents ask for clarification about what the child just said, and they also repeat the child's utterance. Examples of clarification/repetition include the following parent responses:

(1)   Child: We went to Nana's.
      Parent: To Nana's?

(2)   Child: I made a picture.
      Parent: You made a picture.

Parents also make statements that do not require a child response, such as "And then we went to the beach and saw the iceberg." The average number of narratives elicited by parents as well as the average number of utterances per narrative are shown in Table 12.1.

RESULTS

First, we present data on the narratives that the children told to the researcher. Table 12.2 shows the percentage of their narratives that included information on global *when* and *where*. Children show a developmental improvement in their inclusion of such contextual orientation as they get older.

We next turn to the parent-child interactions in which the parents are eliciting narratives from their children. Quantitative measures of parental utterances are the crucial data to analyze (Fivush & Fromhoff, 1988; McCabe & Peterson, 1991), partly because parents often repeat the same question over and over before it is either answered by the child or the parent gives up (Olson-Fulero & Conforti,

TABLE 12.2
The Percentage of Children's Narratives That Spontaneously Include Orientation to When and Where (Including *SD*s and Range of Variation Between Children) at 3 Age Intervals

	Age of Children					
Category	2;2 - 2;7		2;8 - 3;1		3;2 - 3;7	
% of narratives with:						
When (SD)	7.3%	(8.11)	18.6%	(9.73)	32.0%	(12.39)
Range	0-24%		7-38%		16-60%	
Where (SD)	29.1%	(11.94)	39.8%	(6.30)	41.3%	(9.41)
Range	6-44%		31-49%		27-50%	

TABLE 12.3

Frequencies of Parent Utterance Categories per Narrative During 3 Age Intervals of Their Children

Category	Age of Children		
	2;2 - 2;7	2;8 - 3;1	3;2 - 3;7
Wh-content questions	4.05	3.75	2.63
Range	1.5-7.6	0.5-11.4	0.4-5.1
Yes/no context questions	0.99	1.51	0.66
Range	0.1-2.5	0.0-8.3	0.0-1.6
Other content questions	3.56	1.92	2.33
Range	0.6-3.8	0.0-4.3	1.0-5.0
Other yes/no questions	1.59	1.30	1.44
Range	0.6-4.4	0.1-4.3	0.0-2.5
Clarifying questions and repetitions	4.04	3.37	3.08
Range	2.3-6.1	0.0-8.1	0.9-8,0
Statements	1.43	2.17	1.77
Range	0.2-3.9	0.0-4.7	0.0-3.8
Total parent utterances	16.82	15.85	13.62
Range	10.9-25.8	4.1-37.1	4.5-25.0

1983). Or, they may ask a number of questions with similar form, such as "Who was there? Who else was there? And who else was there? And who else?" Because one context-prompting question in a narrative elicitation is not equivalent to an elicitation in which many context-prompting questions are embedded, the appropriate measure is the number of various types of questions that were asked by the parent during each narrative elicitation. The number of each type of parental utterance is shown in Table 12.3.

Next, we calculated correlations between the parents' frequencies of each type of utterance and the child's percent inclusion of *when* and *where* information. We did this for the three age ranges of child data and the three age ranges of parent data. Almost all of the significant correlations between child skill and parent utterances involved child skill when the children were between 3;2 and 3;7. This is the oldest age range included in our study. Thus, there seems to be a maturational component; the narratives of the younger children show little relationship with the parents' elicitation techniques.

Recall the predictions of Vygotskian theory. First, parental questions about context (of whatever syntactic form) should be related to children's skill at providing contextual orienting information in their stand-alone narratives. In contrast, parental noncontext questions (i.e., questions about actions or evaluations) or clarification questions/repetitions should not show the same relationship with children's skill at providing contextual orientation spontaneously when talking to the researcher. Second, there should be a time-lagged relationship between parental context questions and child tendencies to provide spa-

TABLE 12.4

Significant Correlations Between Frequencies of Questions About Context and Children's Provision of Where and When

	Child Performance		
Parent Behavior	Age 1	Age 2	Age 3
Wh-context questions			
		where	
Age 1	-.65, *p* = .020		
Age 2			.54, *p* = .024
Age 3			.68, *p* = .015
		when	
Age 1			.57, *p* = .042
Age 2			.69, *p* = .013
Age 3		.74, p = .007	.66, *p* = .019
Yes/no context questions			
		where	
Age 1			.76, *p* = .005
Age 2			.57, *p* = .042
Age 3			
		When	
Age 1			.64, *p* = .022
Age 2			.78, *p* = .004
Age 3			

Note. Significance level if < .05.

tial/temporal context. That is, parent utterances at Age 1 (when the children were 2;2–2;7) should be related to child context-setting skill at Age 2 (when the children were 2;8–3;1). In addition, parent utterances at Age 1 should be related to child context-setting skill at Age 3 (when the children were 3;2–3;7), and parent utterances at Age 2 should be related to child context-setting skill at Age 3.

The significant correlations between parental *context* questions and children's provision of *when* and *where* information in their narratives to a researcher are shown in Table 12.4. In contrast, only two correlations between parental *NON-context* questions and children's *when* and *where* are significant (and these differ from the correlations for *context* questions): Parental *yes/no noncontext* questions at age 2 correlated negatively with child *when* performance at age 1 (−.72, *p* = .009); at age 3 they correlated positively with child *when* performance at age 2 (.75, *p* = .006). Clearly, children's likelihood of spontaneously including temporal/spatial information is related to how many questions were asked by their parents that specifically focused on context. Questions about actions or evaluations did not play the same role; nor did clarifying questions or repetitions, since these too showed no relationship with children's provision of *when* and *where*. Thus, it was not how much parents asked questions that mattered, but rather what sorts of questions they asked. The questions had to be context-eliciting questions to foster context-setting skills in children.

The time-lagged relationships predicted by Vygotskian theory were also found. Although there were no significant relationships between parental context questions at Age 1 with child performance at Age 2, the story was quite different when one assessed the relationship between parent context questions at both Age 1 and Age 2 with the child's performance at Age 3. There are eight relevant cells in Table 12.4, two cells relating earlier (i.e., at Age 1 and Age 2) parental wh-context questions with child *when* performance at Age 3, two cells relating earlier parental yes/no context questions with child *when* performance at Age 3, two cells relating earlier parental wh-context questions with child *where* performance at Age 3, and two cells relating earlier parental yes/no context questions with child *where* performance at Age 3. Of these eight cells, seven have correlations that are significant. This suggests that a 3-year-old's skill at providing temporal/spatial context is related to parental behavior both 6 months and a year previously.

DISCUSSION

The question underlying this research is why there is substantial variation between children in their ability to provide orientative context in their narratives. We suggest that the discourse style of parents when eliciting personal experience narratives from their children is a crucial antecedent of children's skill at embedding narratives within a spatial/temporal context.

Various parents might emphasize different aspects of a narrative, such as the actions that occurred, contextual orientation, emotion, or other sorts of information. In the present study, we focused on only one of these aspects: orienting context. Our results showed that parents who ask many context-eliciting questions foster context-setting skill in their children. That is, parents who interlace their narrative elicitations with lots of questions like, "*When* did you scrape your knee? *Where* were you when that happened? *Who* was with you? *Who* else was there? *What* did you scrape it on?" and "*Where* did you go for help?" have children who are sensitive to the importance of contextually embedding the events about which they narrate.

It might well be that parents who emphasize other aspects of narration might also foster the development of that aspect in their children's narratives. Such a relationship was suggested by Peterson and McCabe (1992) in their case study of two parent–child dyads. They found that one parent emphasized action and plot, and she had a child who subsequently was good at this aspect of narration. In contrast, another parent emphasized contextual orientation, and she had a child who was subsequently good at this quite different aspect. Other research has documented relationships between topic-extending, elaborative parental styles and longer, more elaborated child narratives (Fivush, 1991; Fivush & Fromhoff, 1988; Hudson, 1990; McCabe & Peterson, 1991). These interrelationships between parental interaction styles and child skill require further research.

A sociocultural account of children's ability to orient their listeners to the context of their narratives was supported, consistent with the framework articulated by Vygotsky. A prediction of this theory is a time-lagged relationship between parental behavior and subsequent child performance. In our data, earlier parent behavior is correlated with later child skill, as predicted. Those parents whose scaffolds when the children are younger include lots of prompts for context have children who, when they are older, can provide such information spontaneously.

Other patterns of correlations might have been found. The performance of the children might have been most highly correlated with the questions of their parents contemporaneously. Thus, the children would be reflecting in their researcher-elicited narratives the sorts of questions they were currently being asked by their parents. This synchronous pattern of correlations was not found. Alternatively, the parents might have been responding to their children's lack of orienting skill by increasing the number of relevant questions they asked later, when their children were older. If so, then earlier child performance would have been highly and negatively correlated with later parent behavior. This parent–response pattern was not found either. Rather, the most consistent interpretation of the pattern of correlations we found is that the earlier questioning style of the parents fostered later development of orienting skill.

An important contrast to parental context questions are questions about other aspects of a narrative event, that is, questions about actions and evaluations. In addition, parents ask clarifying questions and repeat their children's utterances. These questions that focused on noncontextual aspects were *not* related to children's subsequent context-setting skills. Furthermore, sheer talkativeness of the parents was not the crucial variable fostering contextual orientation in child narratives. It was not how *much* parents talked, but rather what they talked *about*. If they encouraged their children to talk about contextually embedding their narrated events, then their children learned to do just that.

This research suggests that children's skill at narration partly develops as a response to others. It thus meshes with the increasing body of literature suggesting that parent–child discourse patterns play an important role in the language development of their children.

ACKNOWLEDGMENTS

The authors would like to thank Pamela Dodsworth for collecting data, and especially the parents and children who allowed us to visit them so frequently and participated so helpfully. We would also like to thank Penny Voutier for data analysis and Michael Bruce-Lockhart for technical assistance. This research was supported by Natural Sciences and Engineering Research Council of Canada grant OGP0000513 to the first author.

REFERENCES

Brewer, W. (1985). The story schema: Universal and culture-specific properties. In D. Olson, N. Torrance, & A. Hildyard (Eds.), *Literacy, language and learning* (pp. 167–194). Cambridge, England. Cambridge University Press.

Brown, R. (1973). *A first language: The early stages.* Cambridge, MA: Harvard University Press.

Bruner, J. S. (1983). *Children's talk: Learning to use language.* New York: Norton.

Bruner, J. S. (1986). *Actual minds, possible worlds.* Cambridge, MA: Harvard University Press.

Cazden, C. (1985). Classroom discourse. In M. C. Wittrock (Ed.), *Research on teaching* (3rd. ed., pp. 432–463). New York: Macmillan.

Eisenberg, A. R. (1985). Learning to describe past experiences in conversation. *Discourse Processes, 8*, 177–204.

Feagans, L. (1982). The development and importance of narratives for school adaptation. In L. Feagans & D. C. Farran (Eds.), *The language of children reared in poverty* (pp. 95–116). New York: Academic Press.

Fivush, R. (1991). The social construction of personal narratives. *Merrill-Palmer Quarterly, 37*, 59–81.

Fivush, R., & Fromhoff, F. A. (1988). Style and structure in mother-child conversations about the past. *Discourse Processes, 11*, 337–355.

Hickmann, M. (1985). The implications of discourse skills in Vygotsky's developmental theory. In J. V. Wertsch (Ed.), *Culture, communication and cognition: Vygotskian perspectives* (pp. 236–257). Cambridge, England: Cambridge University Press.

Hickmann, M. (1986). Psychosocial aspects of language acquisition. In P. Fletcher & M. Garman (Eds.), *Language acquisition* (2nd ed., pp. 9–29). Cambridge, England: Cambridge University Press.

Hudson, J. A. (1990). The emergence of autobiographical memory in mother-child conversation. In R. Fivush & J. A. Hudson (Eds.), *Knowing and remembering in young children* (pp. 166–196). Cambridge, England: Cambridge University Press.

Labov, W. (1972). *Language in the inner city.* Philadelphia: University of Pennsylvania Press.

Labov, W., & Waletzky, J. (1967). Narrative analysis: Oral versions of personal experience. In J. Helm (Ed.), *Essays on the verbal and visual arts* (pp. 12-44). Seattle: University of Washington Press.

McCabe, A., & Peterson, C. (1991). Getting the story: A longitudinal study of parental styles in eliciting oral personal narratives and developing narrative skill. In A. McCabe & C. Peterson (Eds.), *Developing narrative structure* (pp. 217–253). Hillsdale, NJ: Lawrence Erlbaum Associates.

McLane, J. B. (1987). Interaction, context, and the zone of proximal development. In M. Hickmann (Ed.), *Social and functional approaches to language and thought* (pp. 267–285). New York: Academic Press.

Menig-Peterson, C., & McCabe, A. (1978). Children's orientation of a listener to the context of their narratives. *Developmental Psychology, 14*, 582–592.

Olsen-Fulero, L., & Conforti, J. (1983). Child responsiveness to mother questions of varying type and presentation. *Journal of Child Language, 10*, 495–520.

Paris, S. G., Newman, R. S., & Jacobs, J. E. (1985). Social contexts and functions of children's remembering. In C. J. Brainerd & M. Pressley (Eds.), *The cognitive side of memory development* (pp. 81–115). New York: Springer-Verlag.

Peterson, C. (1990). The who, when and where of early narratives. *Journal of Child Language, 17*, 433–455.

Peterson, C., & McCabe, A. (1983). *Developmental psycholinguistics: Three ways of looking at a child's narrative.* New York: Plenum.

Peterson, C., & McCabe, A. (1992). Parental styles of narrative elicitation: Effect on children's narrative structure and content. *First Language, 12*, 299–321.

Polanyi, L. (1982). Linguistic and social constraints on storytelling. *Journal of Pragmatics, 6*, 509–524.

Polanyi, L. (1985). *Telling the American story.* Norwood, NJ: Ablex.

Ratner, H. H. (1980). The role of social context in memory development. In M. Perlmutter (Ed.), *Children's memory: New directions for child development* (Vol. 10, pp. 49–67). San Francisco: Jossey-Bass.

Ratner, H. H. (1984). Memory demands and the development of young children's memory. *Child Development, 55*, 2173–2191.

Snow, C. E. (1983). Literacy and language: Relationships during the preschool years. *Harvard Educational Review, 53*, 165–189.

Snow, C. E., & Goldfield, B. A. (1983). Turn the page please: Situation-specific language acquisition. *Journal of Child Language, 10*, 551–569.

Umiker-Sebeok, D. J. (1979). Preschool children's intraconversational narratives. *Journal of Child Language, 6*, 91–109.

13

Narrative Space Structuring at the Preschool Age: Findings on Monologic and Dialogic Discourse

Barbara Bokus
University of Warsaw, Poland

What exactly is a narrative? Although definitions differ in detail, all agree on central properties. Primarily, a narrative is a verbal representation of events that follow one another in time. Some consider a narrative to be any recounting of temporally sequenced changes in reality (e.g., Labov, 1972; Labov & Waletzky, 1967; Peterson & McCabe, 1983). Others refer to an additional property. According to Polanyi (1985), a story must include not only main line event clauses, but also contextualizing state clauses. Main line event clauses, which have been frequently described as the backbone or "bare bones" of a narrative, what happened, whereas contextualizing clauses include identification of participants, setting, explanation, evaluation, and collateral information (Peterson & McCabe, 1991). Longacre stated that a narrative "involves a distinction between on-the-line or backbone material and supportive, explanatory, tributary or what-have-you material in the balance of the discourse" (1983, p. 99). Bokus (1991, 1992a) distinguished between *narrative line* and *narrative field* in the narrative text. A narrative line reflects changes in referenced reality over time, whereas a narrative field reflects the state of reality at a given moment within a given spatial area to which the narrator is attending.

In the narrative literature, considerable attention is devoted to the *story line* (e.g., Mandler, 1984), the *narrative line* (e.g., Bokus, 1991, 1992a; Sachs, Goldman & Chaille, 1984), the *main line event clauses* (Polanyi, 1982, 1985), or *on-the-line material* (Longacre, 1983). Much less attention has been given to *contextualizing state clauses, tributary material* in the discourse, and *narrative field*—in other words, to what constitutes the background of the developing narrative line.

The purpose of this chapter is to explore this second dimension of narrative text—the narrative field. My analyses will make use of the differentiation of two narrative landscapes introduced by Bruner (1986): the landscape of action and the landscape of consciousness.

BASIC CONCEPTS: NARRATIVE TEXT, REFERENCE SITUATION, NARRATIVE LINE, AND NARRATIVE FIELD

The conceptual framework adopted in the present paper derives from Halliday and Hasan's (1976) definition of *text,* a construct "best regarded as a semantic unit, a unit not of form, but of meaning" (p. 2). The text is realized in utterances of discourse. The discourse in turn is treated as a pragmatic unit of language (Bokus, 1991, 1992b). A text can be analyzed as a chain of *reference situations,* or states of reality, conceived of by the speaker (here, the narrator) from the perspective of a situational subject. Reference situations constituting a text are distinguished according to: (a) the situational subject (every situation is assumed to have some subject, animate or treated as animate), and (b) state of the situational subject—experiencer and/or agent of action.

The state of activity of any subject can embrace: (a) the state of the subject's external activity directly accessible to observation (coded in the *landscape of action* in Bruner's terms), and/or (b) the state of the subject's mental activity, which is not directly accessible to observation but is inferred by the narrator (coded in the *landscape of consciousness*).

The states of reality—external and internal—of any subject can cohere, as in example (1), supplement each other, as in (2), or be divergent, as in (3):

(1) Z.A., 4;4
     Jacek fruwał wysoko i wiedział , że fruwa wysoko.
     'Jacek flew up high and (he) knew (he) was flying up high.'[1]

(2) K.R., 4;6
     Misio płakał. Siedział na polance i płakał. Myślał o swojej mamusi.
     'The little bear was crying. (He) was sitting in the little field and was crying. (He) was thinking of his mummy.'

(3) B.L., 4;5
     Misio myślał, że wcale nie płacze. No płakał bardzo i bardzo ten misio.
     'The little bear thought that (he) wasn't crying at all. But (he) was crying very hard, the little bear was.'

---

[1]English translations of Polish narrative utterances are close approximations. Pronouns in parentheses are not expressed in the children's text. In Polish, the verb morphological structure gives the person and number of the pronominal subject.

Reference situations representing states of reality temporally ordered and therefore connected either chronologically only, or else causally or teleologically as well, form what is called the *narrative line*. The narrative line presents the course of events and episodes (see Bokus, 1992b; Peterson & McCabe, 1983) in referenced reality.

The situation of any subject belonging to the narrative line can be treated by the narrator as a single and sufficient representation of the state of referenced reality at a given moment in time (t_n). But this is not always the case. Sometimes, in order to define the state of reality at t_n, the narrator introduces two or more reference situations into the textual chain. These situations are states of referenced reality at t_n that the narrator apprehends from the perspectives of different subjects copresent in a given spatial area or in various such areas singled out by the narrator and juxtaposed. These reference situations reflect what at a given moment in time (t_n) is happening in the space "controlled" by narrator and comprise what is called the *narrative field*. Dominating the narrative field at t_n is usually the dynamic situation of the subject who is the agent of change (agent of action) in this field, or else the static situation of the subject who "evokes" a reaction in other subjects at the next moment in time (t_{n+1}), that is, a situation belonging to the narrative line. Constructing a narrative text is therefore not restricted to developing the narrative line but also includes extending the narrative field.

In introducing subjects of situations that extend the narrative field, the speaker relates them in some way to the subjects of the narrative line. Such connections give the narrative field a kind of structure that makes it more or less compact. It is to this question, that is, the structuring of narrative space, that the present work is devoted. In this chapter I examine the way the child builds up the narrative field, both independently in monologic discourse and together with a peer conarrator in dialogic discourse.

PROBLEM

The basic research problem of this work can be formulated as two questions, as follows: (a) How do children elaborate the narrative field in the process of monologic discourse? in the process of dialogic discourse? (b) Do changes occur in the structure of the narrative field with narrator's age (3 to 7 years)?

METHOD

Subjects and Research Design

A total of 384 children between ages 3 to 7 took part in the investigation in solo narrator and conarrator roles. They recounted to a peer listener the adventures of two heroes of three picture books. Two variants of peer participant structure were designed. One variant was composed of two children, a solo narrator and a listener, and the other of three children, two conarrators, and a listener. The research design was balanced for age, gender, and order of participation in the two variants. The data consisted of 379 solo narrations and 191 conarrations.

Analyses

Following Peterson and McCabe's (1983) procedures, modified by Bokus (1991, 1992b), reference situation chains constituting the text were described on the dimension of narrative reference reality, that is, narrative line developing over time. In performing the analysis, I identified a different kind of reference situation that did not fit into the narrative line, a kind of situation that revealed a second, spatial, dimension of the narrative. The latter was found to elaborate narrative fields (Bokus, 1991, 1992a). An analysis was made of the relationships between the subjects of situations expanding the narrative field and the subjects of situations comprising the narrative line.

I found that children elaborated narrative fields by introducing situational subjects linked in a given relation to subjects in the narrative line, as follows:

1. Spatial relation

   a. Direct, for example, K.A., 3;8:
      Jacek i Wacek grali w piłkę. A ślimaczek szedł blisko nich.
      'Jacek and Wacek were playing ball. A little snail was coming up close to them.'
   b. Indirect (i.e., by reference to some common point or object in space), for example, R.W., 4;5:
      Jacek leżał pod skałą, brudny był . . . I . . . i na czubku skały siedziała sobie myszka, mała myszka sobie siedziała.
      'Jacek was lying under the cliff, (he) was all dirty . . . And . . . and at the top of the cliff there was a little mouse sitting, a little mouse sat there.'

2. Observer–observed relation, for example, J.R., 4;7:

   Jacek wyciągał Wacka z wody. A muchy się przyglądał, jak wyciągał.
   'Jacek was pulling Wacek out of the water. And the flies were watching how (he) was pulling.'

3. Evaluator–evaluated relation in categories of good–bad, nice–not nice, pretty–ugly, for example, K.W., 6;4:

   Jacek fruwał. Wacek patrzył, że Jacek tak dobrze fruwał.
   'Jacek was flying. Wacek was watching how well Jacek was flying.'

4. Explainer–explained (object of clarification) in categories of cause, goal, effectiveness of action, etc., for example,

B.S., 5;7:
Misio płakał. Ptaszki się dziwowały, dlaczego płakał.
'The little bear was crying. The birdies were wondering why (he) was crying.'

S.C., 6;8:
Jacek pożyczył skrzydełka. Muchy patrzyły na Jacka, że ma skrzydełka, i nie wiedziały wcale po co.
'Jacek borrowed the wings. The flies saw that Jacek had wings and (they) didn't know at all what for.'

Z.R., 5;7:
Misio szukał mamusi. A inne niedźwiadki nie wiedziały, czy znajdzie.
'The little bear was looking for his mummy. And the other bears didn't know whether (he) would find (her).'

These four types of relation between subjects of situations elaborating narrative field and subjects of narrative line situations were sometimes presented in a more complex way than described so far, differently for the landscape of action and for the landscape of consciousness (cases of so—called "double relations"), as follows:

1. Spatial relation (near–far) coded differently in the landscape of action and in the landscape of consciousness, for example, A.G., 5;4, and Z.L., 5;8:

    Jacek i Wacek grają w piłkę nad rzeką. Są daleko od domu, bez mamy . . . [No].[2]
    Mama gotuje obiadek w domu . . . [No]. I myśli . . . Myśli, co chłopcy się bawią przed domem w piłkę.
    'Jacek and Wacek are playing ball by the river. (They) are far away from home, without their mummy . . . [Uhhuh]. The mummy was cooking dinner at home . . . [Uhhuh]. And (she) was thinking . . . (She) was thinking that the boys were playing ball in front of the house.'

2. Observer–observed relation

    (a) Subjects have different roles in the landscapes of action and consciousness, for example, Z.W., 5;6, and B.A., 5;5:
    On patrzył, że Jacek fruwa . . . I tak sobie patrzył i myślał, ze to może on fruwa i Jacek się patrzy . . . [Może Jacek się patrzy.]
    'He was watching Jacek fly . . . And (he) was watching and thinking that maybe he would fly and Jacek would watch . . . [Maybe Jacek would watch.]'
    (b) The object of observation is different in the landscape of action and in the landscape of consciousness (subject's state of activity in the narrative line is displaced in time and space), for example, B.S., 5;3, and T.W., 5;8:

---

[2]The conarrator's contributions are included in square brackets.

Jacek machał w skrzydełka . . . w piasku. [Wacek widział . . .] Wacek widział, co Jacek w piasku . . . Ale tak sobie umyślał, co Jacek jeszcze lata . . . [W powietrzu] Nie spadnął.
'Jacek was waving his wings on the sand. [Wacek saw . . .] Wacek saw Jacek on the sand. And (he) made believe that Jacek was still flying . . . [In the air] (He) didn't fall down.'

3. Evaluator–evaluated relation: divergency of evaluations (bad–good, slow–quick) of the subject's situation in the landscape of action and the landscape of consciousness, for example, K.W., 6;8, and G.L.,6;4:

Wacek płynie do piłki powoli. A żabka się patrzy . . . , że tak źle płynie Wacek . . . [Wacek . . .] Taki ciaptak . . . [No . . . ciaptak] I sobie myśli: Może Wacek bardzo dobrze . . . do piłki . . . szybko płynie. . jak pływak. [Jak pływak.]
'Wacek is swimming slow to the ball. And the froggie is looking . . . how bad Wacek is swimming . . . [Wacek . . .] What a clumsy kid . . . [Uhhuh . . . clumsy] And (he) thinks to himself: Maybe Wacek (is swimming) very well . . . to the ball . . . swimming fast . . . like a swimmer. [Like a swimmer.]'

4. Explainer–explained: different categories (manner of action, goal of action) of explanation of the subject's situation in the landscape of action and the landscape of consciousness, for example, I.B., 6;9, and G.N., 6;7:

Jacek i Wacek idą do lasu . . . bez taty [No . . .] A motyl się martwi, jak znajdą drogę do lasu bez taty . . . [Bez swojego tatusia] I tak sobie patrzy w głowie motylek, co idą z tatą do lasu [Do lasu] Ale . . . po co idą? Na grzyby?
'Jacek and Wacek are going to the woods . . . without their daddy [Uhhuh . . .] And the butterfly is worrying how (they)'ll find the path to the woods without daddy . . . [Without their daddy] And the butterfly sees in his head, that (they) are going with daddy to the woods. [To the woods] But . . . what for? To pick mushrooms?'

In these cases, the narrative field could embrace some areas of subjects' real actions (presented in the landscape of action) and other areas of subjects' hypothesized actions (presented in the landscape of consciousness).

RESULTS

Results showed that development of the narrative field takes place differently in the solo narrator—listener discourse process and in the conarrators—listener discourse process. This is shown in Figures 13.1 and 13.2, which present the frequencies of different types of relations between subjects of situations elaborating narrative field and subjects of narrative line situations in monologic discourse (Fig. 13.1) and dialogic discourse (Fig. 13.2).

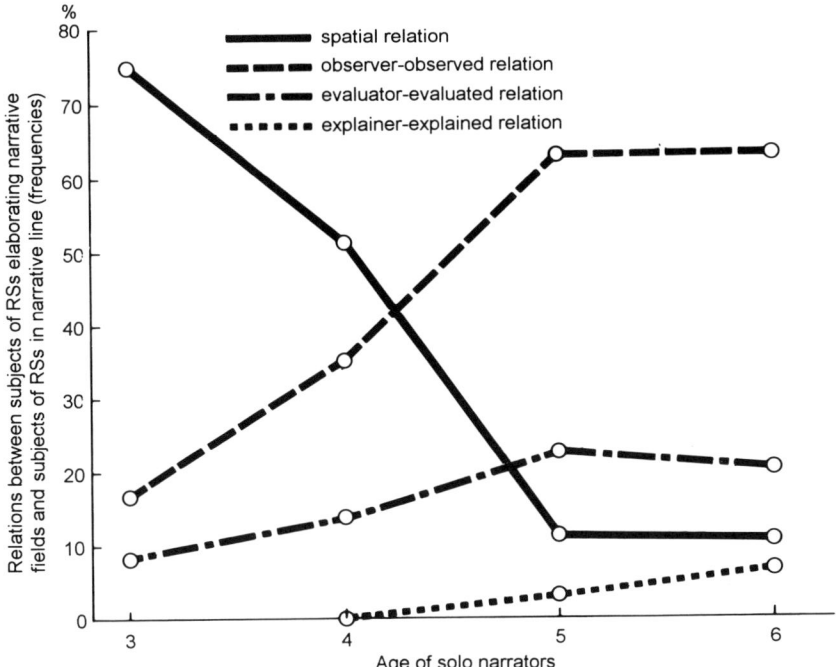

FIG. 13. 1. Narrative space structuring at the preschool age: findings on monologic discourse. Frequencies of different relations between subjects of Reference Situations (RSs) elaborating narrative fields and subjects of RSs in narrative line.

Monologic Discourse

For 3- and 4-year-olds, relations between subjects of situations elaborating narrative field and subjects of narrative line situations were predominantly spatial (75% and 51%, respectively). For 4-year-olds as compared to 3-year-olds, however, the frequency of the spatial relation dropped in favor of the perceptual one, that is, the observer–observed relation ($z = 3.525, p < .01$). The proportion of the latter relation increased from 17% for the 3-year-olds to 35% for the 4-year-olds ($z = 2.946, p < .01$). As concerns the 5- and 6-year-olds, the perceptual relation was most important in the organization of the narrative field. There were observer–observed relations between subjects in the narrative line and those outside it (63% for each age group). Their frequency for 5-year-olds as compared to the 4-year-olds increased from 35% to 63% ($z = 4.558, p < .01$). There was also an increase in the evaluator—evaluated relation (13.5% and 22.6% for the 4- and 5-year-olds, respectively, $z = 1.836, p < .05$).

At the age of 5 the relation of explainer–explained makes its first appearance

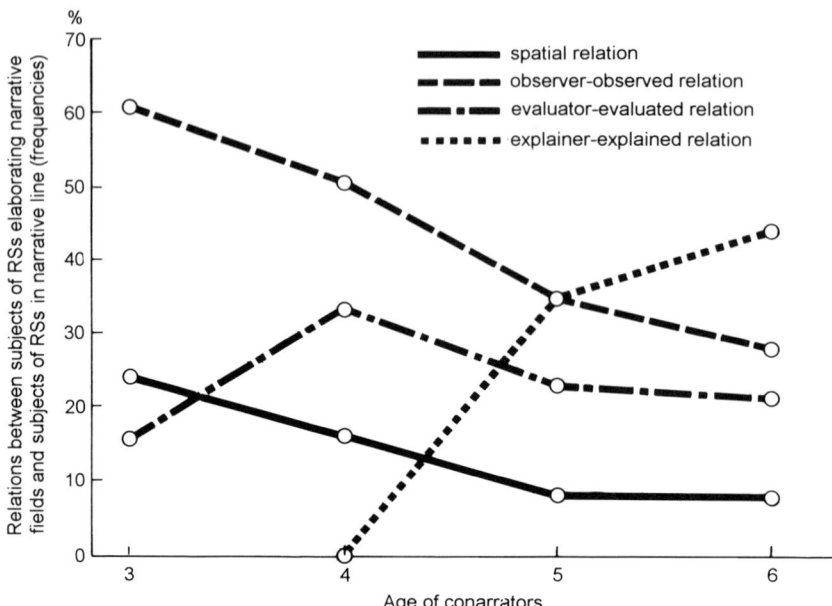

FIG. 13.2. Narrative space structuring at the preschool age: findings on dialogic discourse. Frequencies of different relations between subjects of Reference Situations (RSs) elaborating narrative fields and subjects of RSs in narrative line.

(3%). At this age, there is a decided drop in the frequency of spatial relations between subjects in the narrative line and those outside it (from 51% for 4-year-olds to barely 11% for 5-year-olds, $z = 6.744$, $p < .01$). This level is maintained for the 6-year-olds (ca. 11%, n.s.). The frequencies of the remaining relations in the narrative fields do not differ between 5- and 6-year-olds (see Fig. 13.1).

Dialogic Discourse

For 3- and 4-year-old conarrators, the most frequent situations introduced to elaborate the narrative field were those of subjects in the observer role, watching the events in the narrative line (61% and 51% of all situations in the narrative fields for these age groups, respectively). However, the 4-year-olds as compared to the 3-year-olds more often introduced subjects in the observer role who also evaluated what was happening in the narrative line (an increase from 15% for 3-year-olds to 33% for 4-year-olds, $z = 2.749$, $p < .01$).

In elaborating narrative fields (see Fig. 13.2) 5-year-olds introduced situations with subjects in the observer role alone as often as they introduced subjects in this role who also explained what was happening in the narrative line (35% for each). Six-year-old conarrators most frequently introduced into the narrative field new subjects who tried to explain the events presented in the narrative line (44%). These subjects "put questions to themselves" (thought about some matter, wondered about it, had doubts about something, etc.). Their questions concerned the causes and intentions behind acts and the effectiveness of subjects' actions in the narrative line.

Two Landscapes of Narrative: Both Monologic and Dialogic Discourse

The relations that we see in Figs. 13.1 and 13.2 between subjects of situations elaborating the narrative field and subjects of situations in the narrative line were sometimes presented in the narrative text as double ones, different for the landscape of action and for the landscape of consciousness. These clear differentiations between the reality as presented in the narrative line and the "mistaken" representation of this reality in the minds of the subjects in the narrative field were apparent in the texts of the 5- and 6-year-olds, more often in conarrated than in solo narrated text. The frequencies of the contrasted structures of the narrative field in landscapes of action and of consciousness amount to 3% and 16%, respectively, for monologic and dialogic discourse in the 5-year-old group, and 9% and 25%, respectively, in the 6-year-old group. The detailed data for types of double relations between subjects of situations elaborating narrative fields and subjects of narrative line situations are presented in Table 13.1.

In monologic discourse double representations concern most frequently the observer–observed type of relation and in dialogic discourse the explainer–explained type, that is, those relations that are more often chosen for structuring narrative space by the 5- and 6-year-olds, both as solo and as conarrators.

DISCUSSION

It has turned out that in elaborating narrative fields children introduced situational subjects linked in a spatial relation with subjects in the narrative line or linked additionally in relations of observer–observed, evaluator–evaluated, or explainer–explained. These different modes of narrative space structuring were found to have a formative role in developmental changes in both monologic and dialogic discourse. What was noted is that the last mentioned mode—introducing field situational subjects as explainers or interpreters of states and events occurring in the narrative line—had a direct effect on the building of the narrative line; what was added to the process of narrative text construction were information categories within which the subjects of narrative field situations could look at the state of reality presented in the narrative line. In the framework of these categories the narrator (solo or conarrator) could be shown what reference situations might next occur in the textual chain as a development of the narrative line.

TABLE 13.1
Contrasted Structures of Narrative Fields (Different in Landscapes of Action and of Consciousness) in Solo Narration and Conarration. Frequencies of Double Relations Between Subjects of Reference Situations Elaborating Narrative Fields and Subjects of Reference Situations in Narrative Line

	5-Year-Olds		6-Year-Olds	
	Solo Narration	Conarration	Solo Narration	Conarration
Type of Double Relations	N	N	N	N
Spatial relations	0	2	2	1
	(0.00)	(2.67)	(1.13)	(0.95)
Observer-observed	4	3	9	6
	(3.01)	(4.00)	(5.08)	(5.71)
Evaluator-evaluated	0	0	2	4
	(0.00)	(0,00)	(1.13)	(3.81)
Explainer-explained	0	7	3	15
	(0.00)	(9.33)	(1.70)	(14.29)
All double relations	4	12	16	26
	(3.01)	(16.00)	(9.04)	(24.76)
All noted relations	133	75	177	105
	(100)	(100)	(100)	(100)

Narrative space structuring discussed in terms of landscapes of action and of consciousness (Bruner, 1986) shows that children aged 5 to 6 are capable of producing stories with a dual landscape. This result is of interest in light of the issue of children's ability to consider two landscapes: what is going on in the real world, and what is going on in the minds of story characters. Leondar (1977) claimed that "attributes of thought, feeling, or motive are entirely absent from primary narratives that are characteristic of 5 to 7 year olds" (p. 181). However, Astington (1990) showed that a cursory reading of the stories recorded by Pitcher and Prelinger (1963) from children 2 to 5 years of age yields a number of examples of such attributions, especially in 4- and 5-year-olds' stories. Astington emphasized the special importance of children's theory of mind for their under-standing of narrative with two landscapes: landscape of action and landscape of consciousness. The findings presented here show the importance of children's developing theory of mind for their production of text with dual landscapes of narrative.

ACKNOWLEDGMENTS

The data analyzed in this chapter came from studies supported by Grant RPBP.III.31 from the Ministry of National Education in Poland. The author's participation at the Congress was partially supported by the Stefan Batory Foundation. Grateful acknowledgment is due to Professor Grace Wales Shugar and Professor Tadeusz Tomaszewski. Both read an earlier version of this article and made many helpful suggestions.

REFERENCES

Astington, J. W. (1990). Narrative and the child's theory of mind. In B. K. Britton & A. D. Pellegrini (Eds.), *Narrative thought and narrative language* (pp.151–171). Hillsdale, NJ: Lawrence Erlbaum Associates.

Bokus, B. (1991). *Tworzenie opowiadań przez dzieci. O linii i polu narracji* [Children building stories. Narrative line and narrative field]. Kielce, Poland: Energeia.

Bokus, B. (1992a). Children building stories: Peer interactive spoken discourse. *Polish Psychological Bulletin, 23,* 121–138.

Bokus, B. (1992b). Peer co-narration: Changes in structure of preschoolers' participation. *Journal of Narrative and Life History, 2,* 253–275.

Bruner, J. (1986). *Actual minds, possible worlds.* Cambridge, MA: Harvard University Press.

Halliday, M. A. K., & Hasan, R. (1976). *Cohesion in English.* London: Longman.

Labov, W. (1972). *Language in the inner city.* Philadelphia: University of Pennsylvania Press.

Labov, W., & Waletzky, J. (1967). Narrative analysis: Oral version of personal experience. In J. Helm (Ed.), *Essays on the verbal and visual arts* (pp. 12–44). Seattle: University of Washington Press.

Leondar, B. (1977). Hatching plots: Genesis of storymaking. In D. Perkins & B. Leondar (Eds.), *The arts and cognition* (pp. 172–191). Baltimore, MD: Johns Hopkins University Press.

Longacre, R. (1983). Vertical threads of cohesion in discourse. In F. Neubauer (Ed.), *Coherence in natural language texts* (pp. 99–113). Philadelphia: John Benjamins.

Mandler, J. M. (1984). *Stories, scripts, and scenes: Aspects of schema theory.* Hillsdale, NJ: Lawrence Erlbaum Associates.

Peterson, C., & McCabe, A. (1983). *Developmental psycholinguistics: Three ways of looking at a child's narrative.* New York: Plenum.

Peterson, C., & McCabe, A. (1991). Linking children's connective use and narrative macrostructure. In A. McCabe & C. Peterson (Eds.), *Developing narrative structure* (pp. 29–53). Hillsdale, NJ: Lawrence Erlbaum Associates.

Pitcher, E. G., & Prelinger, E. (1963). *Children tell stories.* New York: International Universities Press.

Polanyi, L. (1982). Linguistic and social constraints on storytelling. *Journal of Pragmatics, 6,* 509–524.

Polanyi, L. (1985). *Telling the American story.* Norwood, NJ: Ablex.

Sachs, J., Goldman, J., & Chaille, C. (1984). Narratives in preschoolers' sociodramatic play: The role of knowledge and communicative competence. In L. Galda & A. Pellegrini (Eds.), *Play, language and story: The development of children's literate behavior* (pp. 45–62). Norwood, NJ: Ablex.

14 Language Input and Attentional Behavior

Anne E. Baker*
Beppie van den Bogaerde
University of Amsterdam, The Netherlands

During the last 10 years we have seen a great increase in the use of crosslinguistic comparison as a test for universalist hypotheses about language acquisition. Comparing languages gives an indication of the validity of these hypotheses, and also possibly of the validity of the interaction of innate language acquisition mechanisms with other factors.

The study of sign language acquisition is interesting for purposes of crosslinguistic comparison for two reasons. First, a sign language can have structures that are comparable with those of some spoken languages, so it enters into the general crosslinguistic data pool. Second, sign languages provide evidence for the influence of modality on acquisition, that is, the influence of the fact that a sign language is in a visual–spatial modality compared to an audio-oral modality.

The visual-spatial modality has a clear influence on attentional behavior: Sign language utterances have to be seen by the child, as opposed to being heard. The requirement of gaining visual attention from the child on the part of the signing adult implies differences in the type of interaction because, for example, attention cannot be split visually between the referent and the communication. The child has to learn to give visual attention to communication (see also Harris, Clibbens, Tibbitts, & Chasin, 1987; Kyle, Ackerman, & Woll, 1987).

In this chapter we aim to describe the language input offered by deaf mothers to two deaf and three hearing children. This study forms part of a larger longitudinal study, conducted at the University of Amsterdam, in which three deaf and three hearing children and their deaf mothers are being followed longitudinally. Earlier studies within the project showed that the mothers use Dutch (NL), Sign

---

*Formerly Mills.

Language of the Netherlands (SLN), and simultaneous communication[1] (SC: signing and speech at the same time) with all children. This chapter focuses on the proportional language use in relation to the attentional behavior of the mothers and children. A comparison will be made between the deaf and hearing children.

The deaf child must pay visual attention in order to have access to the linguistic information. Because it seems improbable that paying visual attention is an innate skill, deaf children will have to learn to divide their attention between objects and actions that are going on and linguistic information (Swisher, 1991). They must learn to check back with their conversational partners. For deaf children this is, of course, also true for spoken language. The expectation is that deaf children will look up at their mothers more often as they grow older.

Hearing children need not give *visual* attention to spoken language, but in order to have access to SLN they do have to pay visual attention. We know from earlier research (van den Bogaerde & Mills, 1994) that, in the majority of simultaneously signed and spoken utterances, the mothers provide the same semantic information in the two modalities, which implies that hearing children need only hear the spoken part in order to have access to the information that is being offered. Even so, we expect hearing children to look up at their mothers for SLN and simultaneously signed and spoken utterances, increasingly so as they grow older.

In this chapter we discuss the various ways in which the deaf mothers gain or hold the attention of their children, and how these attentional strategies may relate to the language they chose to use; we also describe some aspects of the attentional behavior of deaf and hearing children as they grow older. The following questions will be addressed:

1. Do deaf mothers attract their children's attention *explicitly* less often as the children grow older?
2. Is there a change over time in the use of strategies by the deaf mothers, related to the hearing status of the children?
3. Is the use of a particular strategy related to language choice; that is, is a particular strategy significantly linked to a particular language?
4. Does the attentional behavior of the hearing children develop differently from that of the deaf children?

First, we present some information on the subjects participating in this study and how the data were gathered and analyzed. Subsequently, we look briefly at the language input offered to the children by the deaf mothers, after which we discuss the research questions and the results.

---

[1]Simultaneous communication has been given various definitions in the literature on sign linguistics. We have used the following definition: all utterances in which optional spoken components and signs co-occur (see also Coerts, 1992; Pimiä, 1990; Schermer, 1990).

SUBJECTS PARTICIPATING IN THE STUDY

The mothers in this study are all prelingually deaf and use Sign Language of the Netherlands as their first language. The two deaf children are named Laura and Mark and the three hearing children Jonas, Sander, and Alex. Relevant information on each child and his or her family is as follows. Laura was born severely hearing impaired ($\geq$ 70 dB hearing loss in best ear). This diagnosis was made at 10 months; later a far greater loss was measured (120 dB). Laura's father is a hearing child of deaf parents and a native signer. Her mother is deaf and has hearing parents and one deaf sister. Laura has one deaf twin brother and a hearing older brother. Mark was born deaf ($\geq$ 90 dB hearing loss in best ear). He is the brother of Laura and Jonas. Jonas is the hearing older brother of Mark and Laura. Sander is a hearing child of deaf parents. Both his maternal and his paternal grandparents are deaf, as well as many uncles and aunts in his family. He has two older hearing brothers, who are twins. Alex is a hearing child of a deaf mother, who became deaf after meningitis at the age of 2;6; his father has a severe hearing loss. Alex has one older hearing sister and one older hearing brother. There are no other deaf members in his family.

PROCEDURE AND ANALYSIS

The five children and their mothers were filmed monthly at home in a freeplay situation; the filming was done using a Panasonic Camcorder M7 CCD with a JVC monitor. The tapes were transcribed using a JVC monitor (TM 150 PSN) and a Panasonic (AG-6200) videorecorder. Mother and child had a free choice of toys and books; no specific instructions were given to the mothers. For the analysis presented in this chapter two videorecordings were chosen of each mother-child dyad: one when the child was 0;11 and one when the child was 1;11, to show development over one year.

Analysis of the interaction between mother and child began 5 minutes after starting the tape. Ten minutes of each video sample have been transcribed. All of the mother's utterances were transcribed, as well as her nonverbal behavior, that is, all gestures and acts that could be considered an attentional strategy, such as moving a toy or tapping the child (see also the following section on attentional strategies). For the child all attentional shifts to the mother were registered. For all statistical analyses chi-square values were calculated (Everitt, 1986).

Attentional Strategies Used by the Deaf Mothers

Every utterance of the mother was coded for one of the following strategies:

Nonexplicit attentional strategies:

Strategy A: The mother does not actively try to gain the child's attention before an utterance is produced. The mother starts signing and/or talking after the child has looked up at her.

Strategy B: The mother starts signing and/or talking when the child is not looking at her, assuming that the child will look up. Through peripheral vision the deaf children become aware that signing is going on and look up (Siple, 1978); the hearing children perceive movement and/or hear their mother's voice and may or may not look up.

Explicit attentional strategies:

Strategy C: The mother assumes responsibility for the visibility of her signing in an explicit way. Signs are normally made in front of the body or on the body; if the child is, for instance, looking down at a picture in a book, the mother may choose to *dislocate* a sign within the visual field of the child, thus making the sign near the book, or on the body of the child. *Strategy D*: The mother tries to attract the child's visual attention before signing and/or talking by moving an object, by calling the child's name, by tapping the child, or waving an arm or hand in the child's visual field.

Attentional Behavior of the Children

The attentional behavior of the children is coded in order to indicate spontaneous looks. This is related to strategy A of the mothers, because here the mothers have the visual attention of the child before communicating. It is expected that the number of spontaneous looks from all children will increase over time. Positive reactions to strategy B and strategy D were coded in order to indicate the success of these strategies.

A shift in eye gaze direction to the mother after the mother started signing/talking was registered as a positive reaction for strategy B. A shift in eye gaze direction to the mother after an explicit signal for attention was registered as a positive reaction for strategy D. It is expected that the number of positive reactions will increase with time.

LANGUAGE INPUT TO THE DEAF AND HEARING CHILDREN

Before turning to the research questions, we present the necessary background information on the language input that the deaf mothers offer to their children. As Table 14.1 shows, at 0;11 the deaf children are offered predominantly simultaneously signed and spoken utterances, some SLN, and hardly any Dutch.

The mother of Jonas, Mark, and Laura addresses her hearing child, Jonas, mainly in Dutch or offers him simultaneously signed and spoken (with use of voice) input; no SLN is offered to him at this age. This pattern can also be observed with the mother of Alex, although the percentages of Dutch and simultaneous communication do not differ as much as with Jonas's mother. Sander's mother offers him slightly more simultaneous communication than Dutch, and

TABLE 14.1

Percentages of NL, SLN, and SC Utterances in the Input of the Deaf Mothers to the Children at Ages 0;11 and 1;11

	0;11			1;11		
Mother of	*NL*	*SLN*	*SC*	*NL*	*SLN*	*SC*
Laura	2	26	72	0	41	59
Mark	3	35	62	3	41	55
Jonas	70	0	30	19	3	78
Sander	45	2	54	11	5	84
Alex	59	0	41	33	5	63

also some SLN. At the age of 1;11 simultaneous communication has become the predominant form of address with all children, although more so with the hearing children. The deaf children are offered signs (with or without simultaneous mouthing) at least 97% of the time, and the hearing children at least 68%; for these utterances one would also expect the hearing children to look up at their mothers, even though it may be the case that hearing children are more focused on the spoken input (Mayberry, 1976). For all children at both ages it was established that an average 75% of all signed utterances was seen.

RESEARCH QUESTIONS

Attentional Strategies Used by the Mothers

The first question was whether deaf mothers attract their children's attention *explicitly* less often as the child grows older. Table 14.2 shows that the use of nonexplicit strategies A and B (where the mother waits until the child looks up and where she starts signing and/or talking while the child is not looking) increases significantly over time for all children, compared to the use of the explicit strategies C and D, where signs are dislocated and the child's attention is actively sought. This is mainly due to an increase in the number of utterances per turn of the mothers, such as when the child is looking at the mother for the first utterance within a turn, and while the child is still looking, the mother produces another utterance.

Change in Use of Strategies Over Time

The next question we addressed was whether there is a change over time in the use of strategies by the deaf mothers related to the hearing status of the children.

TABLE 14.2

Percentage and (Number of Occurrences) of Strategies A + B Versus Strategies
C + D Used by the Deaf Mothers With All Children, at Ages 0'11 and 1;11

Age of the Children	Nonexplicit A + B	Explicit C+ D
0;11	62 (205)	38 (90)
1;11	76 (388)	24 (136)

With the deaf children there is a shift from strategy B (mothers signs while child is not looking—Laura) and strategy C (dislocation—Mark) to the use and increase of strategy A (wait for child to look up). Among the hearing children we found that, with Jonas and Alex, the mother starts signing/talking when the child is not looking (B) at both ages; this also happens with Sander at age 0;11, but at age 1;11 his mother waits until he looks up at her (strategy A). With all three hearing children the use of strategy A increases.

Strategy Linked to One Particular Language

The third research question asked whether the use of a particular strategy is related to language choice, that is, whether a particular strategy is significantly linked to a particular language? With the deaf children, there is no difference in the use of strategies per language; in other words, the different strategies are used indiscriminatively with Dutch, SLN, or simultaneous communication. This is also true for the mothers of the hearing children; the mothers use strategy B (i.e., giving linguistic information when the child is not looking), both with Dutch and simultaneous communication equally.

Attentional Behavior of the Deaf and Hearing Children

The final question we addressed was whether the attentional behavior of the deaf children develops differently from that of the hearing children. As far as the spontaneous looks at the mothers are concerned, there is considerable individual variation, as shown in Table 14.3. Although all children show an increase in the number of times they look up spontaneously at their mothers, there is a significant difference between Laura, Mark (both deaf), and Sander (hearing) on the one hand, and Jonas and Alex (hearing) on the other. Jonas and Alex do not change their attentional behavior as they grow older, even though their mothers' language input does change (see Table 14.1). The fact that their mothers use their voices in simultaneous utterances cannot be the main reason behind Jonas and

TABLE 14.3
Number of Spontaneous Looks by All Children ($n = 5$) at Ages 0;11 and 1;11

Child	0;11	1;11
Laura	15	32
Mark	14	52
Jonas	19	20
Sander	9	40
Alex	10	13

Alex's attentional behavior, because Sander's mother also always uses her voice in simultaneously signed and spoken utterances. Thus Sander would have the same access to (spoken) linguistic information as the two other hearing children, yet he shows the same spontaneous attentional behavior as the two deaf children, Laura and Mark, who are dependent on visual information. We come back to this later in the chapter.

When the mother started signing and/or talking while the child was not looking at her (strategy B), we expected both the deaf and the hearing children to respond by looking up at their mothers. Table 14.4 shows the children's responses. As can be seen, this strategy is used less with the deaf children than with the hearing children, but the deaf children react significantly more often ($p \leq 0.01$; $df = 3$; $X^2 = 11.345$).

The fact that each hearing child responds relatively little to his mother beginning to sign and/or talk while he is not looking at her raises the following question: When he does look up at his mother, is this more the case when the mother is simultaneously signing and speaking than when she is speaking only? Although at least 68% of the language input to the hearing children is offered with signs, we can see from Table 14.5 that there is no direct link between the response of the hearing children and the signed input offered by their mothers. Only for Jonas at age 0;11 does there seem to be a higher response to simul-

TABLE 14.4
Percentages of Positive Reactions to Strategy B; ( ) is Number of Occurrences of Strategy B

Age	Deaf Children	Hearing Children
0;11	48 (27)	39 (112)
1;11	73 (26)	33 (139)

TABLE 14.5
Percentages of Positive Reactions of the Hearing Children to Strategy B, for NL
and SC Utterances

Children	0;11		1;11	
	NL	*SC*	*NL*	*SC*
Jonas	35	63	23	32
Sander	57	46	33	32
Alex	25	37	38	29

taneously signed and spoken utterances than to Dutch utterances. At age 1;11 he shows the same visual response to Dutch and simultaneous utterances, as do Sander and Alex. In this respect, then, there is no difference among the hearing children.

CONCLUSIONS

As the children grow older, the deaf mothers change their attentional strategies. With Laura (D), Mark (D), and Sander (H) there is less need to attract their visual attention because they look up spontaneously more often at the age of 1;11. Jonas (H) and Alex (H) do not show this attentional pattern; however, their mothers make use of their attention (once obtained, and in whatever manner) to expand the number of utterances per turn. This is also true for the deaf twins and Sander, although to a lesser extent.

The attentional behavior of Sander is especially interesting; although his mother offers him linguistic input comparable to the input offered by the other deaf mothers to their hearing children, he shows attentional behavior similar to the deaf children, Laura and Mark. This may well be due to the fact that in his extended family he has more opportunity to encounter SLN than the other hearing children. Although one might expect the same for Jonas, the fact that he has a hearing father might influence his language development to such an extent that he is more focused on spoken input (see Mayberry, 1976), despite the fact that he has two deaf siblings with whom signing is used predominantly.

When the mothers actively try to attract the attention of their children, the deaf children react positively more often than the hearing children at 0;11 and 1;11. With the hearing children, no relation was found between positive reactions to an attentional strategy and the language used by their mothers; they did not give more visual attention to signing. These findings confirm Mayberry's, that hearing children focus on the oral language when both signing and speech is used by deaf parents. The attentional behavior of the deaf children seems to develop along different lines than that of the hearing children; they check back more with their mother, which suggests that they are more alert to the fact that their conversational partner might offer them signed input. This is also true for one hearing child. Because of the observed variation, hearing status of the child alone cannot explain attentional behavior, nor can the form of linguistic input. Sociolinguistic factors, including extended family hearing status and language use, may also play a part. This should be the focus of future research.

REFERENCES

Bogaerde, B. van den, & Mills, A. E. (1994). Word order in language input to children: SLN or Dutch. In M. Brennan & G. H. Turner (Eds.), *Word-order issues in sign language working papers* (pp.133–157). England: University of Durham, International Sign Linguistics Association, Deaf Studies Research Unit.

Coerts, J. (1992). Nonmanual grammatical markers: An analysis of interrogatives, negations and topicalisations in SLN. Unpublished doctoral dissertation, University of Amsterdam.

Everitt, B. S. (1986). *The analysis of contingency tables.* London: Chapman & Hall.

Harris, M., Clibbens, J., Tibbitts, R., & Chasin, J. (1987). Communication between deaf mothers and their deaf infants. In P. Griffiths, A. Mills, & J. Local (Eds.), *Proceedings of the Child Language Seminar* (pp. 227–240). England: University of York.

Kyle, J. G., Ackerman, J., & Woll, B. (1987). Early mother-infant interaction: Language and pre-language in deaf families. In P. Griffiths, A. Mills, & J. Local (Eds.), *Proceedings of the Child Language Seminar* (pp.217–226). England: University of York.

Mayberry, R. (1976). An assessment of some oral and manual language skills of hearing children of deaf parents. *American Annals of the Deaf, 121*, 507–512.

Pimiä, P. (1990). Semantic features of some mouth patterns in Finnish Sign Language. In S. Prillwitz & T. Vollhaber (Eds.), *Current trends in European sign language research* (pp. 115–118). Hamburg: Signum.

Schermer, T. M. (1990). *In search of a language. Influences from spoken Dutch on Sign Language of the Netherlands.* Delft: Eburon.

Siple, P. (1978). Visual constraints on sign language communication. *Sign Language Studies, 19*, 95–110.

Swisher, M. V. (1991). Conversational interaction between deaf children and their hearing mothers: The role of visual attention. In P. Siple & S. D. Fischer (Eds.), *Theoretical issues in sign language research, Vol. 2: Psychology* (pp.111–134). Chicago: The University of Chicago Press.

15 Language Development by Deaf Children With Cochlear Implants

Jane A. Coerts
*University of Amsterdam and University of Nijmegen,
The Netherlands*

Anne E. Baker*
University of Amsterdam, The Netherlands

Paul van den Broek
University of Nijmegen, The Netherlands

Jan Brokx
Instituut voor Doven, St. Michielsgestel, The Netherlands

In 1990, two deaf children aged 5 years received cochlear implants.[1] These were the first such operations in the Netherlands on young children. Prior to that, a number of cochlear implant operations had been carried out, but exclusively on adolescents and adults. The two children involved had become deaf at the age of 2;9 as a result of meningitis. The implantation was carried out 2 years and 3 months later. Before the operation, both children had a hearing loss greater than a PTA of 140 dB SPL in the better ear; after activation of the speech processor this

---

*Formerly Mills.

[1]There are different types of cochlear implants on the market. The children in this research project were implanted with a 22 channel Nucleus device (MSP-type). The cochlear implant bypasses the damaged middle and inner ear and stimulates the auditory nerve directly. Before the central nervous system can process the auditory information it must be analyzed and decoded. A microphone located behind the ear transforms the sound waves into an electrical signal that is then modulated by a speech processor worn externally. This modulated signal is then conducted to a transmittor that is also located behind the ear. This is then picted up via induction by a subcutaneous receiver, which in turn transmits the signal to the electrodes (22 in this case) located in the cochlea. These electrodes stimulate the auditory nerve so that sound is perceived.

loss was reduced to a PTA of approximately 50 dB SPL.[2] It is to be expected that the increase in access to auditory information will have a positive effect on the development of the children's spoken language.

SUBJECTS, DATA COLLECTION, AND TRANSCRIPTION

In order to investigate the effects of the increase in access to auditory information on the development of spoken Dutch, the spontaneous language production of the children, both girls, was videorecorded over a period of 2 years. The conversation partner for one girl (child 1) was her father, for the second girl (child 2), her mother. Seven videorecordings were made with each child: two before activation of the speech processor and five afterwards. The recordings prior to activation were used to determine the baseline in the language development of the children in the following areas: intelligibility, morphology, syntax, semantics, and pragmatics.[3] The videorecordings after activation were used to determine whether development took place in these areas and, if so, the type and rate of development. Results that are presented here were taken from four recordings: one immediately prior to activation and one each at 7, 12, and 18 months postactivation. In total, 100 analyzable utterances in spoken Dutch were transcribed from each recording; if this number was not achieved within 20 minutes of recording, transcription stopped at this point.[4] Two transcribers transcribed each recording.

According to recent research, it appears that most children who become deaf in an early stage of their language development not only continue to develop spoken language, but also develop a knowledge of a sign language. They therefore become, to a certain extent, bilingual. Research with bilingual hearing children has shown that if a number of conditions are fulfilled, the development of one spoken language does not have a negative influence on the development of a second spoken language (Appel & Muysken, 1987; Cummins, 1984). Research with bilingual deaf adolescents in England has shown that those who were further developed in British Sign Language (BSL) in general were also further developed in English (Conrad, 1979). Thus there appears to be a relationship between the development of a sign language and the development of a spoken language.

---

[2]It is assumed that there is a functional difference with respect to the perception of speech between children with a cochlear implant and children without a cochlear implant with comparable hearing losses. This difference is the result of the limitations of the speech processor with respect to the transmission of speech cues necessary for the understanding of speech. Therefore, it is estimated that the speech perception of cochlear-implanted children with an aided threshold of 50 dB is comparable to that of hard-of-hearing children without an implant with a hearing loss of approximately 80 dB when fitted with conventional hearing aids.

[3]A description of the phonological development of the children will be reported at a later date.

[4]This procedure is in accordance with the conventions used for a language profiling instrument for spoken Dutch: GRAMAT (Bol & Kuiken, 1990). This instrument will be used for the analysis of morphology and syntax.

Both children in this research produced utterances in Sign Language of the Netherlands (SLN) as well as Dutch, although the school and home language environment for both children was predominantly oral. It was therefore decided to also transcribe all SLN utterances produced by the children within the transcription limits described earlier; a native signer assisted with the transcription where necessary. This decision was taken in order to give a complete picture of the communicative development of the children pre- and postactivation.

The number of utterances in Dutch and SLN which the children produced in each recording are set out in Table 15.1. It can be seen that the children produced 100 analyzable utterances in Dutch in each recording with the exception of the preactivation recording for child 1. The number of analyzable SLN utterances is smaller than the number of Dutch utterances in the postactivation period. This could be a result of the child making greater use of the increase in auditory information to produce more spoken language. However, it is also possible that this occurs under the influence of the increased emphasis on the production of spoken language from the part of the parents.

Table 15.1 creates the incorrect impression that the children produced utterances that consisted exclusively of spoken words or utterances exclusively in signs. However, a considerable proportion of the children's language production consisted of utterances in which signs and words were simultaneously produced. These utterances will be referred to as *simultaneous utterances*. The proportion of such utterances was on average 32% for child 1 and 49% for child 2. There was a considerable amount of lexical overlap in the simultaneous utterances; that is, the same proposition was expressed in both the spoken and the signed modality. It was therefore decided to consider a simultaneous utterance, for some analyses, as two separate utterances: a spoken and a signed utterance. This categorization was used for the analysis of intelligibility, morphology and syntax,

TABLE 15.1
Number of Analyzable Utterances in Dutch and SLN per Recording

Number of Months Pre- or Postactivation		Dutch	SLN
Child 1			
Preact.	0 m	21	74
Postact.	7 m	100	46
	12 m	100	48
	18 m	100	58
Child 2			
Preact.	0 m	100	101
Postact.	7 m	100	89
	12 m	100	41
	18 m	100	83

and semantics. The total number of utterances the children produced was therefore in fact less than the sum of the Dutch and SLN utterances as presented
separately in Table 15.1. For the pragmatic analysis, the utterances are split into
three categories: Dutch, SLN, and simultaneous, because there appeared to be a
relationship between category and language function (see later discussion).

All utterances of the adult partner were also transcribed. Like the children,
they produced Dutch, SLN, and simultaneous utterances, although the proportion
of SLN utterances was considerably smaller than that of the children.

ANALYSIS AND RESULTS

Intelligibility

As a result of the increase in access to auditory information, it is to be expected
that the intelligibility of the spoken utterances should increase. For this purpose
the percentage of intelligible spoken utterances was calculated for each recording. This was also calculated for sign utterances in order to give a complete
picture of the language development. An utterance was considered intelligible if
all words and/or signs in the utterance could be assigned meaning by the adult
conversational partner or the transcribers. The results of this analysis, presented
in Table 15.2, show that the intelligibility of utterances in spoken Dutch increases
for both children over the postactivation period, with the children achieving a
high rate of intelligibility in the last recordings. The intelligibility level of the
sign utterances remains at a high level.

TABLE 15.2
Percentages of Intelligible Utterances in Dutch and SLN

Number of Months Pre- and Postactivation		Dutch	SLN
Child 1			
Preact.	0 m	63	100
Postact.	7 m	80	99
	12 m	93	96
	18 m	94	96
Child 2			
Preact.	0 m	72	100
Postact.	7 m	70	100
	12 m	92	100
	18 m	95	99

Morphosyntactic Development

The children's morphosyntactic development—that is, the development of morphology and syntax considered together—was determined using two quantitative measures: the mean length of utterance (MLU) and the mean length of the five longest utterances (MLUL). Both measures were calculated on the basis of the number of morphemes in the utterance. According to Wells (1985), the MLU and MLUL reflect the general level of morphosyntactic development in spoken languages up to an approximate age of 3;6. Whether this is true for sign languages as well is not yet established. The measures MLU and MLUL allow development to be measured within one language. It is not correct to compare these measures across languages because, whether spoken or signed, languages vary considerably in their morphological structure (Hickey, 1988). Therefore, it is not possible to compare the MLU and MLUL measures of spoken Dutch with those of SLN.

Table 15.3 presents the results for MLU and MLUL in Dutch and SLN. For Dutch both children show a clear increase in MLU over the whole postactivation period. There is a temporary drop in the recording at 7 months (child 1) and 12 months (child 2) postactivation. The total picture is that of clear morphosyntactic development for Dutch. In SLN, child 1 shows no increase in MLU(L). This could indicate that child 1 is not developing in morphosyntax. Child 2 shows a clear increase at 18 months, which might indicate that her knowledge of SLN is still increasing. A more detailed analysis of the morphosyntactic development in SLN, presented later, supports this interpretation.

TABLE 15.3
Development of MLU and MLUL for Dutch and SLN

Number of Months Pre- and Postactivation		MLU		MLUL	
		Dutch	SLN	Dutch	SLN
Child 1					
Preact.	0 m	1.14	1.28	1.60	3.00
Postact.	7 m	1.04	1.48	1.80	3.20
	12 m	1.25	1.40	2.40	2.60
	18 m	1.69	1.22	4.20	2.00
Child 2					
Preact.	0 m	1.13	1.32	2.40	3.00
Postact.	7 m	1.63	1.30	3.00	2.80
	12 m	1.31	1.34	3.00	2.20
	18 m	1.87	1.84	5.00	4.40

TABLE 15.4
Morphosyntactic Development of Dutch

Number of Months Pre- and Postactivation		Chronological Age	Phase 1 1;0 - 1;6	Phase II 1;6 - 2;0	Phase III 2;0 - 2;6
Child 1					
Preact.	0 m	5;3	+		
Postact.	7 m	5;10	+		
	12 m	6;3		+	
	18 m	6;9		+	
Child 2					
Preact.	0 m	5;4	+		
Postact.	7 m	5;11		+	
	12 m	6;4		+	
	18 m	6;10			+

The morphosyntactic development of Dutch was further analyzed using the language profiling instrument GRAMAT, a method of analysis for spontaneous language production with norms for Dutch-speaking children with a language production level between 1 and 4 years (Bol & Kuiken, 1987, 1988, 1990). The norms are based on 100 analyzable utterances. On the basis of such a sample it is possible to place a child in a developmental phase for morphosyntax at both the level of clause and phrase. The morphosyntactic structures the children use are entered on a profile sheet; the developmental level is determined according to the type of structures used and the frequency of occurrence.

The SLN utterances were analyzed on the basis of the GRAMAT profile for the purposes of convenience; a comparable profiling instrument is not yet available for SLN. From the results of this analysis it is not possible to place the child in a language developmental phase, but it does make it possible to chart the development of the child across time. With a small number of variables it is also possible to compare development in Dutch and SLN, namely, where this is related to clause complexity.

Table 15.4 presents a summary of morphosyntactic development in terms of the developmental phase the child is placed in on the basis of the profile for Dutch. Both children distinctly show development: child 1 from 12 months postactivation and child 2 from 7 months postactivation.

Both children began in Phase I during the preactivation recording, that is, the one-word phase. During this recording child 1 only produced utterances in terms of clause structure that were related to Phase I; she did, however, produce features at phrase and morphological level that came from Phases II and III. These were not frequent enough to justify her classification in a later developmental phase. Child 2 also produced structures from following phases and at all levels, but again with too low a frequency to justify a classification in Phase II.

Child 2 is clearly already further in her development of Dutch in the preactivation recording, and it is not surprising that she is in Phase II in the following recording, which is 7 months postactivation. Caution is necessary in interpreting this jump as being solely due to the cochlear implant.

From the recording at 7 months postactivation it can be seen that child 1 is still in Phase I; there was no perceivable development at any level. Child 2 is in Phase II and is also producing structures from Phases III and IV. Her development is clearly rapid at this point. One year after implantation both children are in Phase II. Child 1 shows development at clause level towards Phase III; child 2 is not clearly any further in her development than in the previous recording. In the last recording, at 18 months postactivation, child 1 is still in Phase II, although she is now producing structures at the phrase and morphological level of Phase III. Child 2 has moved into Phase III and is producing structures from Phases IV and V.

In summary, child 2 was slightly ahead of child 1 in her morphosyntactic development of Dutch at the beginning of the recordings, that is, at 0 months preactivation. She remains ahead of child 1 and develops at a faster rate, taking 18 months to attain a level for which a hearing younger child takes 12 months. Child 1 is slower and takes 18 months for a 6-month development.

As discussed earlier, the SLN utterances were also analyzed using the GRAM-AT profile. During the preactivation recording both children produced predominantly one-sign utterances. They also produced utterances that were more complex: Both children produced 12 such utterances. The growth in complexity was assessed in terms of combinations of constituents rather than individual signs in accordance with the clause level analysis of GRAMAT. For example the constituent Subject can be realized using one or more than one sign (or word). In *I like cookies* three constituents are present, namely Subject (*I*) Verb (*like*) Object (*cookies*), with each constituent consisting of one word. In *The cookie monster likes chocolate cookies*, there are also three constituents, but here both the Subject and Object consist of more than one word.

In the recording 7 months postactivation both children produced several new structures at different levels, and the proportion of combinations of constituents increased (see Table 15.5). At 12 months postactivation neither child shows development in the frequency and variation in types of combinations at clause level. There is, however, an increase in the marking of negative utterances, assertions, and yes-no and question-word questions using nonmanual grammatical markers. The form and use of these markers in SLN is described in Coerts (1992b). It is striking that both children use these nonmanual markers in both spoken and signed utterances.

During the recording at 18 months postactivation child 1 shows no clear development, compared with the previous recording. Child 2 does clearly show development; she produces more utterances consisting of three constituents (see Table 15.5) and a greater variation in the use of grammatical marking.

Table 15.5 presents a survey of the percentage of utterances consisting of

TABLE 15.5
Development of Complexity in Dutch and SLN Expressed as a Percentage of
Analyzable Utterances per Language

Number of Months Pre- and Postactivation		2 Constituents		3 Constituents	
		Dutch	SLN	Dutch	SLN
Child 1					
Preact.	0 m	0	16	0	0
Postact.	7 m	0	24	0	2
	12 m	20	17	1	0
	18 m	24	22	4	0
Child 2					
Preact.	0 m	2	10	0	2
Postact.	7 m	25	16	3	1
	12 m	13	5	0	0
	18 m	22	31	7	8

more than one constituent in both Dutch and SLN. From this table it can be seen that at the beginning of the study both children are further in their development of SLN than Dutch in terms of number of constituents. In the first recording, both children produce more combinations of signed constituents than spoken constituents; child 1, in fact, only produces utterances of one constituent in Dutch.

Both children show a clear development in the complexity of their utterances in Dutch. Child 1 starts to produce combinations of two constituents from 12 months postactivation on and shows a clear increase in the number of spoken utterances with three constituents at 18 months postactivation. The development of child 2 is similar, but somewhat faster. Combinations of spoken constituents are already clearly evident at 7 months postactivation, and combinations with three constituents are proportionally more frequent at 18 months postactivation than those produced by child 1.

In SLN, only child 2 shows any development in terms of constituent complexity: the percentage of SLN utterances with two constituents generally increases over the four recordings, and at 18 months postactivation utterances with three constituents have become frequent. Child 1 does not show any clear development. This finding for both children agrees with the findings presented earlier for MLU(L) in SLN, which suggests that MLU(L) is an adequate global measure for morphosyntactic development in a sign language as well as a spoken language.

On the basis of the analysis using the measures MLU(L), the GRAMAT profile, and the number of constituents per utterance, it can be concluded that both children show a clear development in the morphosyntax of Dutch. The morphosyntactic development of child 2 is more pronounced than for child 1. Only child 2 shows any development in morphosyntax for SLN. This leads to the interesting conclusion that the rate of development in SLN does not have a negative effect on the development of spoken Dutch. It is possible that it, in fact, has a positive effect; that is, child 2 shows a more rapid development in spoken Dutch than child 1 because she continues to develop in SLN.

Semantic Development

According to research into the semantic development in children acquiring spoken languages, there appears to be a relationship between lexical growth and the structural complexity in the early phases. Children show a leap in semantic growth at the beginning of the phase where they produce utterances with two constituents, and again when they start to produce utterances with three constituents (Lenneberg, 1967). In the latter phase, children also show marked lexical growth in those words that have a predominantly grammatical function, so called *function words* (Besien, 1985; Schaerlaekens & Gillis, 1987).

The lexical growth of the cochlear implant children was determined on the basis of the development in the number of different words or signs (types) produced per recording. These were further divided into two categories: the number of types of function word/sign and the number of types of content word/sign. In the category *content types* the following were included: nouns, lexical verbs, adjectives, adverbs and numerals. *Functions types* included articles, prepositions, connectives, copula, auxiliaries and all pronouns.

On the basis of the results of the morphosyntactic analysis, in particular the results in Table 15.5, it is to be expected that child 1 will show a spurt in lexical growth for Dutch at 12 months postactivation (the beginning of the two-constituent phase) and again at 18 months (the beginning of the three-constituent phase). For child 2 this should be at 7 and 18 months postactivation. Both children should show a clear increase in the number of function words at 18 months postactivation. For SLN, only child 2 is expected to show a spurt in lexical growth, and that should be at 18 months postactivation (the beginning of the three-constituent phase); this should be accompanied by an increase in the number of function signs.

Table 15.6 presents the results of the analysis of the number of types of content and function words/signs in Dutch and SLN. It is not possible to compare the results for Dutch and SLN with each other, because fundamental differences in the structure of the languages lead to a much smaller number of function signs in SLN than function words in Dutch; SLN is a language that does not have the category article or copula, for example. The figures in the table allow only comparison across the recordings for each language separately.

Child 1 shows the predicted spurt at 18 months postactivation for both content and function words. There is no evidence of a spurt at 12 months. The figures

TABLE 15.6
Semantic Development for Dutch and SLN: Number of Content and
Function Types

Number of Months Pre- and Postactivation		Dutch		SLN	
		Content	Function	Content	Function
Child 1					
Preact.	0 m	21	2	28	4
Postact.	7 m	46	0	19	1
	12 m	45	2	19	1
	18 m	84	9	22	1
Child 2					
Preact.	0 m	46	7	26	2
Postact.	7 m	58	7	26	1
	12 m	63	10	16	2
	18 m	73	13	46	4

appear to suggest that this spurt took place earlier, at 7 months postactivation, but this would be an incorrect interpretation, because the absolute figures for the preactivation recording are based only on 21 analyzable utterances (see Table 15.1). Child 2 shows no evidence of a spurt at 7 or 18 months postactivation; her development is continuous. This suggests that the relationship between morpho-syntactic development and lexical growth is not as close as other research suggests.

In SLN, child 1 shows no development, which is in agreement with the general picture of stagnation in this language. Child 2 does appear to show a spurt at the beginning of the three-contituent phase, but this is partly the result of the relatively few SLN utterances produced in the recording at 12 months post-activation. In this recording child 2 showed an unexplained dip in the number of SLN utterances produced (see Table 15.1). Nevertheless, the number of content types at 18 months is considerably higher than in the recording at 7 months, which is based on a comparable number of utterances. Child 2 is clearly developing in SLN in general.

Pragmatic Development

The pragmatic development of the children was explored on the basis of two quite different analyses: visual attention of the children for the spoken utterances of the adult and the different types of turns produced by the children. Although these analyses are so dissimilar, both give insight into the quality of the interaction between the children and their parents.

In relation to the visual attention for the spoken utterances of the adult, it is to be expected that the children after implantation show an increase in their spontaneous visual attention for the Dutch utterances and for the spoken part of the simultaneous utterances.[5] The increase in auditory perception should mean that the children become aware that they are spoken to and therefore give visual attention in order to profit from speech reading. It is not assumed that the children can understand speech on the basis of auditory information alone, because they still have a definite hearing loss and because the speech processor is still limited with respect to the transmission of all characteristics necessary for the understanding of speech.

In order to determine the development in visual attention, each spoken utterance, whether an exclusively Dutch utterance or a spoken part of a simultaneous utterance, was scored as *seen* or *not seen*. An utterance was scored as seen even if only the last part was visually perceived. At this point attentional strategies used by the parents have not been considered in the analysis, although they are most probably highly relevant in determining the number of utterances seen by the child.

From Table 15.7, it can be seen that child 1 initially increases her visual attention for spoken utterances. At 18 months postactivation, there is an apparent drop in the amount of visual attention given to the Dutch utterances and no increase in the attention given to the spoken part of the simultaneous utterances. This might be the result of the activity in which parent and child were engaged during a large part of the recording, namely, looking at photographs. First, the child was clearly stimulated by the material to initiate a large part of the conversation (see following analysis) and therefore did not appear to pay so much attention to the adult's contributions. Second, the photographs themselves held her visual attention so that she seemed reluctant to shift the focus of her attention to her father. Child 2 shows an increase in visual attention for both Dutch and the spoken part of the simultaneous utterances, as was expected.

The visual attention of child 2 was already at a higher level for Dutch-only utterances in the preactivation recording than that of child 1. This might be the result of the attentional strategies used by the mother of child 2; further research is needed to support this interpretation.[6] It is also striking that child 1 has much better visual attention for the spoken part of simultaneous utterances than for Dutch-only utterances. This may be the result of the child more often giving spontaneous visual attention to the signed part of the simultaneous utterances

---

[5]An analysis was carried out for the visual attention given to SLN utterances, but because this was at a high level from the very first recording, the results are not further discussed here (Coerts, 1992a).

[6]See van den Bogaerde (1994) for the use of attentional strategies and the resulting visual attention in children of deaf parents.

TABLE 15.7
Percentages of Seen Utterances in Dutch Only and Spoken Part of Simultaneous
Utterances

Number of Months Pre- or Postactivation		Dutch	Simultaneous (Spoken Part)
Child 1			
Preact.	0 m	18	60
Postact.	7 m	44	65
	12 m	71	80
	18 m	48	78
Child 2			
Preact.	0 m	60	57
Postact.	7 m	88	86
	12 m	99	94
	18 m	94	100

when the signed part is articulated in the same visual field as the face of the adult. Again, further analysis is necessary to establish whether the higher level of visual attention for signed utterances in general improves the visual attention for simultaneous utterances.

The second aspect analyzed for pragmatic development was the communicative contribution of the child in the conversation. The communicative contribution was analysed in terms of turn type. Three types were distinguished: imitation turns, reaction turns, and initiation turns. These were analyzed for Dutch, SLN, and simultaneous communication. An *imitation turn* is defined as a repetition of the adult's utterance that immediately precedes the turn and which the child has seen (see previous analysis and footnote 5) or a repetition of the child's own preceding turn. Reaction and initiative turns are defined using the criteria set out by Heim (1989). A *reaction turn* is a turn in which the contextual focus is the same as that of the previous utterance of the adult, for example, answers to questions. An *initiation turn* is one in which a new topic is introduced or in which the current topic is expanded.

From previous research into the interaction between normally developing hearing children and adults, it appears that the number of initiation turns increases with the language ability of the child (Blank & Franklin, 1980). Heim (1992) has also shown a similar relationship between the development of communicative ability using augmentative and alternative communication forms (AAC) and the number of initiative turns produced by nonspeaking children with cerebral palsy. This was also related to a decline in the proportion of imitation turns. For the two children studied here, therefore, it is predicted that in total the number of initiation turns should increase and the number of imitation turns should drop. It is not clear that a specific prediction can be made for the

TABLE 15.8
Percentage of Turn Types per Recording

Number of Months Pre- or Postactivation		Imitation	Reaction	Initiative
Child 1				
Preact.	0 m	12	50	38
Postact.	7 m	26	55	19
	12 m	39	33	28
	18 m	13	36	51
Child 2				
Preact.	0 m	14	48	38
Postact.	7 m	15	43	42
	12 m	19	66	15
	18 m	16	42	42

Dutch-only turns, the SLN turns, or the simultaneous turns considered separately. The prediction will be tested for communicative ability in general.

Table 15.8 shows that child 1 has an initial increase in the percentage of imitation turns up to 1 year postactivation, after which there is a decline. The reaction turns decline over the period, whereas the initiation turns increase, with a dip in the first recording postactivation. This pattern is as predicted. Child 2 shows little change over the whole period. She begins with a low percentage of imitation turns and this remains. There is more or less an equal distribution across reaction and initiation turns, with the exception of the recording at 12 months postactivation, when she was more passive than usual due to illness. The fact that little change can be seen in child 2 would seem to be the result of the higher level of communicative ability at which she begins. It is to be expected that the percentage of imitation turns would further decrease as the children's language becomes more complex.

A closer analysis of the development of turn types in relationship to the communication mode (Dutch only, SLN, or simultaneous) indicates that both children over the whole period have the most initiative turns in simultaneous communication. Child 1 produces on average 48.5% of her initiation turns in simultaneous communication (as opposed to 24.5% in Dutch and 27% in SLN). Child 2 has on average 62.5% initiations in simultaneous communication (as opposed to 23.8% in Dutch and 13.8% in SLN). The assumption is that an initiation turn will be realized in the communication mode in which the child feels most comfortable, because an initiation requires a greater contribution on the part of the child. Apparently, at this point in the communicative development of these two children simultaneous communication—that is, utterances which are made up of both speech and sign—is the most accessible mode.

CONCLUSIONS AND INTERPRETATION
OF THE RESULTS

In summarizing the results for Dutch in both children, it can be said that the intelligibility of their spoken utterances increased over the period studied and that the morphosyntax and lexicon also developed over the whole period. The development of visual attention for spoken utterances of the adult was evident for child 2 over the whole period, but for child 1 only until 12 months postactivation; the figures for 18 months were possibly influenced by the predominant activity during that recording. In SLN, child 1 showed no development over the period studied, whereas child 2 showed clear development in both morphosyntax and lexicon. The communicative contribution of child 1 changed with a decrease in imitations and an increase in the percentage of initiation turns. Child 2 showed no change, but she began with a low percentage of imitation turns.

The development in spoken Dutch can be attributed, at least in part, to the increase of auditory information as a result of the cochlear implantation. However, two other factors must be taken into consideration when interpreting the size of the effect: natural maturation and the knowledge of the second language, SLN. It could certainly be expected that the children would show development in morphosyntax and lexicon in Dutch without implantation as a result of maturation, but the question is whether this would have taken place at the same rate. Without the possibility of comparing these children with deaf children of the same age but with no implantation, it is impossible to evaluate more precisely the influence of implantation on the development of the spoken language.

It is also possible that the knowledge of SLN has a positive influence on the process and rate of development of spoken Dutch. It is often thought that bilingualism is an unusual language-learning situation and that the bilingual child necessarily must have problems in language development. This biased view is predominant in those parts of the world where most people are monolingual, that is, use one language in their daily lives. In fact, the majority of the world's population is bi- or even multilingual and shows no problems in the development of the languages spoken, unless one of these languages is socially suppressed. For the two children studied here, the level of language development in SLN was higher at the beginning of the study than their level of spoken Dutch, on the basis of morphosyntactic complexity. This was the case even though both children have a predominantly oral language environment. The development of a sign language was not impeded by any physical handicap, whereas the children's deafness was a barrier for their development of Dutch. It is possible that initially both children used their knowledge of SLN alongside their increased auditory possibilities to acquire spoken Dutch. Two observations—first that child 2 developed in SLN during the whole period under study, and second, that child 2 developed more rapidly in spoken Dutch than child 1—suggest that child 2 continues to use her SLN knowledge for her development of spoken Dutch. It is certainly the case that her knowledge of SLN does not negatively influence her development in spoken Dutch.

In conclusion, it can be stated that, on the basis of our research into the language development of two children with cochlear implants, it is difficult to exactly determine the contribution of the factors Increased Auditory Possibilities, Natural Maturation, and Knowledge of SLN on the spoken language development of both children. All factors probably play a part. The use of two control groups consisting of children with hearing losses comparable to those of the implanted children pre- and postactivation is necessary to gain more insight in the precise contribution of the cochlear implant on the one hand and natural maturation on the other. In order to establish the role of knowledge of SLN in the development of spoken Dutch, it is necessary to describe the total language development of children with cochlear implants, instead of solely their spoken language development. The research described in this chapter can be seen as a first step in this direction. Contrary to popular beliefs of researchers in the cochlear-implant field, knowledge of a sign language does not seem to be a factor that impedes the development of a spoken language. More detailed analyses of the total language development of children with cochlear implants should lead to more insight into the extent to which knowledge of one language can contribute to knowledge of another.

ACKNOWLEDGMENTS

This study is part of a larger project on the language perception and production of young deaf children with cochlear implants carried out by the Department for General Linguistics of the University of Amsterdam, the University Hospital of Nijmegen, and the Institute for the Deaf in Sint Michielsgestel. We are grateful to the University of Amsterdam and the Mgr. van Overbeekstichting for their financial support of this study. We also wish to thank the following students of the Department of General Linguistics of the University of Amsterdam for their important contributions to this study: Jane Ayal, Marta Balboa, Françoise Pauluis, Madeleine Peters, Gerti Rijpma, Hilda Schouten, Jeanette Stronks, and Karin Veeneman.

REFERENCES

Appel, R., & Muysken, P. (1987). *Language contact and bilingualism.* London: Edward Arnold.

Besien, F. van (1985). *Kindertaal. De verwerving van het Nederlands als moedertaal.* Amersfoort: Acco.

Blank, M., & Franklin, E. (1980). Dialogue with preschoolers: A cognitively-based system of assessment. *Applied Psycholinguistics, 1,* 127–150.

Bogaerde, B. van den (1994). Attentional strategies used by deaf mothers. In I. Ahlgren, B. Bergman & M. Brennan (Eds.), *Perspectives on sign language usage. Papers from the 5th International*

Symposium on Sign Language Research (Vol. 2, pp. 305–317). Durham, England: University of Durham, Deaf Studies Research Unit.

Bol, G., & Kuiken, F. (1987). Development of morphosyntax in Dutch children from one to four years old. *Belgian Journal of Linguistics, 2,* 93–107.

Bol, G., & Kuiken, F. (1988). *Grammaticale analyse van taalontwikkelingsstoornissen* [Grammatical analysis of language development disorders]. Unpublished doctoral dissertation, Institute for General Linguistics, University of Amsterdam, The Netherlands.

Bol, G., & Kuiken, F. (1990). *Handleiding GRAMAT. Methode voor het diagnostiseren en kwalificeren van taalontwikkelingsstoornissen* [GRAMAT manual. Method for the diagnosis and description of language development disorders]. Nijmegen, The Netherlands: Berkhout Nijmegen Uitgeverij.

Coerts, J. A. (Ed.) (1992a). *Het effect van een cochleaire implant op de taalontwikkeling van jonge dove kinderen* [The effect of a cochlear implant on young deaf children's language development]. Unpublished manuscript, University of Amsterdam, Institute for General Linguistics.

Coerts, J. A. (1992b). *Nonmanual grammatical markers. An analysis of interrogatives, negations and topicalisations in Sign Language of the Netherlands.* Unpublished doctoral dissertation, Institute for General Languistics, University of Amsterdam, The Netherlands.

Conrad, R. (1979). *The deaf school child: Language and cognitive function.* London: Harper & Row.

Cummins, J. (1984). *Bilingualism and special education: Issues in assessment and pedagogy.* Clevedon, England: Multilingual Matters.

Heim, M. (1989). *Kommunicatieve vaardigheden van niet of nauwelijks sprekende kinderen met infantiele encephalopathie: Een analyse van de kommunikatieve interaktie tussen niet-sprekende kinderen en hun dagelijkse konversatiepartners* [Communicative development of nonspeaking children with cerebral palsy: An analysis of the interaction between nonspeaking children and their daily interaction partners] (Final Report for the Prinses Beatrix Foundation). University of Amsterdam, Institute for General Linguistics.

Heim, M. (1992). Beurtwisseling in ondersteunde comminicatie [Turntaking in augmented communication]. *Tijdschrift voor Logopedie en Foniatrie, 64,* 100–107.

Hickey, T. (1988). Mean length of utterance and the acquisition of Irish. In G. Collis, A. Lewis, & V. Lewis (Eds.), *Proceedings of the Child Language Seminar* (pp. 217–226). York, England: University of York.

Lenneberg, E. H. (1967). *The biological foundation of language.* New York: Wiley.

Schaerlaekens, A., & Gillis, S. (1987). *De taalverwerving van het kind. Een hernieuwde oriëntatie in het Nederlandstalig onderzoek* [Language acquisition by children. A renewed orientation of research into the acquisition of Dutch]. Groningen: Wolters-Noordhoff.

Wells, G. (1985). *Language development in the pre-school years.* Cambridge, England: Cambridge University Press.

16 A Path to Literacy Through ASL and English for Deaf Children

Philip M. Prinz
San Francisco State University

Michael Strong
University of California, San Francisco

Marlon Kuntze
California School for the Deaf, Fremont

James Vincent
Jerry Friedman
Priscilla Poynor Moyers
Elliot Helman
San Francisco State University

Probably the single most important problem facing deaf children in the United States is the acquisition of the English language. For many years, failure in this area has been defined by poor written English skills and low reading levels. The reading level of deaf high school graduates in the United States continues to remain at the third- or fourth-grade level (Allen, 1986). However, the relationship between deafness and depressed levels of ability in English language and literacy is complex. The problem is not related to intellectual abilities because, as has been pointed out by educators and researchers in the field of deafness, the distribution of nonverbal intelligence among deaf persons is well within the average range recorded for hearing persons. In fact, when nonverbal, performance-type tests of cognitive ability are used to measure deaf persons' intelligence, there is no difference between deaf and hearing individuals in performance IQ (Braden, 1989, 1992; Furth, 1966; Vernon, 1967).

In a further attempt to unravel the complex relationship between deafness, language and literacy some researchers (see Nelson, Loncke, & Camarata, 1993) have postulated that higher academic performance specifically in terms of reading and language may be related to either: (a) the transfer of communication skills between deaf children of deaf parents and earlier exposure to ASL as a first

235

language; (b) the effects of educational approaches relying on some form of manual communication, which might lead to greater achievement in language and literacy; and/or (c) the connection between accessible learning environments and literacy developments. These hypotheses are briefly reviewed later.

Hearing Status of Parents and Deaf Students' Academic Performance

Not all deaf students are equally underachieving in school, even when degree of hearing loss is taken into account. For example, during the 1960s and 1970s a number of researchers compared the performance of children from deaf and hearing families. Their studies showed that deaf children of deaf parents tended to outperform deaf children of hearing parents in measures of academic achievement, communication skills, and social adjustment (Brasel, 1975; Corson, 1973; Meadow, 1968; Stevenson, 1964; Stuckless & Birch, 1966; Vernon & Koh, 1970), and that deaf parents seem better prepared than hearing parents to cope with deaf children and consequently provide better emotional and educational support (Corson, 1973).

Exposure to ASL and Academic Performance

It has been hypothesized that the superior performances of deaf children of deaf parents might be explained by their early exposure to natural sign languages (e.g., American Sign Language—ASL),[1] thus allowing them to acquire a first language according to developmental timelines. This first language base allows for easy communication with family and members of the Deaf community, thus facilitating and enhancing socialization and also providing a foundation from which to learn English as a second language. Although such an explanation is consistent with theories of social and language development, it has not been tested scientifically. There is, however, some recent evidence that earlier exposure to sign language during childhood results in a greater advantage for sign language acquisition (Mayberry & Eichen, 1991). The researchers in this study found that exposure to sign language prior to 13 years of age resulted in significant effects at all levels of linguistic structure, with greatest effects at the level of sign sentence formulation.

---

[1]American Sign Language is a formal, visual-gestural, rule-governed language, whose components consist of chereme combinations that form signs (rather than phoneme combinations that form words, as in spoken languages). The linguistic units of ASL consist of movements, shapes, and positions of specific body parts, including hands, arms, eyes, face, and head. The grammar of ASL is not derived from English, although it is influenced by it, given its coexistence as a minority language within the majority-language culture of North America. ASL has no written form. It should be distinguished from a number of artificial sign codes of English (such as Signing Exact English, known as SEE 2), which were developed as educational tools and are used in conjunction with spoken English (simultaneous communication).

SIGN LANGUAGE AND EDUCATIONAL ACHIEVEMENT

Since the widespread adoption in the United States during the 1970s of total communication programs for educating deaf children (where teachers speak concurrently with some form of English signing), a small number of researchers have attempted to demonstrate that educational approach might account for some of the variance in English literacy. Studies that compared total communication with oral programs tended to show superior academic results for the signing programs (e.g., Brasel & Quigley, 1977; Chasen & Zuckerman, 1976; Moores, Weiss, & Goodwin, 1978; Weiss, McIntyre, Goodwin, & Moores, 1975). The teachers' use of Signed English, SEE 1, SEE 2, and other forms of manually coded English systems have demonstrated positive impact on the English language development of deaf students (Bornstein & Saulnier, 1981; Brasel & Quigley, 1977; Crandall, 1978).

Attempts to isolate the effects of the different English signing systems that have been developed to represent English grammar, such as SEE 1, SEE 2, and Signed English (e.g., Luetke Stahlmann, 1989), have been largely inconclusive because it is difficult to find subjects who have been exposed consistently to one system, and also because it is difficult, if not impossible, for even skilled teachers to present these systems consistently and completely while speaking, and many deaf students are instructed in the form of pidgin signing or Englishlike signing (Kluwin, 1981; Marmor & Petitto, 1979; Maxwell & Bernstein, 1985; Strong & Charlson, 1987).

Because ASL rarely, if ever, plays a significant role in educational programs for deaf children, its effects have been only minimally tested. However, there are some studies of the use of ASL in the classroom (e.g., Goldberg & Bordman, 1975; Sallop, 1973; Stewart & Hollifield, 1988) that reveal the effectiveness of ASL in enhancing language comprehension and student comprehension of instructional materials. Morariu and Bruning (1984) investigated the influence of language modality and syntax on tests involving the free recall of meaningful passages. Students recalled ASL contexts better than English contexts in both the signed and print modalities. Furthermore, Stewart (1988) found that students comprehended manual-only presentation of ASL stories better than Signed English stories.

Hatfield, Caccamise, and Siple (1978) used story retelling tasks to test the relative competence of students who were bilingual in ASL and English. They found that proficiency in ASL corresponded to retelling ability in both languages. However, because the English versions were in manually coded English, one cannot conclude with confidence from this research that ASL skills are related to English abilities—the manual English used in the study included many ASL-like structures.

Stewart (1990) developed a demonstration total communication project with the goal of teachers becoming consistent in the role of modeling English and ASL. English was the primary language of classroom and ASL was used as an intervention tool to disambiguate discourse situations, facilitate comprehension of instructions, and enhance the meaning of English phrases. Preliminary evaluation of this program indicates that the use of ASL facilitated the acquisition of communication and English literacy skills.

With the recent gathering interest in the application of bilingual educational approaches for deaf children and the use of ASL to teach English (e.g., Grosjean, 1992; Johnson, Liddell, & Erting, 1989; Paul & Quigley, 1987; Strong, 1988, 1990), the question of the relationship between ASL proficiency and English literacy is especially relevant. As reported here earlier, only limited research has been performed to show that instruction in ASL facilitates English, or that knowledge of ASL is related to English literacy. Some advocates of a bilingual/bicultural approach stress the significance of the educational use of ASL by quoting second language acquisition theory on crosslinguistic transfer of skills (e.g., Cummins, 1979), the negative results obtained by alternative methods, and the superior performance of deaf children of deaf parents.

Language Input and Literacy Development

Some researchers have emphasized the connection between accessible learning environments and literacy, specifically, the role of social interaction in the individual's spoken and written language development (Bruner, 1977; Vygotsky, 1978). Related to this is the role of social interactionist theories in understanding literacy development in children (Cazden, 1988; Dyson, 1989; Garlon & Pratt, 1989; Heath, 1983; Ramsey, 1990; Schieffelin & Gilmore, 1986; Taylor, 1983; Tharp & Gallimore, 1988). The notion is that thought and intellectual development depend on language that is culturally and historically created through social interaction. Meaningful discourse, social interaction, and cultural dialogue appear to be essential for the development of literacy.

DESCRIPTION OF THE CURRENT STUDY

The current study comprises the first phase of a 4-year research project designed to investigate the relationship between American Sign Language (ASL) competence and English literacy in school-aged deaf students. The rationale for conducting such a study stems from the research that showed deaf children of deaf parents outperforming deaf children of hearing parents on a number of educational measures including reading levels. This finding led to the hypothesis that the children of deaf parents were benefiting from fluency in ASL. This hypothesis has never been confirmed or denied, and is particularly relevant in the light of current moves toward bilingual/bicultural models of education for deaf children and recommendations for greater use of ASL and deaf teachers in the classroom.

Specifically, in the current study the hypothesis that competence in ASL facilitates the acquisition of English literacy was tested by measuring gains in

TABLE 16.1
Subject Profile

Subject	Age	Sex	Parental Hearing	ASL	R/D
1	13;3	F	H[a]	L[b]	R[c]
2	12;3	F	D	H	R
3	12;3	M	D	H	R
4	12;3	F	H	L	R
5	12;11	M	H	L	D
6	11;11	F	D	H	D
7	11;7	F	D	H	D
8	12;7	F	H	H	R
9	12;9	M	H	L	D

[a]H = Hearing; D = Deaf
[b]L = Low ASL Fluency; H = High ASL Fluency
[c]R = Residential Student; D = Day Student

English literacy (reading and writing) and comparing it to proficiency in ASL. In order to control for the influence of cognitive ability on English literacy, IQ was also measured.

Subjects

The sample consisted of 6 girls and 3 boys with a mean age of 12;3. All participants exhibited severe to profound bilateral hearing losses (see Table 16.1). Five students were rated by teachers as "high" ASL users and four were rated as "low" ASL users. The sample included five residential students and four day students. The subjects participating in the research were randomly selected from deaf students attending the California School for the Deaf in Fremont (CSDF) with the only proviso being that they have no complicating mental or physical impairments. Parental consent was obtained prior to any testing, which was conducted after school hours and consisted of three measures: tests of ASL, English literacy, and cognitive abilities.

Methodology and Test Procedures

The ASL, English reading and writing, and cognitive measures are described in this section and in Table 16.2.

TABLE 16.2
Test Instruments

Instrument	Purpose	Source
ASL Test	Test productive grammatic competence in ASL	Prinz & Strong, 1993
The Woodcock-Johnson Psycho-Educational Test Battery-Revised (WJ-R)	Test English reading & writing	Woodcock & Johnson, 1990
Matrix Analogies Test-Short Form (MAT)	Test cognitive skills	Naglieri, 1985

ASL Test

In order to determine the influence of students' knowledge of ASL on English literacy, it was necessary to document their underlying linguistic competence in ASL. In the absence of any adequate ASL measures, an ASL Test (Prinz & Strong, 1993) was developed to assess basic competence in production of ASL. The test was used to assess competence in ASL grammar (e.g., indexing, subject-verb agreement, embedding, sign chaining) and the ability to use ASL classifiers in complex descriptions (a description of ASL grammatical structures is located in Appendix A). The test used an edited, 9-minute excerpt from a primarily nonverbal animated cartoon. The student was initially asked to view the entire cartoon. The story was then divided into 10 different episodic segments (ranging between 5 and 10 seconds in duration), which were replayed one by one to the student, who then was asked to describe what had happened in each segment. The student's story description was videotaped by a deaf researcher, who coded the grammatical structures according to a predetermined ASL checklist (see Appendix A). A second deaf researcher independently coded the grammatical structures, and interrater reliability was established at .91.

Assessment of Reading, Writing, and Cognitive Abilities

English literacy was assessed using the Woodcock-Johnson Psycho-Educational Test Battery, Revised (Woodcock & Johnson, 1990). In order to control for nonverbal intelligence, the Matrix Analogies Test (Naglieri, 1985) was administered. Both tests were adapted for administration to signing deaf children by presenting the instructions initially in ASL followed by Pidgin Signed English (PSE) for those students who indicated that they did not understand the instructions.

The Woodcock-Johnson Psycho-Educational Test Battery-Revised (WJ-R) (Woodcock & Johnson, 1990).   The WJ-R is a standardized test that is widely used in educational settings for measuring cognitive abilities, scholastic aptitudes, and achievement. The WJ-R was normed on individuals between the ages of 2 and 95 years and has a high reliability rating (median reliability coefficients for reading and writing clusters of .89 or above). Similarly, the concurrent validity figures range from .79 to .83. The WJ-R yields a wide range of scores including age and grade equivalents, percentiles and standard scores for individual subtests, and clusters of subtests that assess the same curriculum area (e.g., reading and writing). Additionally Compuscore, a computer scoring program, is available for the WJ-R. The Compuscore printout yields a full range of scores for each subtest and cluster as well as an analysis of discrepancies between ability and achievement. Subtests specifically selected from the Standard and Supplemental Batteries of the WJ-R are described in Appendix B.

Assessment of Cognitive Abilities: Matrix Analogies Test-Short Form (MAT) (Naglieri, 1985).   The Matrix Analogies Test (MAT), a nonverbal intelligence test, was selected to assess and rule out any significant cognitive problems in the participants in the study. It was selected because it has a broad North American standardization and researchers have found the MAT to be useful in predicting deaf children's achievement.

RESULTS

All of the participants in the study performed within the average range of intelligence on the (MAT). A two tailed t test was utilized to determine the significance of proficiency in ASL for performance in English literacy (reading and writing). Analysis of the data indicates there is evidence for a positive correlation between broad reading and writing achievement and fluency in ASL such that higher ASL users performed at a significantly higher level on English literacy tests (see Table 16.3). Broad reading is composed of letter-word identification and reading comprehension subtests. Broad writing encompasses dictation and writing samples subtests. A significance level of .10 ($p < .10$) was selected for the data analysis. A significant difference ($t = 2.83, p = .06, p < .10$) was found on broad reading achievement when comparing the performance of the high ASL users ($n = 5$) and the low ASL users ($n = 4$) on the reading subtests of the WJ-R (Woodcock & Mather, 1990) (mean score of 87 for the high ASL users versus 68.8 for the low ASL users). Similarly, a significant difference ($t = 1.51, p = .26, p < .10$) was found on broad writing achievement when comparing the performance of the high ASL users ($n = 5$) and the low ASL users ($n = 4$) on the writing subtests of the WJ-R (mean score of 89 for the high ASL users versus 69.2 for the low ASL users).

TABLE 16.3
Performance on English Literacy Tests and Fluency in ASL

	High ASL Users	Low ASL Users
Literacy Tests	Mean Score	Mean Score
Broad reading	87	68.8
t test on difference between 87 and 68.8 $t = 2.83^a$		
Broad writing	89	69.2
t test on difference between 89 and 69.2 $t = 1.51^b$		

$^a p < .10.$
$^b p < .10.$

DISCUSSION

Results of the current study indicate there is preliminary evidence for a significant correlation between broad reading and writing achievement and fluency in American Sign Language (ASL), suggesting that proficient ASL users perform at higher levels on English literacy tests. In previous studies, it has been demonstrated that cognitive capacities of deaf children without any additional sensory, motoric, or cognitive deficits are normal, and so, of course, are adequate for learning, memory, and language acquisition (Bellugi, 1991; Bonvillian, Charrow, & Nelson, 1973; Martin, 1991). Some researchers have argued further that deficits in achieved levels of language or educational performance may be more appropriately attributed to limitations in the availability of learning opportunities allowing for deafness (Nelson, Loncke, & Camarata, 1993). These researchers further argue that severe problems of linguistic deprivation of deaf children born into hearing families are caused by access difficulties, and that educational approaches should focus on lifting access barriers and emphasizing natural, self-directed language structure exploration in the child's first language and then, later, in a second language.

Some researchers have argued that total communication programs have created more appropriate communication environments, but that they are not adequate (Erting, 1992; Johnson, Liddell, & Erting, 1989). These researchers maintain the notion that only a natural language can function as a first-order, complex symbol system for deaf children. They also stress that social interaction with adults and peers fluent in natural sign language can provide deaf children with the symbolic and cognitive tools needed to learn the second-order symbolic processes in reading, writing, and engaging in meaningful discourse through English.

It has been previously hypothesized that with linguistic competence and efficient teacher-student interaction in a natural sign language, translation from the domain of everyday concepts to the domain of inschool concepts becomes possible. Translation from one language (i.e., sign language) to another language (i.e., written English) can be systematic. Meaningful discourse focused on history, science, literature and mathematics can occur. This is the current practice in Sweden, Denmark, Venezuela and Uruguay (Bergman, 1994; Davies, 1991; de Lujuan, 1994; Hansen, 1990; Wallin, 1994). Similar ideas have been advanced in the United States (Erting, 1992; Kannapell, 1974, 1978; Paul, 1988; Quigley & Paul, 1984; Stevens, 1980; Strong, 1988; Supalla, 1994; Woodward, 1978). However, prior to the present research there have been no systematic studies to adequately assess the relationship between American Sign Language and educational achievement—specifically, English literacy.

The current research represents the first phase of a 4-year study investigating the relationship between American Sign Language (ASL) competence and English literacy in school-aged deaf students. In the second phase of the research study, the relationship between ASL competence and English literacy will be examined both diachronically and synchronically over a 3-year time period.

Approximately 200 deaf participants between 8 and 15 years will be randomly selected from students attending the California School for the Deaf in Fremont, California. Parents of the participants will complete a Home Communication Survey providing information on communication and language behavior at home that will supplement formal testing. Specifically, the hypothesis that early competence in ASL facilitates the acquisition of English literacy will be tested by measuring gains in English literacy from the testing at Time One to the testing 1 and 2 years later and comparing them with ASL competence at Time One. The hypotheses that at a given point in time there is a positive relationship between ASL ability and English literacy among a group of deaf school children will be measured by comparing ASL competence and English literacy at each of the three testing times. In order to control for the influence of cognitive ability on English literacy, performance IQ will also be measured.

If ASL competence is found to be related to English literacy, it is also important to teachers, parents, and deaf children to know at what ages this relationship is strongest. One would expect that, as children get older, any correlation would diminish. This hypothesis will also be tested. Because a number of the participants will be expected to make significant gains in ASL competence between the first and subsequent testings, it is also to be expected that the correlation between ASL competence and English literacy will weaken over the 3-year period. Continued research on this topic will contribute to an understanding of the relationship between proficiency in a natural sign language and academic achievement in reading and writing. Additionally, this research will contribute to the further refinement of second language acquisition theories on crosslinguistic transfer of skills from a native language to a second language (Cummins, 1979), and theories of second-language learning and literacy (Wong-Fillmore, 1989a, 1989b). This information will assist educators in developing effective bilingual and second-language acquisition programs for deaf children.

ACKNOWLEDGMENTS

The present study was supported by a 4-year Field-Initiated Research Grant (No. HO23C30074) from the U.S. Department of Education, Office of Special Education and Rehabilitative Services. The project is cosponsored by the California School for the Deaf (CSD) in Fremont, CA. The authors would like to thank the students, parents, administrators, and teachers at CSD for their cooperation in implementing the study.

REFERENCES

Allen, T. (1986). Patterns of academic achievement among hearing impaired students: 1974 and 1983. In A. Schildroth & M. Karchmer (Eds.), *Deaf children in America* (pp. 161–206). Boston: Little Brown.

Bellugi, U. (1991). The link between hand brain: Implications from a visual language. In D. Martin (Ed.), *Advances in cognition, education, and deafness* (pp. 11–35). Washington, DC: Gallaudet University Press.

Bergman, B. (1994). Sign language in society: Part I. In C. Erting, R. Johnson, D. Smith, & B. Snider (Eds.), *The deaf way: Perspectives from the International Conference on Deaf Culture* (pp. 309–317). Washington, DC: Gallaudet University Press.

Bonvillian, J., Charrow, V., & Nelson, K. E. (1973). Psycholinguistic and educational implications of deafness. *Human Development, 16,* 321–345.

Bornstein, H., & Saulnier, K. (1981). Signed English: A brief follow-up to the first evaluation. *American Annals of the Deaf, 126,* 69–72.

Braden, J. (1989). Deafness as a natural experiment: A meta-analytic review of IQ research. In D. Martin (Ed.), *Second international symposium on cognition, education, and deafness: Working papers* (Vol. 1, pp. 42–60). Washington, DC: Gallaudet University Press.

Braden, J. (1992). Intellectual assessment of deaf and hard-of-hearing people: A quantitative and qualitative research synthesis. *School Psychology Review, 21,* 82–94.

Brasel, K. (1975). *The influence of early language and communication environments on the development of language in deaf children.* Unpublished doctoral dissertation, University of Illinois.

Brasel, K., & Quigley, S. (1977). The influence of certain language and communication environments in early childhood on the development of language in deaf individuals. *Journal of Speech and Hearing Research, 20,* 95–107.

Bruner, J. (1977). Early social interaction and language development. In H. Schaffer (Ed.), *Studies in mother-child interaction* (pp. 271–289). New York: Academic Press.

Cazden, C. (1988). *Classroom discourse.* Portsmouth, NH: Heinemann.

Chasen, B., & Zuckerman, W. (1976). The effects of total communication and oralism on deaf third-grade "rubella" students. *American Annals of the Deaf, 121,* 394–402.

Corson, H. (1973). *Comparing deaf children of oral deaf parents and deaf children using manual communication with deaf children of hearing parents on academic, social, and communicative functioning.* Unpublished doctoral dissertation, University of Cincinnati.

Crandall, K. (1978). Inflectional morphemes in the manual English of young hearing impaired children and their mothers. *Journal of Speech and Hearing Research, 21,* 372–386.

Cummins, J. (1979). Linguistic interdependence and the educational development of bilingual children. *Review of Educational Research, 49,* 222–251.

Davies, S. (1991). Bilingual education of deaf children in Sweden and Denmark: Strategies for transition and implementation,. *Sign Language Studies, 71,* 169–195.

de Lujan, M. (1994). Early intervention with deaf children: A bilingual experience. In C. Erting, R. Johnson, D. Smith, & B. Snider (Eds.), *The deaf way: Perspectives from the International Converence on Deaf Culture* (pp. 122–137). Washington, DC: Gallaudet University Press.

Dyson, A. (1989). *Multiple worlds of child writers: Friends learning to write.* New York: Teachers College Press.

Erting, C. (1992). Deafness and literacy: Why can't Sam read. *Sign Language Studies, 75,* 97–112.

Furth, H. (1966). *Thinking without language: Psychological implications of deafness.* New York: The Free Press.

Garton, A., & Pratt, C. (1989). *Learning to be literate: The development of spoken and written language.* Cambridge, MA: Basil Blackwell.

Goldberg, J., & Bordman, M. (1975). The ESL approach to teaching English to hearing-impaired students. *American Annals of the Deaf, 120,* 22–27.

Grosjean, F. (1992). The bilingual and the bicultural person in the hearing and in the deaf world. *Sign Language Studies, 77,* 307–320.

Hansen, B. (1990). Trends in the progress towards bilingual education for deaf children in Denmark. In S. Prillwitz & T. Vollhaber (Eds.), *Sign language research and application* (pp. 51–62). Hamburg: Signum.

Hatfield, N., Caccamise, F., & Siple, P. (1978). Deaf students' language competency: A bilingual perspective. *American Annals of the Deaf, 123,* 847–851.

Heath, S. (1983). *Ways with words.* New York: Cambridge University Press.

Johnson, R., Liddell, S., & Erting, C. (1989). *Unlocking the curriculum: Principles for achieving access in deaf education* (Working Paper 89–3). Washington, DC: Gallaudet University, Gallaudet Research Institute.

Kannapell, B. (1974). Bilingual education: A new direction in the education of the deaf. *The Deaf American, 26,* 9–15.

Kannapell, B. (1978). Linguistic and sociolinguistic perspectives on sign systems for educating deaf children. In F. Caccamise & D. Hicks (Eds.), *ASL in a bilingual, bicultural context: The proceedings of II. NSSLRT* (pp. 219–232). Silver Spring, MD: National Association of the Deaf.

Kluwin, T. (1981). The grammaticality of manual representations of English in classroom settings. *American Annals of the Deaf, 126,* 417–421.

Luetke Stahlmann, B. (1989, March). *An investigation of the English language abilities of hearing-impaired students exposed to various instructional languages and systems.* Paper presented at the annual meeting of the American Education Research Association, San Francisco, CA.

Marmor, G., & Petitto, L. (1979). Simultaneous communication in the classroom: How well is English grammar represented? *Sign Language Studies, 23,* 99–136.

Martin, D. (Ed.). (1991). *Advances in cognition, education, and deafness.* Washington, DC: Gallaudet University Press.

Maxwell, M., & Bernstein, M. (1985). The synergy of sign and speech in signed communication. *Applied Psycholinguistics, 6,* 63–82.

Mayberry, R., & Eichen, E. (1991). The long-lasting advantage of learning sign language in childhood: Another look at the critical period for language acquisition. *Journal of Memory and Language, 30,* 486–512.

Meadow, K. (1968). Early manual communication in relation to the deaf child's intellectual, social, and communicative functioning. *American Annals of the Deaf, 113,* 29–41.

Moores, D., Weiss, K., & Goodwin, M. (1978). Early education programs for hearing-impaired children: Major findings. *American Annals of the Deaf, 123,* 925–936.

Morariu, J., & Bruning, R. (1984). Cognitive processing by prelingual deaf students as a function of language context. *Journal of Educational Psychology, 76,* 844–856.

Naglieri, J. (1985). *Matrix analogies test-Short form (MAT).* San Antonio, TX: The Psychological Corporation.

Nelson, K. E., Loncke, F., & Camarata, S. (1993). Implications of research on deaf and hearing children's language learning. In M. Marschark & M. Clark (Eds.), *Psychological perspectives on deafness* (pp. 123–151). Hillsdale, NJ: Lawrence Erlbaum Associates.

Paul, P. (1988). American Sign Language and English: A bilingual minority-language immersion program. *CAID - News 'n' Notes.* Washington, DC: Conference of American Instructors of the Deaf.

Paul, P., & Quigley, S. (1987). Using American Sign Language to teach English. In P. McAnally, S. Rose, & S. Quigley (Eds.), *Language learning practices with deaf children* (pp. 219–253). Boston: Little Brown.

Prinz, P., & Strong, M. (1993). Test of American Sign Language (ASL). Unpublished test. San Francisco: San Francisco State University, ASL Literacy Project.

Quigley, S., & P. Paul (1984). ASL and ESL? *Topics in Early Childhood Special Education, 3,* 17–26.

Ramsey, C. (1990, June). Language and literacy learning among mainstreamed deaf students. Paper presented at the annual meeting of the American Anthropological Association, New Orleans, LA.

Sallop, M. (1973). Language acquisition: Pantomime and gesture to signed English. *Sign Language Studies, 3,* 29–38.

Schieffelin, B., & Gilmore, P. (Eds.). (1986). *The acquisition of literacy: Ethnographic perspectives.* Norwood, NJ: Ablex.

Stevens, R. (1980). Education in schools for deaf children. In C. Baker & R. Battison (Eds.), *Sign language and the deaf community* (pp. 14–23). Silver Spring, MD: National Association of the Deaf.

Stevenson, E. (1964). A study of the educational achievement of deaf children of deaf parents. *California News, 80,* 143.

Stewart, D. (1988). *A model communication and language policy for total communication programs for the hearing impaired* (Occasional Paper No. 125). East Lansing: Michigan State University, Institute for Research in Teaching.

Stewart, D. (1990). Rationale and strategies for ASL intervention. *American Annals of the Deaf, 135* (3), 205–210.

Stewart, D., & Hollifield, A. (1988). A model for team teaching using ASL and English. *Perspectives for Teachers of the Hearing Impaired, 6,* 15–18.

Strong, M. (1988). A bilingual approach to educating deaf children: ASL and English. In M. Strong (Ed.), *Language learning and Deafness.* (pp. 113–129). Cambridge, England: Cambridge University Press.

Strong, M. (1990). Bilingualism and deaf children. In M. Garretson (Ed.), Eyes, hands, voices: Communication issues among Deaf people [Monograph]. *Deaf American, 40,* 125–127.

Strong, M., & Charlson, E. (1987). Simultaneous communication: Are teachers attempting an impossible task? *American Annals of the Deaf, 132,* 376–382.

Stuckless, E., & Birch, J. (1966). The influence of early manual communication on the linguistic development of deaf children. *American Annals of the Deaf, 111,* 425–460, 499–504.

Supalla, S. (1994). Equality in educational opportunity: The deaf version. In C. Erting, R. Johnson, D. Smith, & B. Snider (Eds.), *The deaf way: Perspectives from the International Conference on Deaf Culture* (pp. 427–435). Washington, DC: Gallaudet University Press.

Taylor, D. (1983). *Family literacy.* Portsmouth, NH: Heinemann.

Tharp, R., & Gallimore, R. (1988). *Rousing minds to life: Teaching, learning and schooling in social context.* New York: Cambridge University Press.

Vernon, M. (1967). Relationship of language to the thinking process. *Archives of General Psychiatry, 16,* 319–323.

Vernon, M., & Koh, S. (1970). Effects of manual communication on deaf children's educational achievement, linguistic competence, oral skills, and psychological development. *American Annals of the Deaf, 115,* 527–536.

Vygotsky, L. (1978). *Mind in society: The development of higher psychological processes* (Edited by M. Cole, V. John-Steiner, S. Scribner, & E. Souberman). Cambridge, MA: Harvard University Press.

Wallin, L. (1994). Sign language in society: Part II. In C. Erting, R. Johnson, D. Smith, & B. Snider (Eds.), *The deaf way: Perspectives from the International Conference on Deaf Culture* (pp. 318–330). Washington, DC: Gallaudet University Press.

Weiss, K., McIntyre, C., Goodwin, M., & Moores, D. (1975). Characteristics of young deaf children and intervention programs (Research Rep. No. 91). University of Minnesota, Research Development, and Demonstration Center in Education of Handicapped Children.

Wong-Fillmore, L. (1989a). Language learning in social context: The view from research in second language learning. In R. Dietrich & C. Graumann (Eds.), *Language processing in social context* (pp. 277–302). Amsterdam: Elsevier.

Wong-Fillmore, L. (1989b). Teachability and second language acquisition. In M. Rice & R. Schiefelbusch (Eds.), *The teachability of language* (pp. 311–332). Baltimore: Paul H. Brookes.

Woodcock, R., & Johnson, M. B. (1990). *Woodcock-Johnson psycho-educational battery-Revised.* Allen, TX: DLM Teaching Resources.

Woodcock, R., & Mather, N. (1990). WJ-R tests of achievement: Examiner's manual. In R. W. Woodcock & M. B. Johnson (Eds.), *Woodcock-Johnson psycho-educational battery—Revised.* Allen, TX: DLM Teaching Resources.

Woodward, J. (1978). Some sociolinguistic problems in the implementation of bilingual education for deaf students. In F. Caccamise & D. Hicks (Eds.), *ASL in a bilingual, bicultural context: The proceedings of II. NSSLRT* (pp. 120–133). Silver Spring, MD: National Association of the Deaf.

APPENDIX A

ASL Grammatical Structures

1. a. *Indexing.* This grammatical process assigns entities (objects, persons, animals, or ideas) to specific reference points in space. They can be present in the real world or in the mind of the signer (i.e., abstract). Indexing is sometimes referred to as "linguistic pointing." It uses the "G," "B," and "A" pronoun signs to indicate spatial agreement. The "G" handshape is used for person pronouns, the "B" handshape is used for possessive pronouns, and "A" for reflexive ("self") pronouns. Levels of indexing include real-world indexing where a child refers only to present entities. Semi-real-world indexing involves using present objects as substitutes for nonpresent objects. At higher levels the child begins to refer to nonpresent entities and consistently indexes for multiple referents. b. *Perspective shift.* In addition to indexing, a signer can "become" the person, animal, or thing being described (i.e., the signer takes on a "role).

2. *Verb agreement.* This is a grammatical process that shows the relationships between a verb and its arguments (i.e., nouns or noun phrases functioning as subjects and objects). Agreement between a verb and arguments can mark location (the verb moves from place X to place Y); person (the verb shows relationships between 1st person, 2nd person, and 3rd person; number (the verb agrees with an argument that is singular, dual, or plural).

3. *Morphological modification—nouns.* Through this process, noun signs are altered to show various adjective concepts (size, shape, and spatial arrangement). This process involves augmentation (enlarging) and reduplication of the sign (e.g., GLASS + BIG-GLASS). Specific facial expressions are also produced along with the sign modifications.

4. *Classifiers.* These are specific handshapes that function similar to pronouns. They represent the physical characteristics, meaning or function of the nouns that they represent. They combine with verbs to become part of a verb phrase or predicate. The three main types of classifiers include SASS (size and shape specifier), which shows the size and/or shape of an object (e.g., rectangular, cylindrical, thin) and is used in a motion/location verb. It generally is a classifier that is used with a sign that modifies or describes the object (e.g., BLUE SQUARE or METAL PIPE).

5. *Embedding.* This is a process that embeds or inserts signs within signs. An example of a verb embedded within another verb is a vehicle skidding on an icy road. An example of multiple morphological modulations within a single verb is signing to continually give something to each of many people where the sign GIVE is made with repeated circular motion and moves to each of three points in space successively.

6. *Sign chaining.* This is a process that allows the signer to maintain a specific focus during a segment of signing. Topic chaining allows the signer to hold (usually on the nondominant hand) a sign in place while signing a series of signs on the other hand. Verb chaining involves using the same classifier across a series of signs (e.g., holding the VEHICLE classifier while describing a series of activities in which a driver engages).

7. *Negated sentences.* This can be shown by a headshake or by a negative sign accompanied by a headshake.

8. *Questions.* This can be shown by specific facial expressions (e.g., eyebrow raise, body tilted forward).

ASL Production Checklist

1.   Indexing and Perspective Shift

_____ Shifts body to assume a different role
_____ Shift in perspective
_____ Shifts perspective to that of other character or role

2. Verb Agreement

_____ Location
_____ Person
_____ Number

3. Pluralization

_____ By repetition of same noun
_____ Through classifiers
_____ Through morphological modification of verb

4. Modifying Nouns

_____ By augmentation or diminuation
_____ Through facial expression

5. Classifiers

_____ DCL (Descriptive size and shape specifiers)
_____ LCL (Location or spatial relations)
_____ SCL/LCL (Verbs of motion)
_____ BPCL (Different body parts as verbs of motion)
_____ BCL (Mimetic recreation of action)
_____ CL (Hands as agent of action)
_____ ECL (Elements as verbs of action and location)

6. Embedding

_____ Verbs within verbs
_____ Multiple morphological modulations

7. Sign chaining

_____ Topic chaining
_____ Verb chaining

8. Negated Sentences

_____ Headshake
_____ Negative sign

9.   Question

_____   Eyebrow raise
_____   Body tilt forward

APPENDIX B

Selected Subtests of the Woodcock-Johnson Psycho-Educational Test Battery-Revised (Woodcock & Johnson, 1990).

Subtests specifically selected from the Standard Battery of the WJ-R included:

1. *Letter-word identification:* Matches pictographic representations of words within actual picture of an object and identifying isolated letters and words.

2. *Passage comprehension:* Matches of a picture a printed phrase and secondly reading a short passage and identifying a missing key word.

3. *Dictation:* The first part measures prewriting skills such as drawing lines and copying letters. The second section measures skill in providing written responses to a variety of questions requiring knowledge of letter forms, spelling, punctuation, capitalization, and word usage.

4. *Writing samples:* Measures skill in writing responses to a variety of requests involving various formats (e.g., sentence completion, picture description, paragraph completion). The written responses are then scored with respect to spelling, grammar, and the completeness of expression.

The following subtests were administered from the WJ-R Achievement Supplemental Battery:

1. *Reading vocabulary:* Measures skill in reading words and supplying appropriate meanings (synonyms and antonyms).

2. *Proofing:* Measures skill in identifying and correcting a mistake in a typewritten passage. These errors are in the areas of punctuation, capitalization, inappropriate word usage, or misspellings.

3. *Writing fluency:* Assesses skill in formulating and writing simple sentences within a 7-minute time frame. Each item consists of a stimulus picture accompanied by a set of three words.

4. *Spelling:* Uses spelling items from the Dictation and Proofing subtests. It targets skill in producing correct spellings and in detecting incorrect spellings in written passages.

5. *Usage:* Uses items from the Dictation and Proofing subtests. It assesses skill in producing grammatically correct language usage and in detecting usage errors in written passages.

17 Sentence Production Models: Explaining Children's Filler Syllables

Barbara Bernhardt
Carolyn E. Johnson
University of British Columbia

In the early stages of language development, some children supplement their words to fill out phrasal units with apparently meaningless fillers. These fillers are phonetically consistent morphemelike forms that are not semantically interpretable but are an integral part of the phrasal intonation contour. These forms have variously been designated, for example, *empty forms* (L. Bloom, 1973; Leonard, 1975), and *phonetically consistent forms* (Dore, Franklin, Miller, & Ramer, 1976). Although some take the shape of idiosyncratic polysyllables, such as Allison's [widə], reported by L. Bloom (1973), they are more typically underspecified vowels or syllabic nasals; hence, following Peters (1977), we will refer to them as *filler syllables*.[1]

Children who produce filler syllables where morphemes should be demonstrate that they have some knowledge of the existence of sentence constituents and their linear ordering. This is evidence that their competence is relatively greater than their performance indicates; there is something about the process of sentence production that needs to be explained. To date, there are no real models of children's sentence production; researchers who judge filler syllables to be a processing phenomenon (e.g., L. Bloom, 1973) do not describe how such fillers might arise during the production process.

In this chapter, we consider whether a well-developed adult sentence production model can account for children's filler syllables, specifically, the nasal filler syllables used by two preschool children with age-appropriate language comprehension but delayed language production. We briefly review Garrett's (1975,

---

[1]Peters (1977) used the term *filler syllable* to designate what she interprets to be "place-holders to fill out not yet analysed parts of a phrase" (p. 564; 1983, p. 72), as did Peters and Menn (1993).

1980, 1984) model, as the most familiar and widely cited sentence production model, and use it to motivate hypotheses about the possible loci and functions of children's filler syllables. We then test these hypotheses with data from the two children, who have severe phonological and language production disorders.[2] Our main objectives are to (a) determine how and at what point filler syllables might arise in sentence production, given an assumption of linguistic competence, and (b) evaluate Garrett's model in terms of its relevance to filler syllable data and child sentence production.

Sentence Production Models

The encoding of a message requires the interaction of conceptual, pragmatic, semantic, syntactic, and phonological components. The precise nature of these various components and how they relate in real time processing—whether serially or in a parallel interactive mode[3]—are the subject of output modeling debate. In serial models such as Garrett's (1975, 1980, 1984), Fromkin's (1971, 1993), Caramazza and Berndt's (1985) and Levelt's (1989), a conceptual message level encoding precedes linguistic sentence encoding, and both precede motor articulatory control levels of output. Because all serial models are essentially similar, we present here an overview of the main features of Garrett's model, the most widely examined serial model of sentence production, and then derive predictions for filler syllables.

Based primarily on his analysis of types of speech errors, Garrett's model has three major parts: (a) the message level, which responds to linguistic and non-linguistic facts and serves as input to the sentence processor; (b) the sentence processing level, which is the focus of the model; and (c) an articulatory level that controls motor realization of the phonological and phonetic representations (the output of the sentence processing component).

Sentence processing includes two main levels of representation: functional and positional. At the functional level, the first level in the processing sequence, lexical items are selected, specified for functional structures, and assigned to structural role positions. Thus, major class elements (nouns, verbs, adjectives) are assigned to phrasal roles. Speech errors supporting this level are meaning-based substitutions and whole-word exchanges between phrases. Encoding at the functional level appears to be "controlled in terms of verb-dominated groups of simple phrases," which are not specified for surface order.

The subsequent positional level of encoding involves "a transition from a logic-oriented to a pronunciation-oriented representation" (1984, p. 177). Seg-

---

[2]The use of production data from children with language disorders to inform models of speech production is in keeping with existing discussion of these models, several of which are based on production data from adults with aphasia (see, e.g., Caplan, 1985; Caramazza & Berndt, 1985).

[3]Due to space constraints, we will not review parallel interactive models, such as Stemberger's (1985), in this chapter. This does not eliminate them as candidate "best model" for describing children's sentence production.

mental structure (phonological form) of lexical items is retrieved, and surface phrasal geometry is determined. The latter arises through assignment of lexical formatives to phrasal positions and interpretation and siting of grammatical formatives in the surface sequence. Garrett differentiates between major category elements (nouns, verbs, adjectives) and minor category elements (both bound and free functor morphemes, including adverbs, intensifiers, and determiners) at this level, noting that errors involving minor elements do not include exchange process errors (such as, "room to my door" for the intended "door to my room"; 1980, p. 188). To account for this fact, he assumes that the minor elements occur only as features of the planning frames generated at the positional level. Their forms are specified by the syntactic structure, at the point of access. Phrasal stress is also a feature of surface phrasal structure, generated with the positional planning frames. The last step of sentence processing involves translation from the positional level to phonetic representation, a level which is suggested to account for specific phonetic errors that conform to the phonotactics of the language.

Based on Garrett's model, we can predict the following of filler syllables:

1. If filler syllables have consistent surface positions, they should then have generally interpretable functions, because the assignment of position follows encoding of function.

2. If they appear between major category elements, they might also be interpreted to replace minor category elements rather than major category elements. Again, their function should be interpretable if the surface phrasal geometry is interpretable.

3. If the positional level results from two major unordered processes—lexical form retrieval and surface geometry formation—performance constraints could result in a kind of "competition" between those processes. Across a sample, a child's utterances might show variability reflecting this competition. Some utterances might have sentencelike intonation contours with filler words, reflecting a phrasal geometry encoding. Other productions might have phonetically interpretable words but lack a phrasal intonation (successive single-word utterances).[4]

4. Detailed phonetics of filler syllables should conform to English phonotactics.

Other serial models agree with Garrett's in terms of a basic sequence of encoding, leading to similar predictions about the source of filler syllables. However, major points of difference give rise to different predictions. For example, Caplan (1985) suggested an interpretation (or extension) of Garrett's model

---

[4]This type of difference evokes the referential/expressive distinction across language learners described by, for example, Nelson (1973) and Peters (1977). Some children appear to use word division error phrases with often uninterpretable phonetic form early in their language development, whereas others tend to use successive and interpretable single words.

in which functors actually trigger the phrasal geometry. This predicts that if filler syllables replace function words, surface phrasal geometries would not be constructed, leaving only sentencelike utterances without phrasal categories (i.e., linearly ordered lexical items labeled for major lexical categories but not labeled NP, VP, etc., and not part of hierarchical phrase structures). In Fromkin's (1971, 1993) utterance generator model (from which Garrett developed his model), generation of phrasal intonation contour follows semantic-syntactic encoding but precedes lexical selection. This implies that the prosodic form of utterances is the primary phonetic form. It follows that fillers are predicted any time semantic-syntactic categories are activated but specific lexical forms are not retrieved; some kind of default segmental form is necessary to fill out the specified phrasal contour. Levelt's (1989) model focuses on the incremental nature of sentence production, which means there can be some feedback from the phonological to the syntactic encoding level, affecting subsequent positional grammatical encoding within a sentence. Consequently, phonological encoding of lexical items that have reached their surface destination may compete with activation of other lexemes for processing space, resulting in an underspecified phonological form. Note that the locus of syntactic/inflectional encoding varies from model to model. Thus, differences in predictions for filler syllables relate primarily to interpretability of the syntactic function of filler syllables.[5]

METHOD

Data for this study were the nasal filler syllables produced by two preschool boys with language production disorders involved in a phonological intervention study (Bernhardt, 1990).[6] Filler syllables are defined as phonetically consistent forms that are part of the phrasal intonation contour but do not correspond to morphemes in the adult language. These forms, by definition, do not include hesitation phenomena. Filler syllables were analyzed for their positions and functions in the children's utterances.

---

[5]The model differences with respect to syntax may result from the type of evidence used to construct and test the models. Garrett and Fromkin based their models on speech errors by normal speakers; Caplan and Caramazza & Berndt were trying to account for agrammatic speech of adults with aphasia. This source difference for model construction may bear on the results reported in this chapter.

[6]In Bernhardt's study, six children and their parents participated in individual phonological therapy three times a week in three consecutive six-week therapy cycles. Phonological goals and methods were set up in accordance with nonlinear phonological theory and analyses (see Bernhardt, 1990, 1992, 1994). The two boys reported here, Jeremy and Sean (pseudonyms), were S3 and S4 in this study, respectively. In Sean's case, the second and third cycles of therapy included a limited focus on grammatical form in addition to phonological goals, specifically (a) plurals in the word shape CVCVC, and (b) wh-words, in four sessions on word-initial /w/ words. Bernhardt and Gilbert (1992) reported some of S3's phonological data.

Subjects

The subjects were Jeremy and Sean, 3;4 and 3;5, respectively, at the onset of the intervention study. Both boys were the second children of English-speaking Canadian parents and had age-appropriate motor, cognitive (as measured by the Wechsler Intelligence Scale for Children–Revised, Wechsler, 1974), and social skills. Both had normal hearing and demonstrated language comprehension within normal limits as measured by the Auditory Comprehension Subtest of the Preschool Language Scale, Revised (Zimmerman, Steiner, & Pond, 1979), and the Peabody Picture Vocabulary Test, Revised, Form M (Dunn & Dunn, 1981). Both children were delayed in language production, with age scores of 2;6 on the Preschool Language Scale Verbal Ability Subtest, and had severe phonological disorders (see later discussion and Appendix).

Data Collection

The children's initial assessment included an audiorecorded phonological and language sample (elicited with a standard set of objects and pictures) and the battery of standardized tests of language comprehension and production just itemized. Hearing screening, an oral mechanism examination, and a case history filled out by the parents completed the assessment procedures. The sampling methodology was used at the end of each 6-week therapy cycle and at 6-month intervals after the phonological intervention study concluded. All sessions were recorded on Ampex 631 tapes with a Nagra IV reel-to-reel tape recorder and an AKG D202 microphone in a speech-language therapy clinic.

Analysis

The first author phonetically (International Phonetic Association, 1979, plus diacritics) and orthographically transcribed the assessment and end-of-cycle probe tapes using a Revox taperecorder and Videoconcepts F700 dynamic earphones. The second author independently transcribed a random sample of utterances from Sean's tape. Intertranscriber agreement for narrow phonetic transcription was 93% after discussion and resolution of differences; differences involved details of voicing and inclusion of glottal stops.

Data reported here are from sample 1 for Jeremy (age 3;4) and for samples 1, 2, and 3 for Sean (ages 3;5, 4;0, and 4;6). Mean length of utterance (MLU) was calculated for: (a) utterances without fillers; (b) utterances with only open-class words; and (c) all utterances (i.e., including utterances with filler syllables and counting each filler as one morpheme). Type:token ratios (TTR) were calculated for all words in each sample, and for open-class and closed-class items separately.

Transcripts were analyzed for number, distribution, and function of filler syllables. All utterances with filler syllables were coded for position of filler(s), specific lexical items that co-occurred with fillers, the functional categories of these lexical items, phrase structure, and discourse relation to prior utterances. The first analysis determined how production of filler syllables might be related to the children's phonological systems and whether fillers replaced specific lexical items. Each subsequent analysis was motivated by the inability of the prior analysis to account for all the filler data. These analyses were: (a) relevance of general lexical impoverishment or retrieval difficulty, or impoverishment or difficulty in retrieving specific lexical categories, to filler syllable production; (b) predictability of distribution of filler syllables in terms of grammatical role at the phrase or clause level; (c) discourse function of filler syllables, specifically whether fillers were (1) utterance initiators, or (2) distributed according to the given versus new information distinction.

The majority of filler syllables produced by both subjects were syllabic coronal nasals, [n]. Occasionally there was anticipatory place assimilation of the nasal, as shown in the following examples. (In all examples, B = Bernhardt, M = Mother.)

    (1) Jeremy, 3;4
        B: a screwdriver (naming a toy)
        J: yeh, daddy home [ŋ] one
    (2) Sean, 3;5
        [ŋ] go   = where did it go?

Because these examples are few, and predictable from phonetic context where they do occur, we refer to all filler syllables in the following discussion as [n].

RESULTS AND DISCUSSION

MLU and the frequency of the children's production of filler syllables in each sample is shown in Table 17.1. MLU (1.24–1.56, depending on whether or not filler syllables are included) and upper bound (u.b.) of 3 morphemes placed Jeremy at 3;4 in Brown's (1973) stage I; Sean was in stage I–II at age 3;5 (MLU = 1.62–2.39, u.b. = 3), stage II at 4;0 (MLU = 2.02–2.47, u.b. = 7), and late stage III–early stage IV at 4;6 (MLU = 2.97–3.11, u.b. = 7). Although filler syllables were frequent for both boys, Sean produced them twice as often as Jeremy at the lower MLU values, and his utterances with fillers were relatively much longer than his utterances without fillers. Jeremy stopped using filler syllables by the second sample. Sean continued to use them well beyond the period reported here, but their frequency diminished over the period of study.

Filler Syllables and the Phonology

Because both children had severe delays in both syntactic and phonological production, we queried whether the filler syllables were highly underspecified

TABLE 17.1
MLU and Proportion of Utterances With Fillers for Both Subjects

Subject	Sample #	Age	MLU: U with open + closed class	MLU: with open class	MLU: All[a]	%Us with fillers
Jeremy	1	3;4	1.24	1.10	1.56	23.5%
Sean	1	3;5	1.62	1.41	2.39	46.3%
Sean	2	4;0	2.02	1.55	2.47	24.0%
Sean	3	4;6	2.97	--[b]	3.11	16.9%

Note. U = utterances without fillers except in last column, where it designates proportion of utterances with fillers out of total utterances.
[a]Includes utterances with fillers in count, and counts each filler as one morpheme.
[b]There were only two utterances in this category.

phonological substitutions for specific lexical items, as one manifestation of general phonological impairment.

Sean and Jeremy's Phonological Systems

The syllable/word structure of the two boys was characterized by frequent use of CV words, and infrequent use of CVC and CVCV words (see Appendix). Production of the CVC and CVCV forms appeared to be facilitated by overuse of sibilants in C_2 position: for example, Sean's *cherry* pronounced as [tʰæzi], or Jeremy's *bandaid* pronounced as [mɛⁱs]. (For further discussion and examples, see Bernhardt, 1990, 1994; Bernhardt & Gilbert, 1992.)

Similarities in the subjects' phonological systems extended to their segmental inventories. Major places of articulation (labial, coronal, dorsal) were reasonably well established. Manner categories included the developmentally early stops, nasals, and glides, with some use of fricatives: word-final and medial sibilants as described earlier and, in Jeremy's case, word-initial labiodentals. Liquids were absent from both children's systems, with glides and glottal stops (plus [h] in Sean's case) appearing in their place. The glottal [h] was absent from Jeremy's repertoire. Substitution patterns were both typical ([w] for /r/, and, in Jeremy's case, stops for fricatives) and atypical (glottals for liquids and, in Sean's case, also for fricatives).

The use of filler syllables is, then, consistent with the general lack of specified phonological form. The phonological impairment is implicated at least in part in the use of fillers.

Filler Syllables—Specific Word Substitutions?

For Jeremy, [n] appeared to be a specific, if somewhat unusual, phonological substitution for the deictic form *this*. Three facts lead us to that conclusion:

1. The [n] syllable immediately dropped out of use between the fifth and sixth weeks of the phonological intervention project, after a period of radical change in syllable structure, and at the exact time that the deictic form *this* became frequent.[7] (In the first sample of 94 utterances and 147 words, Jeremy used one deictic form [dɪs] immediately after Bernhardt said *that*; otherwise, no examples of *this* or *that* were in the assessment sample, nor were they used generally, according to parental report.)

2. In the assessment language sample, the [n] appeared to have a clear deictic function 15/22 times (with no clear function for the other seven [n] tokens). The filler was often supplemented with a pointing gesture.

3. He had other unusual word substitutions: [ɚ] for *big*, [ˈʌbəm] for *yes*, and [biˈjæbi] for *little* (although the latter is conceivably derivable from *baby,* with diphthong metathesis and lowering).

For Sean, however, the specific word substitution hypothesis does not appear to be sufficient to explain the use of the fillers. Fillers continued to appear in his speech at age 6;6, but much less frequently than at age 3;5. Although they decreased in frequency over time, no particular morpheme(s) specifically replaced them.

Filler Syllables—A General Phonological Source?

Sean's rate of progress in phonological development was similar to Jeremy's during the phonological intervention period. At the end of that period (age 4;0), he had productive and age-appropriate use of English phonology with the exception of /r/, interdentals, and word-final nasal clusters. However, unlike Jeremy, who mastered /r/, the interdentals, and alveopalatals without further intervention, Sean continued to have substitutions for /r/ and /θ/, and difficulty with complex multisyllabic words, even at age 8;0.

The residual phonological difficulty suggests that general phonological impairment was a significant factor in his protracted use of [n] syllables. Further to that explanation, Tables 17.1 and 17.5 show distributional changes relating to filler syllables at the end of the major phonological intervention period (age 4;0). Although MLU increased minimally, from 2.39 at age 3;5 to 2.47 at age 4;0, the number of utterances with fillers decreased by approximately one half, from 46.3% to 24% of the sample. Because the decrease in filler syllable use co-occurred with the period of rapid phonological development, we deduced that the filler syllables arose primarily because of the previously high degree of underspecified phonological representations for words, and/or access to them. How-

---

[7]Jeremy has notable word retrieval difficulty (Test of Word Finding score at the 9th percentile at age 7;0). Although fillers dropped out when *this* became frequent, Jeremy used other compensatory strategies (such as avoidance and circumlocution) to circumvent a continuing difficulty accessing phonological form of known lexical items.

ever, two facts led us to seek additional sources for the filler syllables: (a) their continued frequent use at age 4;0, when the phonological system was relatively intact (24% of utterances; 10.9% of total word tokens), and (b) their decrease in use over time, with plateaued development in phonology.

Filler Syllables for Sean—Partial Result of Lexical Category Impoverishment or Access?

We next examined the possibility that a generally impoverished lexicon (or access to it), or a specific lexical *category* impoverishment or access, was implicated in Sean's filler syllable production. Sean's stable scores across time on standard tests suggest relative lexical impoverishment, at least in comparison with his nonverbal abilities. Test scores for single-word vocabulary comprehension (Peabody Picture Vocabulary Test-Revised, Dunn & Dunn, 1981) and naming (Expressive One-Word Picture Vocabulary Test, Gardner, 1979) were in the average range, with comprehension scores consistently somewhat higher than naming scores. These scores matched his average range scores on the Verbal Scale of the Wechsler Intelligence Scale for Children-Revised (WISC-R) (Wechsler, 1974), but contrasted to above average scores on the Performance Scale of the WISC-R (a 19-point gap between scales).

Word frequencies and lack of lexical variety in the samples also suggested a general impoverishment of the lexicon. Type:token ratios (see Table 17.2) for equivalent numbers of utterances for each of the samples across time were .31, .35, and .38, a low ratio for lexical items (Miller, 1981, suggested .5 is closer to average).

When we divided the sample into closed- and open-class items, other perspectives on TTR emerged. In the first sample, the TTR for open-class items only was .50, compared with a closed-class item value of .16. Adults typically have a 2:1 ratio for open:closed-class item TTRs; children at Stage I/II have different open:closed-class ratios, depending on their style of acquisition (Nelson, 1973). Thus, we cannot assert that the .50:.16 (approximately 3:1) ratio is abnormally disproportionate, but merely note it. For Sample 2, the TTR for open-class items was .36, and for closed-class items was .20, showing a shift in lexical category composition in terms of open/closed-class items. The Sample 3 closed-class item TTR was .37, and the open-class TTR, .51, in other words, a ratio similar to that of Sample 2.

Calculating *token* frequencies only over the whole samples, shifts in category composition are noted that reveal further changes in the open/closed-class distinction (see Table 17.3). Between the first and second samples, filler use decreased by 54.6% (from 24% of total sample to 10.9% of sample = 2:1 ratio), while closed-class morpheme tokens increased by 27.8% (34.2%:43.7%), and open-class tokens increased by only 6.7% (40.6%:43.3%). From Sample 2 to Sample 3, fillers decreased again, from 10.9% to 3.2% of the total sample, while

TABLE 17.2
Type/Token Ratios[a] for Lexical Categories in Utterances With and Without Fillers

Category/Structure Type	Utterances Without Fillers	Utterances With Fillers	Utterances Without Fillers	Utterances With Fillers	Utterances Without Fillers	Utterances With Fillers
	Sample 1	*Sample 1*	*Sample 2*	*Sample 2*	*Sample 3*	*Sample 3*
Nouns	26:43/84[b]	24:27/72	18:36/100	8:19/39	17:34/100	6:8/17
Verbs	5:5/84	8:18/72	15:26/100	9:17/39	16:30/100	6:7/17
Closed-class items	12:30/84	6:32/72[c]	26:70/100	12:28/39	42:125/100	12:19/17

[a]Types: tokens/number of total utterances of that type (*yes, no* excluded from closed-class tally).
[b]25/32 tokens = *that.*
[c]Overall TTRs for equivalent numbers of utterances across the three samples were .31, .35, and .38.

TABLE 17.3
Percentage of Sean's Word Tokens Categorized as Open Class, Closed Class,
Filler, or Uncodable

Sample	Open Class	Closed Class	Filler	Uncodable
1	40.6	34.2	24.0	1.3
2	43.3	43.7	10.9	2.0
3	36.7	58.8	3.2	1.3

closed-class tokens again increased in frequency by a similar proportion, 34% (43.7%:58.8%), but this time open-class tokens decreased in overall frequency— by 15% (43.3%:36.7%). The consistent relationship between filler syllable decrease and closed-class item increase suggests a possible relationship between fillers and closed-class items. The decrease in overall proportion of open-class tokens reflects the increase in open-class types (.36 to .51), and possibly also a balancing between open- and closed-class categories.

Looking at particular lexical items per equivalent numbers of utterances across the samples, the following were found to be frequent:

Sample 1 frequent words:

1. Closed-class items: *that* (33 tokens), *no* (26), *two* (11), *more* (7), *me* (7), *way* (6). Closed class items with fewer than five tokens were *yeh*, the particle *up*, the progressive verb form *-ing*, pronouns *mine, everybody, you*, and *one*, and the adverbial *too*.

2. Open-class items: *mommy* (11), *go* (9), and *broke* (6).

Sample 2 frequent words:

1. Closed-class items: *that* (24), *yeh* (14), *no* (10), *me* (8), *do* (5), *back* (5). New moderate frequency closed class words were deictics *here, these* and pronouns *I* and *him*. Infrequent new closed class items were auxiliaries *don't, is/are*, the negative *not*, prepositions *for/in/on*, conjunctions *and* and *but*, wh-question words *where/what/(which)*, deictics *there* and *those*, and pronouns *them, it, we*.

2. Open-class items: *mommy* (13), *"peanut-butter-sandwich"* (12), *go* (10), *elephant* (8), *juice* (7), and *way* (5).

Word frequency was similar to that of Sample 1, with two closed-class items (*that, no*) and one open-class items (*mommy*) still being among the most common words. As previously noted, closed-class items increased in type and tokens; the variety is apparent in the forms listed.

Sample 3 frequent words:

1.   Closed-class items: *no* (25), *this* (17), *all* (13), *now* (8), *is* (8), *that* (8), *I* (6), *two* (6), *one* (5), *some* (5). Among the frequent words, more type changes were evident than between Samples 1 and 2: the deictic *this* overtook *that*, *I* replaced *me*, more quantifiers were used (although *two* was frequent from the beginning), and *is*, an AUX form, appeared in the frequent list.

2.   Open-class items: Only three words had five occurrences or more in the portion of the sample studied: *knife* (5), *egg* (5), *know* (5), (*mommy* dropping out of the list).

Specific Lexical Category Impoverishment— Closed-Class Items and Phonological Form

The proportional increase in closed-class items between Sample 1 and Sample 2 coincided with the period of most rapid phonological development. In terms of phonological form, the closed-class items that appeared or increased in frequency in the second and third samples are not similar in their segments. Thus, increased production abilities for a specific set of features and segments cannot directly account for the increase in closed-class item use. However, closed-class items *are* phonologically similar in their prosodic structure, both in syllable number (i.e., they are monosyllabic), and unstressed phrasal position. Therefore, the general acceleration in phonological development (which occurred at both segmental and prosodic levels) may have facilitated their encoding/access. However, several facts suggest that phonological development, particularly in terms of prosodic structure, was not solely implicated in the increase in closed-class item use:

1.   The increase in closed-class items did not occur not across the board, that is, for all closed-class items.

2.   Certain closed-class items were the most frequent words in the samples, suggesting that they were not inaccessible as a class.

3.   Fillers often had strong stress equal to that of the phonetically formed words. Thus, stress itself did not appear to be a clearly implicated factor.

4.   Closed-class items continued to increase in use between Samples 2 and 3, even though the phonology was at that time relatively well-established and stable. Phonological development thus was not co-occurring at the same rate as morphological development, although perhaps the new phonological foundation meant that morphology could develop on that base.

Overall, although contributing, a prosodic explanation does not appear adequate to account for the fillers and the changes, even within a more circumscribed lexical category type, in this case, closed-class. Closed-class items, furthermore, are not uniform as a *category* in filler syllable replacement: Some closed-class items were produced frequently with phonetic form, and others appeared to be replaced by fillers. We need to look both beyond the phonology and the open/closed-class distinction to elaborate our understanding of filler syllable use.

Filler Syllables and Phrasal Structure

Attributing meaning to fillers is a tentative exercise at best, with many interpretations possible. We were only able to attribute very general functions to fillers in the phrasal structure, rather than assign direct meanings or calculate proportions of various possible functions.

Sample 1: For Sean, as for Jeremy, the fillers appeared to have a general reference (pronominal) or deictic (*this, that*) function in many instances, such as:

(3) [n] ice cream

(4) [n] cold

(5) [n] all broken

Such utterances had co-occurring directed eye gaze or pointing. On one occasion the reference appeared to be to himself:

(6) [n] want X (even though he did use *me* in other utterances)

Unlike Jeremy, however, for whom the fillers seemed to specifically replace *this*, Sean did use a deictic word *that*, plus first and second person pronouns. In fact, the word *that* was his most frequent word, appearing in both subject and complement positions, with and without fillers present. It appeared frequently as a complement with a filler in a formulaic expression:

(7) [n] that (interpretable sometimes as a question "what's that,"
       sometimes as a comment, "look at that")

Thus, although the fillers did appear to replace deictic words in many utterances, they also had other reference functions, or may have enhanced deixis, or supported interrogative functions in others. For example, fillers appeared in phrases with *go*, such as:

(8) [ŋ] bee go (looking around, ostensibly meaning "where did the
       bee go?")

Wh-words and third-person pronouns (reference pronouns) did not appear in the Stage I sample, nor would they necessarily be expected at this stage of syntactic development.

Sample 2: Fillers continued to have functions similar to those we assumed in Sample 1. However, only one token of the previously frequent formulaic phrase [n] *that* appeared, even though the word *that* remained the most frequent word. One new function appeared to be as a connective between constituents:

(9) juice [n] cookie

Several [n]s appeared in connective positions both utterance initially and internally, for example:

(10) peanut-butter-sandwich [n] back   = say 'peanut butter sandwich', and he will come back

As mentioned earlier, sample 2 showed an increase in closed-class item use, which reflected increases in previously used forms and emergent forms. Of particular interest for filler syllable decrease is the beginning use of wh-words *where* and *what,* third person pronouns *him, it,* and *them,* and conjunctions *and/but.* These forms are not unexpected, given Sean's Stage II MLU.

Sample 3: Sample 3 fillers have some of the same apparent functions—deictic, referent, connective, or interrogative. Fillers again decreased in use, while grammatical morphemes, including wh-words, pronouns, the word *this,* and conjunctions, appeared or increased in use. Question words *what, where, who* and *why* appeared infrequently. In terms of pronouns, although more types and tokens were present, with the notable emergence of the form *it,* third person pronouns were infrequent. Furthermore, *it* was the only third-person pronoun to appear in subject position (twice, compared with 16 times in object position). The conjunction *and* was more frequent (10 occurrences), and other connectives used were *because, for,* and *to.* Nine fillers could be interpreted as having connective functions, although other interpretations were possible for several, for example:

(11) S: [n] this egg
     [n] more eggs

The filler could be interpreted as having a deictic or connective function, or both. More specific and sophisticated connective functions appear in the following, however:[8]

---

[8]An *if/then*-type function was still in use at age 5;6, when [n] was much less frequent overall, for example:

B: If I don't put my—(prompting for complex sentence with if)
S: what could happen?
B: Okay. And ask me this last one.
S: [n] you don't eat, what can happen?

(12) B: Explain to me what I have to do.
S: [m]-[m] you get one with green, [m] you have to X X do this

(13) B: *If* we cut it in half, what could we do?
S: [n] everybody have it

Sean's language development level at this point was late stage III-early stage IV (MLU of 3.11; use of complex sentences). Frequently used forms that matched the MLU were the first and second person pronouns and *it* in object position, quantifiers, demonstratives, *-ing,* plurals, possessives, and negatives. Expected forms for the MLU that were infrequent were auxiliary and copula forms, wh-words, and third-person pronouns other than *it* in object position. Missing but expected forms were articles. Forms that appeared to be in advance of his stage were conjunctions such as *because.* It is not unusual for some forms to be ahead and some "behind" the MLU level. We merely note the asynchrony to comment that a generalized grammatical morphology impairment seems insufficient to account for Sean's filler syllable usage. This is consistent with our previous comments on closed class items.

Pronouns, Wh-Words, and Connectives

Even though the functions of filler syllables were not clearly unitary in many instances, reference, interrogative, and connective functions (whether the fillers were sole carriers of the function, or enhancements of other linguistic or para-linguistic phenomena) seemed the most plausible. Thus, in terms of the morpho-syntax, the development of pronouns, wh-words, and connectives seems to be most related to the filler syllable usage. Wh-words were the least established category across the samples (appearing infrequently, even after being intervention targets). In typical development, question words are often used in routinized expressions with low phonological form until about Stage III, although the routinized forms may carry some of the phonetic content, as in [sæt] or [wʌsæt] for *what's that* (Johnson, 1980, 1981). Thus, the filler use for wh-words is not unexpected, although somewhat exaggerated in its low phonetic content.

Pronoun use varied across type and person. Both first and second person pronouns appeared from the first sample, which was consistent with the MLU, and became a very frequent closed-class category in Sample 3. The deictic form *that* was the most frequent word in the first two samples, with *this* being a frequent closed-class category in Sample 3 (followed by *that).* As is typical in development, the third person pronouns appeared after the first and second person pronouns. However, the late emergence of *it* is somewhat unusual (*it* usually emerges with the first and second person pronouns in Stage I, according to Chiat, 1986.) The low phonetic content of *it,* particularly the word-final /t/, which Sean often omitted, may be implicated in the delayed emergence of the word. However, very few utterance-final fillers were in the samples, and *it* usually appears postverbally first, as it did for Sean. Thus, fillers did not appear to replace *it* in its most expected postverbal position.

Interpretation of fillers as replacements for connectives is difficult for Sample 1. It is possible that some of the utterance-initial fillers had a connective function (especially because adults use [n] as a rapid speech form of *and*, giving a phonological source for the nasal filler). However, no phrasal units were conjoined with any identifiable connectives. The replacement of connectives does appear to follow development, however, as the Sample 2 and 3 data showed.

Overall, for connectives and pronouns, fillers appeared to follow the grammatical development to a certain extent, more delimited functions being noted over time. Pronouns, wh-words and connectives do not form a syntactic category. However, they do have a similar positional distribution. All can occur phrase initially in surface form, and in Sample 1, fillers were most frequently utterance-initial, an often unstressed phrasal position in English. Again the connection between the prosodic position and fillers seems relevant. However, as we commented earlier, the prosodic explanation is not sufficient to account for the fillers, but interacts with other aspects of the grammar, in this case, reference, interrogative and connective words. (We return to the positional issue in the discourse function discussion.)

Fillers and Phrasal Constituents

All of the previous discussion seems to indicate that fillers replaced single morphemes. However, analysis of contingent utterances also indicated possible elliptical replacement of larger syntactic units, such as S or NP, for example:

(14) M: Are you fixing it?
S: [n] already. me fix already   (replacing subject pronoun and verb)

Where fillers appeared in NP position, a deictic or personal pronoun may have been grammatical in adult English, but we cannot assume that particular replacement for the child's production. Only the replacement of NP itself can be assumed.

Fillers were used in a variety of phrase structures, although primarily in phrasal units rather than in complete sentences, that is, with NPs *or* VPs. Because fillers were more frequent utterance initially, the subject NP appeared to be replaced more frequently than other forms. (In this sense, where other children may have omitted subjects at this developmental point, Sean replaced subjects with fillers.) For our analysis of subject replacement, we only considered those fillers preceding a narrowly defined VP element, that is, a verb or adjective. With this criterion, 25% of total utterances with fillers were of the [n]-VP type in

TABLE 17.4
Pharsal Categories in Utterances With and Without Fillers for Sean

Utterance Type	Sample 1: 3;5	Sample 2: 4;0	Sample 3: 4;6
Without fillers	a. NP elaborations two more dirt b. no + verb or Noun no car	NP elaborations one for mommy and for you	S elaborations I want this be here cause only little boys go on nobody sits
With fillers	Sentences a. [N] Noun + Comp [N] eye dirty b. [n] Noun + Verb (N=pro, N) [N] me do [n] horsie go?	S elaborations [m] back [m] cookies that car go [n] brokey	Complex sentences B: Explain to me what I have to do. S: [m]-[m] you get one with green, [m] you have to <X> do this

Sample 1, 53% in the second, and 47% in the third.[9] Fillers also appeared frequently before NPs: 47% of the total utterances with fillers in Sample 1, 21% in Sample 2, and 15% in Sample 3. (See Table 17.4 for more examples.)

Subject NPs were not always replaced when the filler preceded a VP. Across all three samples, fillers also appeared utterance initially even when subjects were present, as examples (15)-(17) show:

(15) Sample 1:
[ŋ] horsie go?

(16) Sample 2:
B: I can hop like an elephant (pretending elephant finger puppet is a rabbit)
S: [n], no, [n] elephant [n] walking

(17) Sample 3:
[n] four sit
[n] you do this?

Proportionally, utterances with fillers preceding *full* sentences increased from 5.9% in the first sample to 14.7% and 15.3% in the next two samples.

---

[9]The differences between the first sample and the others partly reflect the type of counting convention requiring verbs or adjectives to represent VPs and the general lack of verb use in the first sample. An NP following a filler could also be a VP element, a complement of an unrealized verb, or an auxiliary.

In summary, fillers could not always be considered as replacements of single morphemes. Their roles in the phrasal structure, furthermore, appeared to be different, depending on the constituents with which they co-occurred.

Lexical Category Types and Phrasal Types in Utterances With and Without Fillers

Further analysis of the phrasal constituents themselves in utterances with and without fillers revealed complementary distribution differences for verbs that may be implicated in filler syllable use.

Sample 1 comparison of utterances with and without fillers.   A greater proportion of verb types and tokens appeared in the utterances with fillers (8:17 in 72 utterances) than in those with no fillers (5:5 in 84 utterances) (see Table 17.2). A greater proportion of noun tokens appeared in the utterances without fillers, although type proportion was about the same. Closed-class tokens (not counting *yes* and *no*) were about equally frequent in the utterances with and without fillers. However, proportionally more *types* of closed-class items appeared in utterances without fillers. Major phrasal types found only in utterances without fillers included (see Table 17.4):

1. NP elaborations of the type Determiner + Noun (determiner loosely defined as adjective, quantity marker), for example:

    (18) two more dirt

2. *no* + Verb or Noun, for example:

    (19) no car

3. Verb + ing, for example:

    (20) walking

Major phrasal types found only in utterances with fillers were:

1. [n] N + Comp (Adjective), for example:

    (21) [n] eye dirty

2. [n] Noun + Verb (where N = pronoun or noun), for example:

    (22) [n] me do

3. [n] Noun + Noun + Verb (where the second noun is a complement of VP), for example:

    (23) [m] monkey banana eat

Sample 2 Comparison of Utterances With and Without Fillers.   Sample 2 showed an equalization of lexical category types, although there was still a slightly greater proportion of verb types and tokens in the utterances with fillers than noun types and tokens (Table 17.2). Closed-class types and tokens were essentially equivalent across the two types of utterances. The main distributional difference between the two samples in terms of lexical categories was the proportional expansion of closed-class item *types* in utterances *with* fillers. Recalling that the overall token proportion of closed/open-class items increased from Samples 1 to 2, it is noteworthy that both type *and* token proportion expanded in utterances with fillers. Thus, there is no absolute mutual exclusivity between fillers and closed-class items, as we noted earlier.

Phrase structure in Sample 2 showed expansions in both types of utterances. Noun phrase elaborations in utterances without fillers included conjoined NPs, and NPs with PP, for example:

(24) one for mommy and for you

Utterances without fillers also showed an increase in verb phrase. Sentences of the type Noun + Comp or Noun + Verb (+ Comp) were present, for example:

(25) everybody that way

Utterances with fillers now had the morpheme *-ing*, determiner + Noun phrases, and what appeared to be more complex constructions with utterance-internal fillers, for example:

(26) that car go [n] brokey

Sample 3 Comparison of Utterances With and Without Fillers.   Sample 3 differed in having a roughly equivalent proportion of nouns and verbs. Phrasal units in utterances without fillers included some of the same structures as the previous samples, with expansion both in single sentences and in conjoined or complex sentences, for example:

(27) this red one want go on here
(28) 'cause only little boys go on

Utterances with fillers also included structures seen in the previous samples and longer complex sentences, as in (12).

Across the three samples, phrase structure was more complex in utterances with fillers. Utterances without fillers had more noun phrase elaborations, and utterances with fillers more verb phrase and sentence elaborations. Over time, utterances without fillers "caught up" in terms of sentence structure, but the utterances with fillers advanced again in comparison. This "shifting window" for the fillers again points to the plurifunctionality of the fillers and demonstrates that they had more than a phonological source in the grammar.

Discourse Functions of Filler Syllables

It is enlightening to balance the phonological, lexical category and phrase structure explanations of filler syllables with an analysis of the fillers' discourse functions. We investigated two hypotheses: (a) the fillers were merely utterance initiators, and (b) they replaced, or substituted for, given (versus new) information in the discourse.

The following facts lead to rejection of the first hypothesis (which would amount to the proposal that fillers do not serve the lexical and morphosyntactic functions we have shown they do serve): (a) although fillers were most frequent in utterance-initial position, this frequency decreased over time (see Table 17.5), as (b) fillers appeared utterance internally, utterance finally, or alone, as shown in example (8) at age 3;5 and examples (29)–(31) at 4;6, and (c) sometimes more than one filler was produced in a single utterance, as in examples (29) and (31). (Also see Table 17.5.)

(29) [n] turning [n]

(30) [n] (three tokens, meaning *no, yes, wow*)

(31) [n] [ə] show you all my toys [n]

Given a cautious interpretation, it is not possible to rule out a discourse initiation function for some fillers. However, the complementary distributions noted in the phrase structure discussion suggest that filler syllables represent more than a communication habit. Taking an information-processing point of view, there may be a suppression effect on the phonological form of utterance- or phrase-initial words; as an utterance is sequenced for production, the first words

TABLE 17.5
Distribution of Fillers Over Time in Sean's Utterances

Sample	1	2	3
% [N] utterances with utterance-initial [N][a]	95.5%	82.1%	60.0%
% [N] utterances with more than one [N][b]	3.3%	14.3%	20.0%

[a][N]: Not exclusively utterance-initial.
[b]More than one [N] in some utterances.

may be more subject to breakdown. This type of initiation breakdown does not negate earlier conclusions about phrase structure and is consistent with the notion of performance limitations (see P. Bloom, 1990; Slobin, 1985).

The second hypothesis posits an ellipsis-substitution function for filler syllables, where fillers stand in for information established by a prior utterance. Such given information is often utterance initial in English, and children with production limitations typically leave it out, lexically encoding only new information (see, for example, Greenfield & Smith, 1976; Keenan, Schieffelin, & Platt, 1978).

Reliability of coding Sean's utterances for given/new information was low for Samples 1 and 2; for example, over half the filler syllables in the Sample 1 were ambiguous in terms of reference to given or new information. However, coding reliability for sample 3 was 93% and yielded the following results: 48% of fillers replaced given information; 6% replaced new information; 21% filled other clearly grammatical or emphatic functions, where reference was not apparent; and 25% were ambiguous in their reference or had more than one interpretable function, as shown in example (32):

(32)   [n:]! (expression of amazement, proposition presupposed)
       '[n] can't 'believe it (follows [n:] referring to given information, emphatic,
       replaces *I*)

Although grammatical functions could be attributed to some of the 48% given information substitutions, this could not be done with confidence, as example (32) illustrates.

If the 25% of fillers coded ambiguous are counted as replacing given information, the total in this category becomes 73%, a sizeable majority. The given-new information distinction is a strongly supported explanation for filler syllable production, but it is not sufficient to explain filler use across the sample. Phrase structure explanations continue to be important.

SUMMARY

Phonological impairment is at least partly responsible for both Jeremy and Sean's use of filler syllables. Jeremy's use of [n] ceased precisely at the time he was able to say *this* with ease. Sean's production of [n] decreased dramatically between samples 1 and 2—a period of rapid phonological development—although it continued to be frequent over the period of study. Sean's relative lexical impoverishment is also implicated in his use of fillers. The drop in frequency of filler use between samples 2 and 3 followed language intervention focused on closed-class wh-words, copula, and pronouns. However, the open versus closed class distinction does not hold up as an explanation of filler production because of the different patterns of use for individual closed-class items, some of which were frequent from the outset of the study. Filler syllables appeared to fill specific grammatical and phrase structure roles in many of Sean's utterances, including replacement of deictic terms, wh-words, pronouns, and conjunctions, as well as larger syntactic units such as NP or S. In addition, utterances with and without fillers tended to be in complementary distribution; an interesting contrast here is greater NP elaboration in utterances without fillers versus more verb types and more complex verb phrase and clause structure in utterances with fillers. Although the majority of filler syllables were utterance initial, this in itself does not explain filler production. The majority of fillers replaced given information, often in utterances where their grammatical function was unclear. Some filler syllables were clearly plurifunctional, simultaneously marking, for example, emphasis, given information, and an identifiable grammatical role.

SENTENCE MODEL PREDICTIONS IN LIGHT OF THE FILLER SYLLABLE DATA

Garrett's Model

1. If filler syllables have consistent surface positions, they should then have generally interpretable functions, because the assignment of position follows encoding of function.

Functional level minimally supported: For Jeremy, fillers seemed to have a clear and unitary function, as a deictic form (*this*), function therefore possibly being assigned prior to position. However, for Sean a functional interpretation of fillers was difficult for many utterances. Elements of deixis, reference and questioning were suggested, but it was not clear which of those or other functions applied in each case. Thus, although it may have been encoded prior to positional assignment, function was indeterminate. In contrast, position was reasonably consistent (most fillers were phrase-initial); therefore, perhaps, position was encoded earlier than function, with function left ambiguous due to lack of lexical meaning, phonetic form, or phrasal status. Garrett's distinction between the functional and positional levels is supported by the fact that fillers occurred more often in utterances with verbs, suggesting a phrasal geometry was in place prior to assignment of phonological form.

2. Fillers might also be seen to replace minor category elements rather than major category elements.

Major/minor category distinction unsupported: The model suggests that fillers appearing between major category elements should replace minor category elements. The positioning of the fillers was primarily phrase initial, thus arguably occurring at least some of the time between major category elements. Another aspect of the data suggesting a distinction between minor and major category elements was the concurrent increase in frequency of closed-class elements (minor category elements) and decrease in frequency of filler syllables, in comparison to the small changes in frequency of open class elements.

The prediction does not completely hold, however. Closed class items did not form a unitary category in terms of their relative frequencies or replacement with fillers. Some closed class items were the most frequent words from the outset, and others emerged over time as fillers decreased in use. In addition, we argued that fillers appeared to replace major category elements: single nouns or verbs, entire phrases, or even sentences. In summary, in contrast to what the model predicts, minor and major category elements do not appear to be completely distinguishable, nor do fillers appear to replace minor category elements exclusively.

3. If the positional level results from two major processes—lexical retrieval and surface geometry formation—performance constraints could result in a kind of "competition" between those processes.

Support for a positional level: The complementary distribution of lexical and phrasal categories for utterances with and without fillers suggests possible relevance of the positional level. Utterances without fillers were more commonly noun phrase elaborations than verb phrases or sentences. Utterances with fillers had more complex phrase structure, and fewer noun tokens, suggesting a bifurcation congruent with the positional level (lexical selection versus surface phrasal geometry). Further evidence is the persistence of fillers and their shifting function as Sean's language continued to develop. In each sample there is evidence of competition between different kinds of encoding.[10]

4. Detailed phonetics of filler syllables should conform to English phonotactics.

Partial support for a phonetic realization level: Nasals are logical replacements in that they are early-developing phones in a repertoire. Some of the time, the fillers showed place assimilation to the subsequent consonant, a typical type of place assimilation for nasals in English.

CONCLUSION

The data from these children is unique in the language acquisition/language disorder literature. The use of filler syllables indicates that, underlyingly, the child has some knowledge of the serial ordering of sentences of English, and the need for a variety of grammatical constituents. Pressure of discourse and other restrictions on sentence encoding (phonological, lexical, and syntactic) appeared to limit phonetic encoding of certain types of words, particularly third-person pronominal subject constituents, deictic constituents, wh-words and connective words. The fact that some fillers appeared to have only a discourse function for

---

[10]This aspect of Garrett's model has much in common with connectionist models (see Bates & MacWhinney, 1989; Stemberger, 1985). Our data are indeterminate in choosing between serial and parallel interactive models on this point.

Sean, and that discourse conditions that required rapid or emotional speech increased use of fillers (to the point where it was the only element of the utterance), some version of an interactive activation sentence production model also has some appeal, although an explication of this model and its predictions is beyond the scope of this chapter. At this time, we have only a hint of what a model might look like for children's sentence production. The question does need to be addressed, particularly for intervention with children such as these. Recent applications of Garrett's model for aphasia intervention have resulted in more successful outcomes for aphasia therapy. Learning more about sentence production in children may result in a similar change in intervention strategies for children with language impairments.

REFERENCES

Bates, E., & MacWhinney, B. (1989). Functionalism and the competition model. In B. MacWhinney & E. Bates (Eds.), *The crosslinguistic study of sentence processing* (pp. 3–73). New York: Cambridge University Press.

Bernhardt, B. (1990). *Application of nonlinear phonological theory to intervention with six phonologically disordered children.* Unpublished doctoral dissertation, University of British Columbia, Vancouver, Canada.

Bernhardt, B. (1992). Developmental implications of nonlinear phonological theory. *Clinical Linguistics and Phonetics, 6,* 259–281.

Bernhardt, B. (1994). The prosodic tier and phonological disorders. In M. Yavas (Ed.), *First and second language phonology* (pp. 149–172). San Diego, CA: Singular Publishing Group.

Bernhardt, B., & Gilbert, J. (1992). Applying linguistic theory to speech-language pathology: The case for non-linear phonology. *Clinical Linguistics and Phonetics, 6,* 123–145.

Bloom, L. (1973). *One word at a time.* The Hague: Mouton.

Bloom, P. (1990). Subjectless sentences in child language. *Lingusitic Inquiry, 21,* 491–503.

Brown, R. (1973). *A first language: The early stages.* Cambridge, MA: Harvard University Press.

Caplan, D. (1985). Syntactic and semantic structures in agrammatism. In M. L. Kean (Ed.), *Agrammatism* (pp. 125–152). New York: Academic Press.

Caramazza, A., & Berndt, R. S. (1985). A multicomponent deficit view of Agrammatic Broca's Aphasia. In M. L. Kean (Ed.), *Agrammatism* (pp. 27–63). New York: Academic Press.

Chiat, S. (1986). Personal pronouns. In P. Fletcher & M. Garman (Eds.), *Language acquisition* (2nd ed., pp. 339–355). Cambridge, England: Cambridge University Press.

Dore, J., Franklin, M., Miller, R., & Ramer, A. (1976). Transitional phenomena in early anguage acquisition. *Journal of Child Language, 3,* 13–28.

Dunn, L., & Dunn, L. (1981). *Peabody picture vocabulary test (rev.).* Circle Pines, MN: American Guidance Service.

Fromkin, V. (1971). The nonanomalous nature of anomalous utterances. *Language, 47,* 27–52.

Fromkin, V. (1993). Speech production. In J. Berko Gleason (Ed.), *Psycholinguistics* (pp. 272–300). Fort Worth, TX: Harcourt Brace Jovanovich.

Gardner, M. (1979). *Expressive one-word picture vocabulary test.* Novato, CA: Academic Therapy Publications.

Garrett, M. (1975). The analysis of sentence production. In G. Bower (Ed.), *Psychology of learning and motivation* (Vol. 9, pp. 133–177). New York: Academic Press.

Garrett, M. (1980). Levels of processing in sentence production. In B. Butterworth (Ed.), *Language production I* (pp. 177–220). London: Academic Press.

Garrett, M. (1984). The organization of processing structure for language production: Applications in aphasic speech. In D. Caplan (Ed.), *Biological perspectives on language* (pp. 172–193). Cambridge, MA: MIT Press.

Greenfield, P., & Smith , J. (1976). *The structure of communication in early language development.* New York: Academic Press.

International Phonetic Association (1979). *The principles of the International Phonetic Association* (Handbook of the IPA). London: London University College.

Johnson, C. E. (1980, October). *The ontogenesis of question words in children's language.* Paper presented at the Fifth Annual Boston University Converence on Language Development, Boston, MA.

Johnson, C. E. (1981). *Children's questions and the discovery of interrogative syntax.* Unpublished doctoral dissertation, Stanford University, Stanford, CA.

Keenan, E., Schieffelin, B., & Platt, M. (1978). Questions of immediate concern. In E. Goody (Ed.), *Questions and politeness* (pp. 44–55). Cambridge, England: Cambridge University Press.

Leonard, L. (1975). On differentiating syntactic and semantic features in emerging grammars: Evidence from empty form usage. *Journal of Psycholingujistic Research, 4,* 357–364.

Levelt, W. (1989). *Speaking: From intention to articulation.* Cambridge, MA: MIT Press.

Miller, J. (1981). *Assessing language production in children: experimental procedures.* Assessing Communicative Behavior, Vol. 1. Baltimore: University Park Press.

Nelson, K. (1973). Structure and strategy in learning to talk. *Monograph of the Society for Research in Child Development,38* (1–2, Serial No. 149).

Peters, A. (1977). Language learning strategies: Does the whole equal the sum of the parts? *Language, 53,* 560–573.

Peters, A. (1983). *The units of language acquisition.* Cambridge Series of Monographs and Texts in Applied Psycholinguistics, S. Rosenberg (Ed.). New York: Cambridge University Press.

Peters, A., & Menn, L. (1993). False starts and filler syllables: Ways to learn grammatical morphemes. *Language, 69,* 742–777.

Robbins, J., & Klee, T. (1987). Clinical assessment of oropharyngeal motor development in young children. *Journal of Speech and Hearing Disorders, 52,* 271–277.

Slobin, D. I. (1985). Crosslinguistic evidence for the language-making capacity. In D. I. Slobin (Ed.), *The crosslinguistic study of language acquisition. Vol. 2: Theoretical issues* (pp. 1157–1256). Hillsdale, NJ: Lawrence Erlbaum Associates.

Stemberger, J. (1985). An interactive activation model of language production. In A. W. Ellis (Ed.), *Progress in the psychology of language* (Vol. 1, pp. 143–186). Hove, England: Lawrence Erlbaum Associates.

Wechsler, D. (1974). *Wechsler intelligence scale for children—Revised.* San Antonio, TX: Psychological Corporation.

Zimmerman, I., Steiner, V., & Pond, R. (1979). *Preschool language scale-2 (Rev.).* Columbus, OH: Charles Merrill.

APPENDIX

A. Jeremy's Phonological Profiles and Intervention Targets

Phonolog. Category	Age 3;4	Intervention Targets: Blocks 1, 2, and/or 3	Age 3;10
CVC	Marginal: Only with nasal or default consonant WF [s][a]	Bl. 1 for CVC shape Bl. 2 eliminate assimilaions /dissimilations among stops	√
CVCV	Marginal in common reduplicated forms. No other disyllables.	Bl. 1 for CVCV word Shape	√ Generalized to other multisyllabic words
Glides:	/w/: WI√		√
/w/ and /j/	Others : Developing		
Nasals	/m/: WI, WF√ /n/: WI√	/n/: C2 target for Bl. 1 CVCV word shape	√

Stops: [-voice]	/p,t/: WI√ except for aspiration Others: Developing/Marginal	/p/: C_2 target for Bl. 1 CVC word shape /t/: C_2 target for Bl. 1 CVCV word shape /t/ & /k/: Bl. 2 CVC training	√
Stops: [+voice]	/b/: √ /d/, /g/: Developing WI Others: Marginal or absent	/d/: C2 target for Bl. 1 CVCV word shape	√ except devoiced WF
Fricatives/Affricates	/z/: Default[a] C_2 in disyllables /s/: Default WF consonant Marginal WI affricates, no other fricatives	/f/: Bl. 1 and 2 target /s/: Bl. 2 and 3 WI singleton and cluster target /z/: Bl. 2 plural target	All √ except interdentals
Liquids	None	/l/: Bl. 1 and 2 target /r/: At age 7+	/l/ √; /r/ still developing at age 8
/h/	Developing		√

Note. WI = word-initial; SIWW = syllable-initial, within-word; WF = word-final. √ = 80% + matches with adult target. Developing 30%-79% matches. Marginal: less than 30%.
[a]Default = frequent substitution (if WF consonant present at all).

279

APPENDIX

B. Sean's Phonological Profiles and Intervention Targets

Phonolog. Category	Age 3;5	Intervention Targets: Blocks 1, 2, and/or 3	Age 3;11
CVC	Marginal word shape: WF defaulta consonant [s] or [p]	Bl. 1: CVC word shape	√
Disyllabic words	Developing: SIWW default consonant /z/	Bl. 1: CVCV word shape	√
	Other disyllables marginal	Bl. 2: CVCVC word shape	
Glides: /w/ and /j/	/w/: WI√ only		√
	/j/, SIWW /w/: Developing		
Nasals	/m/: WI, SIWW √	/m/, /n/: C₂ targets for Bl. 1 CVCV and CVD word shapes	√ except in final nasal-stop clusters
	/n/: WI √		

		/l/: Bl. 2 morpheme -ing target	√
Stops: [-voice]	/p, k/: Developing in all word positions; /t/: Developing WI, otherwise marginal	Others: Developing/marginal; /j/: C_2 target for Bl. 1 CVCV word shape	
Stops: [+voice]	WI: √ Developing SIWW Absent WF	/d/: C_2 Target for Bl. 1 CVCV word shape	√ except some devoicing WF
Fricatives/ Affricatives	/f,v/: WI √; No other fricatives	/s/: Bl. 2 and Bl. 3 WI and cluster target; Alveopalatals, interdentals: Bl. 2	All√ except alveopalatals, interdentals
Liquids	None	/l/: Bl. 1 and 2 target; /r/: Bl. 3 target	/l/: √ /r/: marginal
/h/	Absent	Bl. 1 and 2 targets	√

Note. WI = word-initial; SIWW = syllable-initial, within-word; WF = word-final.
√ = 80% + matches with adult target. Developing: 30%–79% matches. Marginal: less than 30%.
[a]Default [s] = WF substitution both for singletons and whole syllables.

Author Index

Subject Index